Don't Divorce Your Children

Don't Divorce Your Children

Children and Their Parents
Talk About Divorce

JENNIFER M. LEWIS, M.D., *and*
WILLIAM A. H. SAMMONS, M.D.

CONTEMPORARY BOOKS

306.8
Lew

Library of Congress Cataloging-in-Publication Data

Sammons, Williams A. H.
      Don't divorce your children : children and their parents talk
about divorce / William Sammons and Jennifer Lewis.
           p.   cm.
      ISBN 0-8092-2793-2
      1. Children of divorced parents.   2. Parenting.
      I. Lewis, Jennifer M.   II. Title.
HQ777.5 .S33   1999
649'.1—dc21
                                                                98-49523
                                                                CIP

Cover design by Jeanette Wojtyla
Cover photograph © Phil Borges/Tony Stone Images
Interior design by Impressions Book & Journal Services

Published by Contemporary Books
A division of NTC/Contemporary Publishing Group, Inc.
4255 West Touhy Avenue, Lincolnwood (Chicago), Illinois 60646-1975 U.S.A.
Printed in the United States of America
International Standard Book Number: 0-8092-2793-2

99 00 01 02 03 04 VG 17 16 15 14 13 12 11 10 9 8 7 6 5 4 3 2

Contents

THE EARLY PHASE OF DIVORCE

Considering Divorce 3
In which Leila's big sister, Terri, age eleven,
confirms Leila's fear that something is wrong

Long before any formal statement is made to the children that their
parents are going to separate, most kids have sensed that something
is wrong, even if they don't understand what it is. In these diaries
the little sister is concerned because of the atmosphere in the
house, but her mother is unsure whether to say anything since no

decisions about separation have been made. The commentary deals with the problems of staying together after the marriage is over emotionally, and how children perceive this limbo period.

Once the decision to separate or divorce has been made, parents find they face a difficult choice: deciding who else has to know and when they get told—before or after the children? The diaries reveal the pain and anguish that occur when a child discovers her parents' secret. The commentary offers guidance on how to build peer and adult support for your children without immediately revealing the divorce, ways to marshal the interest of grandparents and relatives, and suggestions for constructing a list of the other people who should be told before or immediately after the children are told.

Parents often seek to shield the children from the reality of the situation in order to spare them pain. The child's diary exposes the difficulties of being told half-truths. The commentary explains why many of the words intended as reassurance can actually increase anxiety in children and decrease their trust in their parents. We focus specifically on how to handle the period of uncertainty while parents come to a settlement agreement.

Actually telling a child that one parent is going to leave the family home and live elsewhere is an event parents dread. However, it is far better than having the child experience an abrupt departure of one parent without warning. The child's diary expresses her fears on hearing the news while her father grapples with indecision about exactly how much to say. The commentary stresses the importance of what to say, when to say it, and how to plan the sequence of events so that both parents are prepared to meet the children's needs at this difficult time.

A child's description of her reactions to the gift of an expensive mountain bike reveals the mixed emotions many children feel when a parent appears to have used a present as a bribe. The commentary focuses on the pitfalls of buying too much and doing too much for children, especially in the early stages of divorce when they are particularly needy of reassurance and nurture.

Children often think it may be their fault that their parents are separating. Thinking of this sort is shown in a son's diary questioning whether his staying up late to watch television precipitated the argument that led to his dad's leaving. This chapter explains the different ways that children come to believe they are at fault and offers suggestions to enable parents to discuss these feelings in a constructive manner.

In this diary the child voices her annoyance with the visitation plan. The commentary highlights the pitfalls of accepting a visitation arrangement in which time with the children is allocated in short blocks. The experience of children and adults is that short visits often cause more frustration than pleasure. In constructing a schedule, we encourage parents to objectively consider whose emotional and physical needs are being served by the allocation of visitation time.

8 Creating a Schedule

In which Ellen, age twelve, can't anticipate what visitation schedule would work best for her

The diaries show that kids and parents often view the utility and fairness of schedules differently. The commentary describes how a schedule can evolve. We offer general guidelines as well as specific considerations to be weighed for individual children, combined with suggestions for managing the complications of melding the requests of multiple children with the valid needs of parents for space and time. The chapter concludes with the pros and cons of examples of schedules that have worked for other families.

9 Handovers

In which fifteen-year-old Ryan tells what he would like to happen on Friday nights when Mom picks up the kids

The child's diary describes the traditional handover of children from one parent to the other in a face-to-face situation at the house where the children live most of the time. Both diaries make it plain why this is rarely the ideal method and why it complicates the overall transition from the care of one parent to the other. In the commentary, specific suggestions are made as to the time and place of handovers.

0 Transitions

In which Amanda, age eight, describes what happens when Dad returns them to Mom after a visit

Even a whole weekend visit may seem short for parents and children if the transitions from one home to the other are emotionally unsettling. This daughter has come to realize that it takes her time to adjust to being at her father's, so their quality time together is really less than a day. Just as she is beginning to enjoy herself, it is time to go—an event she has come to dread as her younger brother invariably cries and creates a scene when Dad leaves them back at Mom's. Finding a way to make transitions go smoothly and learning to optimize transition times are critical to making the most out of time together. The commentary describes ways to decrease the tension during the period of adjustment and why, from the child's perspective, these work.

11 Telephoning Home   89
In which ten-year-old Sarah wants to call Mom
from Dad's house

After a mutually enjoyable day, a daughter unexpectedly wants to call home to her mother. The intrusion into their time together irritates the father and precipitates a situation in which the daughter wants to go home but her brother does not. The commentary examines whose needs are being served by these telephone calls and encourages the setting up of ground rules in order to maintain the rhythm of the visit. When, and when not, to give in to a child's request to go home is discussed.

12 Why Not on Thursdays?   97
In which nine-year-old Larry talks about Dad's
one-night stand

The exposure of the children to the dating behavior of one parent frequently results in increased animosity between the parents, which in turn can jeopardize the negotiation of an equitable divorce agreement. These diaries illustrate how differently a child and his mother react to his father's one-night stand. The commentary stresses the importance of protecting children from their parents' sexual experimentations and suggests how each parent can do a better job in looking after the best interests of the children.

THE MIDDLE PHASE OF DIVORCE

Keeping in touch with your kids' rapidly changing plans is never easy. Accommodating changes when you only see them sporadically is even harder. This commentary deals with the pros and cons of different communication mechanisms and points out the advantages of having phone, fax, and E-mail available to you and your children.

Just about every parent has been awakened in the middle of the night by a child frightened by a dream, and both have ended up sleeping in the parent's bed or the child's bed. Nurturing behaviors considered natural and comforting before the divorce, however, may now precipitate suspicion and criticism from other adults. This father, concerned about appearances, refuses to let his daughter sleep in his bed. She is unable to understand why what was previously acceptable is now not allowed by her father while still encouraged with her mother. In the commentary, we explore the ease with which normal nurturing activities can be misinterpreted and the problems this can cause for single parents raising children of opposite genders.

At birthdays, neither parent wants to be left out of the celebration. Since birthdays are often celebrated on an occasion other than "the day," unlike Christmas or Thanksgiving, two separate birthday parties would appear to be the answer. As the diaries reveal, however, two parties are not always better than one. In the commentary, we explore the reasons for this and how special days can be celebrated differently after divorce.

Every parent wonders whether, following a divorce, it is better to move with the children and start in a place with no negative memories or to stay in the family home. Often the economic consequences of the decision take priority. The commentary looks at the pros and cons of moving, from the logistic, emotional, and financial points of view of all concerned.

Grandparents, friends, teachers, and neighbors often form an extended family for children involved in divorce. The diary reveals the support and insight this boy gains from his grandparent's non-judgmental listening to his concerns and questions. This is contrasted with the pain and turmoil he feels when other family members take sides and defend one parent or the other. The commentary highlights the advantages to children when grandparents play a constructive role, even when these relationships may limit parent-child time together.

In many divorces, the communication between parents becomes strained and infrequent. In this diary a daughter describes the anguish she feels when once again she gets caught between her parents. While a parent may believe that the child's attempts to get more financial support or to change the schedule may be successful when other approaches have failed, the commentary delineates the pressures and ambivalence children must bear when asked to be a messenger. We offer alternatives to using children as pawns in parental struggles.

Older children are often exquisitely sensitive to the emotional reactions of each parent and may seek to protect a parent from pain or disappointment. When they have an especially wonderful weekend with their father, Kevin's sister asks her brother not to tell their mother. He is unable to keep his adventures secret, kindling an embarrassing situation for everyone. The commentary focuses on the problems caused when children are asked to keep secrets from either parent. It examines the distrust that ensues and the conflict children feel when their own happiness causes adult resentment or serves to incite further parental hostility.

This daughter relates the saga of her brother's visits to the psychologist, beginning with his problems at school and ending with his increasing resistance. His father reveals the reasons why many parents are ambivalent about turning to professional help. The commentary includes a discussion of the positive role mental-health professionals can play in helping families and the importance of setting goals for therapy.

Last-minute cancellations are devastating to children who are
eagerly anticipating a visit and are disruptive to the parent home
with the child. This diary describes both mother and child's reaction to the father's last-minute call. The commentary helps devise
ways of avoiding this occurrence and ways to minimize the damage
caused by unanticipated changes in the schedule.

THE LATE PHASE OF DIVORCE

Children often believe the signing of a document will somehow
remove uncertainty from their lives, and they are puzzled when
they find parents don't always agree on what it says in the divorce
decree. This boy, like many of his peers, wants to see for himself
what it says about finances (who is paying for extracurricular activities or college) and who has the ability to change the visitation
schedule. The reasons for having a plain English (as opposed to a
legalese) version of the document to show children and the ways
this can help them adapt to the reality of the divorce are the major
topics of the commentary.

For kids, one of the most puzzling and exasperating results of the
divorce is that frequently, for the purposes of organizing the schedule, the children are lumped together as a homogeneous group,
irrespective of their ages and needs. From the children's point of
view, there are good reasons to individualize the schedule. The

commentary is based on this child-oriented perspective. It offers suggestions as to how to make schedules flexible and meld the needs of different children with the time and work commitments of parents. The diary reveals why many of these changes come about at the instigation of children, and why they serve to benefit all the siblings, not just one individual.

24 Assuming New Responsibilities 191
In which sixteen-year-old Judy wonders how she'll resolve the conflict between her social life and her home life

Divorce brings many changes in the roles individuals play in the family. This daughter appreciates the opportunity to take on new responsibilities that she feels have helped her become more prepared to be a parent and a self-sufficient adult. Increasingly, however, she feels taken for granted and realizes that her desire for a social life means she can no longer contribute to the household as fully as her mother would like. The commentary looks at ways children can gain self-confidence by making contributions to keeping the household functioning; it also identifies the signs that indicate a child is being overburdened and likely to become resentful.

25 Sleep-Over at Dad's 197
In which Lizzie, age fourteen, faces the social stigma of divorce

Having become comfortable with the back-and-forth visitation over the previous three years, this teenager is ready to reveal to her friends that her parents no longer live together—by having a sleepover at her father's. Stunned by the reluctance of her friends' parents to let them come, she realizes new aspects of the stigma surrounding divorce and the prejudices involved. The commentary acknowledges society's suspicion of single fathers and deals with how to help children anticipate the prejudices they will encounter.

Following a divorce, parents often find there are barriers to being involved in a child's interests and activities—beyond the time and money necessary. This daughter is hurt when she misinterprets her father's reluctance to attend her ballet class as a lack of support for her favorite activity. The commentary directly addresses the gender bias that many men who take a significant parenting role face and points out how to turn this situation to their advantage.

This teenager has a hard time accepting the ways his father spends money while his mother is desperately trying to save for the future. When the economic status of each parent differs dramatically, children are often uncomfortable with the disparity. The commentary discusses what children would see as fair and cautions against either parent behaving in an ostentatious manner if the other parent is not equally advantaged.

Sooner or later most divorced adults are faced with the challenge of introducing their girlfriend or boyfriend to their children. At what stage in the relationship this should occur and how it can be done with the least acting-out from the children is discussed in the commentary. In this diary Robert describes some of his ambivalent feelings toward his dad's girlfriend and what helped the introductory weekend go well.

Being compared to a person your parent despises is never a positive experience. When that person is your other parent, it sets up multiple loyalty issues. Ted is both angry at his mom for failing to see his positive attributes and at his father for having so many shortcomings. Tempting as it is to compare your children with the absent parent, the commentary speaks to the harm it does to the child's self-esteem and both parent-child relationships.

In this diary a teenage girl explains why she no longer wants to be made to visit with her father and why she thinks she should be allowed to make her own decisions. Her mother, while sympathetic, is ambivalent about letting her stay home, as she herself has made other plans. Reasons for visitation refusal are explored in the commentary and advice is offered as to how to decrease the chances of this happening with your child.

This teenager voices the problem many teenagers face: that of knowing how and when to break up with a girlfriend or boyfriend. Raising this issue with his divorced parents brings up all sorts of conflicts for him and them. The commentary advises talking about values and relationships with your children before a teenage crisis precipitates an awkward situation.

32 **The Disappearing Parent** 251
In which Sam, age ten, wonders why Dad has gone to Las
Vegas and hasn't come back after two weeks

Many parents, especially men, end up abandoning their children, emotionally and financially. This ten-year-old tries not to believe it is possible that his father is not coming back for him, while his mother sees it as a predictable continuation of his irresponsible behavior. The commentary, while sympathizing with the urge to get away and start a new life without the hassles of visitation and child support, strongly opposes this action as a solution to divorce frustration and looks at the long-term consequences for the children concerned.

33 **Long-Distance Parenting** 257
In which Tom, age seven, arrives with his reluctant siblings
for a summer vacation with Dad

The difficulties of maintaining a quality relationship with the children when a parent lives out of state or overseas are acknowledged in the commentary. Suggestions for maintaining maximum contact during the year are given and ideas for projects that can be carried on over a distance are offered. The diaries highlight that it takes time, patience, and work to re-establish a comfortable "family atmosphere" after being apart for long periods of time.

Preface

The Rights of Children of Divorce

This book is predicated on our belief that your children deserve:

- Lasting relationships with both parents
- Number-one status in their parents' lives
- Parental cooperation throughout the divorce
- Truthful answers to their questions
- Relief from feelings of guilt and blame
- Freedom from interparental hostility
- Attention to their thoughts and feelings
- Input into the visitation schedule
- Privacy in communication with family and friends
- No displacement by competing relationships
- No requirement to "parent" their parents
- Freedom from the role of messenger
- No coercion to keep secrets
- An understanding of the divorce agreement

Jennifer M. Lewis, M.D.
William A. H. Sammons, M.D.

Acknowledgments

This book could not have been written without the help, advice, and support of our patients, colleagues, families, and friends.

We would like to extend our special thanks to our respective spouses, Carol White-Sammons and John Doggett for their patience and support; and to our uniquely wonderful children Red Sammons, Emma Doggett, and Rebecca Doggett who carry energy, wisdom, and love with them wherever they go. We also wish to thank our own parents, who taught us to value family closeness, communication, and the importance of having two parents who continue to love and believe in their children.

We are especially grateful to our literary agent, Deborah Grosvenor, and to our editor, Kara Leverte, for seeing the value in this project; to Nancy Sommers for her personal support; and to Aaron Kula, Susan Cammer, Joan Bachrach, Rick King, Sarah King, Elaine Putnam, and

Irene George for their thoughtful comments on the manuscript and personal insights into the experiences of divorcing mothers, fathers, and their children.

Jennifer M. Lewis, M.D.
William A. H. Sammons, M.D.

Introduction

Don't Divorce Your Children is a book about the ups and downs of parenting before, during, and after divorce. It celebrates the joys you can garner from lifelong relationships with your children and illustrates how to nurture those relationships with all the strength and energy you can muster. This book will be invaluable whether you are thinking about separating from your spouse, are already negotiating a divorce agreement, or are many years past the divorce itself. It is a book you can turn to for advice whether your children are toddlers or teenagers; whether you loathe the sight of your ex-partner or are on amicable terms. If you are looking for help with solving problems and minimizing the negative consequences of divorce on your children, this is the book that you need.

Children's Rights and Children's Needs

We have written this book on behalf of the children of divorce. As consultants in developmental and behavioral pediatrics, our experience tells us that children express themselves eloquently through their actions and behavior, but not always through their words. For the past twenty years, in our pediatric practices, we have been children's interpreters—to their parents, their teachers, and their peers. Writing this book constitutes a continuation of that role. This book shares with you the information and wisdom we have gained through these interactions with parents and children.

Over time, we have become increasingly aware of the difficulty divorced parents have in recognizing the needs of their children as separate and different from their own. Parents are understandably self-absorbed for months or years, before and after the divorce. Drawing on our understanding of child development and our experience, we have constructed a list of children's rights, which are the cornerstone of our thinking. Recognizing these rights is the key to healthy and joyful post-divorce relationships with your children.

The goal of this book is to help you help your children by increasing your understanding of the pressures all children feel—irrespective of their chronological age: their helplessness to change the family situation; their anger and sadness at their plight; their need for consistent, contingent, and responsive parenting; and their desire to have their questions answered honestly and their suggestions taken seriously. Throughout the book we will explain your children's behaviors, thoughts, and feelings; examine how your children perceive parental behavior; and discuss in what ways you need to change your behavior when things are not going well. Where appropriate, we draw certain distinctions by age or sex of the child. Our emphasis, however, is less on handing out simplistic recipes for your behavior based on your child's age or gender and more on illustrating a consistent approach to making decisions that will work effectively, whether your child is male or female, four or fourteen.

Parents' Questions

Don't Divorce Your Children addresses the questions that many of you think about every day: "Where are my children now?" "Should I phone them or wait for them to phone me?" "What can I do to make them happier?" To fathers and mothers who have never stood in your shoes, these may seem like the sort of humdrum questions any parent might be called upon to resolve; but as a divorced or divorcing parent, you know that in your current life situation the most mundane problems or worries take on added emotional significance and poignancy. This book will answer your questions, resolve lingering doubts, and offer useful advice. We have put before you the spectrum of problems and dilemmas that we have seen affect divorcing families. We have also described to you the thoughts and feelings of the adults and children we have worked with. As every marriage is different, so is every divorce. You can learn from others and learn from us, but we believe you will learn the most from examining your, and your own children's, responses to daily events.

How This Book Is Set Up

In recognition of how different the perspectives of parents and children can be and how critical it is to understand the other's point of view, each chapter comprises paired diary entries of a child and a parent writing about the same event, followed by a discussion of the issues raised, and our recommendations for handling the events described. These diary entries are not taken from actual journals; instead, they reflect our compilation of the experiences our patients have shared with us. As children under the age of ten usually do not express themselves coherently in writing, the diary format may appear to have limited us to only describing the feelings and points of view of children above this age. This is not the case. Although the viewpoints of young children are sometimes poorly articulated, we are convinced, from watching their behavior and listening to them talk, that they are struggling with many of the same issues their older siblings are. We have therefore taken the liberty of composing diary entries on their behalf, reflecting how they think, rather than how they write. The insights you will gain from reading the children's diaries in *Don't Divorce Your Children* will help you be appropriately responsive to even your youngest children's needs.

So that this book should be relevant whether you are male or female, the residential or the nonresidential parent, approximately half the parents' diaries are written by fathers, the other half by mothers. In the great majority of divorces, women assume the burden of becoming the residential parent. They are expected to manage the stress of single parenting, while coping with the economic hardship and emotional turmoil that frequently follow the separation. This constellation of responsibilities can feel overwhelming and unfair. Fathers face a different, but equally challenging, situation. Men are often thrust into an unfamiliar emotional and practical parenting role that they find daunting, whether they are active co-parents or periodic "visitors." They receive little support and are frequently discouraged by their inability to play a "real" father role. By giving voice to both points of view, we wish to highlight mothers' and fathers' problems and stress the importance of both parents staying actively involved with their children. We want to encourage fathers and mothers to understand the separate, but pivotal, roles they each play and to realize that it is essential that both maintain a positive, caring involvement in their children's lives.

Because day-to-day events frequently demand rapid decisions, we have used an events-based approach in this book so you can quickly find the answers to the problems you need to solve. You do not have to read *Don't Divorce Your Children* from start to finish or the chapters in any particular order. By scanning the titles and the short summaries provided in the Table of Contents, you will easily locate the chapters relevant to your questions. Each chapter is self-contained and readable in about ten minutes. The answers and advice you are searching for are incorporated in the discussion sections, and practical guidelines are offered at the end of each chapter.

Although you will pick and choose the chapters you read, no chapters are irrelevant. For example, "Sharing Dad's Bed" (Chapter 14) may not seem, at first glance, to apply to your family—either because you don't have a little girl that age or she doesn't climb into bed with you—but, although the specifics of the event may not seem pertinent, the points discussed are universally relevant. The chapter is not merely about an eight-year-old daughter wanting to climb into bed with her daddy after a nightmare; it is also about all children's need for security, the parent as nurturer, defensive fathering, fear of criticism, and the significance of family rituals. So, even if the event in a given chapter is foreign to your experience, you will find that the emotions and feelings will not seem alien. Through event-based chapters, we will help you focus on behaviors, your own and your children's, and relate these back to the primary goal of the book—to help you help your children thrive, despite the painful experiences of divorce.

We believe strongly in the ability and desire of parents to maintain positive relationships with their children. Parents may want to divorce each other, but they seldom want a divorce from their kids. To avoid this sad and not infrequent event, the parent-child relationship needs to be cared for and to be nurtured. *Don't Divorce Your Children* will be invaluable because it is not just about problem solving but also problem avoiding. In this book, we wish to affirm that your experience has much in common with that of other divorcing parents and, at the same time, offer insights that will allow you to apply our advice to your unique situation.

This book will help you, as a divorcing parent, to:

- share the experience we have gained counseling hundreds of families negotiating divorce,
- look at common events and issues from your children's points of view,
- realize in what ways all the "players" in the divorce drama are affected differently by the same event,
- access helpful advice in a short time, without reading the book cover to cover,
- focus on how to avoid problems rather than merely react to them,
- use suggestions that are practical, anticipatory, and sufficiently thoughtful to match the complex situations you face every day, and
- make decisions that truly serve your children's best interests.

We encourage you to explore this book with an open mind. Read it for information, read it for advice, but, most of all, read it for the sake of your children.

Don't Divorce Your Children

The Early
Phase of
Divorce

Considering Divorce

In which Leila's big sister, Terri, age eleven,
confirms Leila's fear that something is wrong

Child's Point of View: What Is Really Going On?

I had the best day yesterday. Everyone said, "Leila, you were great!" I was the fairy godmother in *Cinderella* and got to wear Aunt Fran's confirmation dress, which she decorated with pink and purple sequins. I sang a solo and didn't even mess up, like I did in rehearsal! Mom and Dad and Terri came, and they said I was the best singer and they were so proud of me. They even phoned Aunt Fran in California to tell her how awesome I was.

But today everything seems different. Mom and Dad are back to not talking to each other, and I'm not sure whether I'm supposed to just hang out in my room or whether I dare ask them to take me to the park to meet my friends. I asked Terri and she said we should try not to annoy them, and then she said something I didn't really understand. Something about hearing them, through the wall of her bedroom, shouting and then crying. I asked who was crying and she said "Both." I've never seen Daddy cry, but I think Mom was crying last week when I went down to tell her I couldn't sleep. I don't think anyone died or anything serious like that, but I must admit, everyone in the house has been acting strange recently . . . except me!

Parent's Point of View: Why Tell the Kids Now?

Terri knows I'm having an affair. I'm sure of it. I sense she is really angry with me, even though she's been extra helpful around the house and overpolite for the past few weeks. I'm not sure how she could have found out. Maybe she saw me with Larry the night he brought me home when Bob was away, or maybe she has overheard the telephone calls I make when I'm "working" in my sewing room. When she's around, Larry and I have tried to be very careful not to look too friendly, but I'm not sure my acting ability is as good as Leila's.

I feel so guilty tonight. Leila was terrific in the musical and so proud to be performing for her whole family. Watching her, I couldn't help wondering how I would tell her Bob and I are splitting up. When we got home, she was bubbling with excitement, and even unemotional Bob hugged her and told her how proud he was. Then we went to bed. I was tired and just wanted to go to sleep, but there followed the nightly argument I dread. Bob became angry and verbally abusive, and all my doubts about whether I should leave him melted away. Now he's sulking and refusing to talk with me. Goodness knows what Leila makes of all this. She's been so bound up in the play I'm not sure whether she's noticed the atmosphere in the house lately. If not, why would I burst her bubble? Maybe I should wait a bit longer before telling her. She's so little and innocent; what's happening is not going to make any sense to her. After all, she just thinks of Larry as her soccer coach.

Making Sense of It All

Children, like Terri, know their parents are considering divorce long before their parents tell them. No matter how well their parents try to keep everything hidden, children rarely miss all the cues that occur as adults go through the process of deciding whether to split up or stay together. Most parents think that the "real" effects of the divorce commence at the time they tell the children that they've made the decision. That is far from reality. Often the children have been making adjustments to the unraveling of the marriage for months or years. Even in marriages ostensibly suddenly torn asunder by infidelity, like the one in the diaries, the children have been coping for some time with the parental coldness and disharmony that leads to or results from an extramarital affair.

That's not to say the children are prepared. Even a sophisticated eleven-year-old like Terri cannot envision all the changes this parental discord will bring to her life. Few, if any, children want to see their parents split up, so they cry when told or sit in stunned silence. Their personal reactions are idiosyncratic, based on more than fear of the unknown or a sense of abandonment. Many children devote serious effort to keeping everyone together and are determined to succeed despite what their parents say. Like Terri, many children become more cooperative and extra helpful. Some are more direct: they beg their parents not to split up and try to make both parents feel guilty. Especially in families where parents have drifted into cool disregard of each other, children may test all the limits and act out negatively in ways designed to elicit attention. Younger children are less manipulative, but their behavior can regress and they may start bed-wetting and thumb sucking.

Occasionally children's actions mobilize parents to address their differences in positive ways. Sometimes children may influence wavering parents to seek further counseling when they come face-to-face with the realities of their children's reactions and what life will be like after the divorce. More frequently, parents decide to stay together out of guilt, out of unwillingness to face the financial costs and losses of divorce, or "for the sake of the children." In the latter case, their children not only realize a certain sense of power, but seek to strengthen their feelings of being in control by taking on the considerable burden of trying to maintain the couple's happiness. If and when these laudatory efforts fail, however, there are inevitable feelings of responsibility for the breakup (see Chapter 6).

Guilt feelings are only one of many problems for children when parents split up after staying "too long" in an unhappy marriage. We think that no one should separate precipitously and without consulting professional help, but too many children have related to us the dismal stories of living for years with parents who have no positive feelings for each other, or worse, who are physically and/or verbally abusive to each other. The kids are subjected to endless "pretenses," lies, and unpleasant discoveries. They are inevitably recruited as confidants to hear about the shortcomings of the other parent or to "approve" affairs. The erosion of trust and security caused by such parental behavior may be as harmful as the negative effects of a divorce itself, especially if the pretending drags on for years. Parents may convince themselves they are still acting in the children's best interests, but such self-serving arguments are frequently delusions. Parents are merely giving in to their need to be needed, trying to avoid the loneliness they believe will be part of the divorce, or refusing to jeopardize the sense of personal validity they derive from having the child as an ally.

Such a "for the children" arrangement leaves many parents feeling virtuous, even though they remain less than happy or satisfied with their own personal lives. No doubt they want to do the right thing for their children, but what they create is a treacherous limbo state. Looking back, many children have told us they hated that time most of all. Uncertainty about the future, and hence, the inability to adapt, creates anxiety that no parental reassurance will assuage. Once the marriage is to the point where nights are consumed by parental hostility and arguments, when surreptitious or angry conversations after the kids have gone to bed are frequent, when affairs are acknowledged to other people or each other, be assured the kids are paying a price.

Some parents who openly admit they no longer wish to cohabit choose to separate while remaining married. Separations, especially ones purportedly "to get back together," often merely perpetuate the limbo state, although they do give an opportunity to test out the realities of living apart. More than one perceptive child has said, "My parents can't get back together if they don't see or talk with one another—or if they just argue about money." Unfortunately, many separations are not constructive, but get consumed in endless manipulations for financial advantage or become a contest to win over the affections of the children.

There is nothing parents can do to protect children from all the pain involved in going through a divorce. Even the prospect of divorce brings sadness. Many children retreat into a shell; their emotions are muted, but punctuated by occasional outbursts. Often when the parents try to induce the reluctant children to talk, the kids flare out with angry protests, especially if they know one parent hasn't been telling them the truth. Faced with an unhappy child, many parents want to reduce their own guilt, and they end up blaming the other parent for causing the divorce, thus precipitating a loyalty crisis for the child. This usually achieves the opposite of the desired effect: a burst of anger directed at the parent who encouraged talking, rather than the parent who is being criticized. On the other hand, when children are sensitively helped to share their feelings, and blame is not a major element of the parental dialogue, emotions can be soothed and children are helped to adapt.

Most adults go through a multistage process when pondering divorce:

1. Emotional distance when affairs or the attainment of career goals seem to provide the necessary balance to enable the marriage to continue.
2. A period of careful calculations of the financial costs and weighing the prospects, good and bad, of living alone.
3. A decision to separate with consideration of whether and when to tell the kids. This phase may overlap or precede the wrangle of trying to work out the details of custody, support, visitation, long-term financial obligations, etc.

While children shouldn't be part of making the emotional decision to end the marriage, when parents are at the stage of contemplating whether the financial costs are worth it, you can assume the kids "know" at some level. Then it's likely to be time to tell the truth, especially if challenged, before the children hear the news through the grapevine (see Chapter 4).

General Guidelines

When a marriage is emotionally strained to the point where divorce is being considered, it's a tough time for everyone in the family, including the children. You can make this a very trying time for the kids, or you can minimize the demands on them if you are aware of the following:

- You will face less distrust and resentment in the future if you always tell the truth. Half-truths and white lies will come back to haunt you.
- Open arguments and hostility create loyalty conflicts. These induce most children to take on the burden of making things better for one parent or the other. Coolness, distance, or lack of caring between parents has an identical effect. If children fail in their peacemaking efforts, they then live with profound guilt feelings, convinced the divorce is their fault.
- If you're having repeated serious discussions after the kids' bedtime, you can be assured that any child over the age of five knows the gist of what is being said. They rarely fail to notice late night arguments or your telephone conversations with friends, even though you think they're totally preoccupied with the television or some other activity. Early in the morning may be a "safer" time to try to work things out, since kids seem to rarely overhear conversations at 5:00 A.M.
- Any parent feels confused, alone, threatened, and concerned about "losing the kids" when divorce is an imminent prospect. It's supporting and flattering to have the children suddenly behave better, be more affectionate, or want to spend more time with you, but don't forget they are doing this because they "know," even though they haven't been "told."
- Telling children the bad news as a sudden confession, in a fit of anger, or a bout of self-pity is as inappropriate as letting them find out from a source other than yourselves.

Whom Do You Tell, and Why?

In which nine-year-old Jenny discovers the big
secret her parents have been keeping from her

Child's Point of View:
Why Am I the Last to Know?

I just want to throw up. I thought Allison was my best friend, but now I hate her. During recess today she was hanging out with Annie and Lindsay, so I went over to join them. When I appeared, they stopped talking and started to walk away. I got really mad when they wouldn't say what they had been talking about. I said I thought it was bad of them to plan things without me and keep secrets, and I said I was going to tell Mrs. Brown that they were being mean. Allison said they weren't being mean and that if I wanted to know, she was talking about how she overheard her parents say my parents were getting divorced. I think I called her a liar before I burst into tears and ran to the office. I was crying so hard the principal couldn't even understand that I wanted him to call Mom at work to come pick me up.

While I was waiting for her, I kept telling myself it couldn't be true. She had told me Dad was on a business trip, and she would never lie to me. When Mom did come, she had to tell me. Dad really isn't out of town; he's looking for a new place to live. I'm so scared and so mad with everybody. I don't want to talk to Dad or Mom ever again. Why do they have to divorce? Why did Mom tell Allison's mom before she told me? Didn't she know everyone else would find out and I would look like a fool? And why did Allison have to tell everyone? I really hate her for that.

Parent's Point of View:
How Did My Daughter Find Out?

I've sometimes wondered what a traitor feels like, and now I know. This morning the principal from the school called and told me that my daughter was sitting in his office crying hysterically about a divorce. For a moment I couldn't believe it—how did she know? But that wasn't really the point. What was I going to tell her now? How was I going to tell her? I suppose I should have called Todd home from the office so we could do it together, but I was too panicked and just rushed over to the school.

When I saw Jenny's face, I felt like our relationship was changed forever. She stared at me and just kept asking if it was true. When I said, "Yes," the conversation was over. Jenny just wanted to go home, and now she's up in her room and keeps telling me to go away.

I gather from the principal that Allison must have heard her parents talking. I called Laurie and was furious with her, since she was the only person I had confided in and I really trusted her not to tell anyone. She claimed she had no idea how Allison knew. She said she hadn't even told Jim until last night when they were talking about ways they could help us . . . and then they were in their bedroom with the door closed, two hours after Allison went to bed.

I know we never should have waited this long to tell Jenny, but it didn't seem to make any sense to tell her before Todd knew where he was going to live. What a disaster! Now the school people will be mad with us because we didn't warn them, and of course the scene means it will be all over town in a flash.

Making Sense of It All

Having made the decision to separate or divorce, parents immediately face a series of difficult choices: whom to tell? For some there is a desire not to tell anybody, in the vain hope that if nobody knows, it won't happen. Others want to tell everybody, hoping that the support of friends and family will make the hurt and pain go away. Neither strategy is realistic or productive. Most adults need to talk to somebody. They initially want to reveal the impending separation to people who will support them; people who will talk about their own experiences; people who will ease their sorrow, sympathize, and reassure them that the divorce is the other person's fault. The reality is there are few friends or family members who are prepared to fill all these roles. Even when told, many choose to remain on the sidelines, hoping the crisis will blow over. This distancing can be a troubling but not uncommon experience for adults considering separation or divorce.

Friends

Because of your need to discuss your life crisis with someone other than your spouse, it is unlikely that your kids will be the first people to know; but it is important to ensure that they are not the last, and that they hear the bad news from you, their parents, not through friends or gossip. As you search about for the support you so badly need, be aware that each person with whom you share information is a walking time bomb until you tell your children. As illustrated in Jenny's diary, unfortunately children often hear either all or snippets leaked from a friend, neighbor, or family member. Gossip has a life of its own, and what adults talk about, kids overhear. If it's going to be a while before the kids know about the divorce (e.g., while new living arrangements are being put in place), confiding in friends and social acquaintances may make you feel less unhappy or alone, but be warned that word tends to spread. Whether it's your friends who say something wrong or their kids who tell, tease, or taunt your unprepared or unknowing children, that's not the way you want them to first hear the news.

Friends and family, if informed in a timely manner, can help you build the support system your children will need. Misguidedly, in anticipation of the loneliness that parents fear separation and divorce will bring, many try to become emotionally closer to their children by spending more time with them, rather than encouraging them to become more involved in outside activities. Your children, like you, need access to people who will be supportive, so try to think of the teachers, coaches, and family members with whom they have good relationships, and increase their contact with the kids. By being prepared to reveal your decision to divorce to people who will be able to extend extra time and extra attention to your children, you can provide your children with a buffer which is invaluable on those inevitable days when you are sullen and emotionally erratic. Don't forget the kids will need people to talk to and have fun with when you're not available or at your best. They need adult relationships in which they feel valued, regardless of the state of the family.

Your children will also probably want to take refuge in peer relationships. Try not to make plans that meet your own needs for time with the kids when it means that they will have less time for activities with others their own age. We've seen parents, in anticipation of the separation, very successfully set up support systems for the future by getting the kids involved in athletics, gymnastics, Brownies or Scouts, or social activities sponsored by community or peer groups. It may be better not to tell all the parents of your kids' friends what is about to happen (if you want to avoid Jenny's predicament), but do try to set up more play dates (maybe sleep-overs or weekend activities) in the weeks before and after the separation.

Family

It is often a challenge to decide when and what to tell the grandparents and other relatives. Don't be surprised if you receive less support than you hoped for from your family, especially if you are perceived to be selfish in your decision to divorce and therefore your children are being "needlessly" hurt in the process. More than one parent has been caught in an awkward situation: first becoming distraught and angry from being rejected or criticized by a family member, and then trying to answer a worried child's questions about "What happened when you talked to Grandma?" without revealing the secret of the pending separation. It is essential to tell relatives to keep their approval or disapproval of the divorce to themselves, even though they may merely be trying to support you. Remind them that you do not want your children in a loyalty bind, and you do not want negative remarks said about either parent in the presence of the kids. Taking sides in front of the children should be clearly out of bounds. Often, the most helpful people are the ones who can simply take part in child-centered activities and not look to play the role of amateur psychiatrist. Sometimes it's aunts, uncles, older cousins, or even more distant relatives who play the key roles at this time, because they feel less pressure to take sides, and they go to the ball game, the dance recital, etc., out of sheer interest in the child and for the joy of the experience.

School

Carefully consider when to inform the school. Sometimes the classroom teacher, sometimes the principal, sometimes a guidance counselor can be of invaluable support. Many schools hold informal lunch groups to talk about family issues and growing-up questions. If the school is aware of the family problems, they can encourage your child's participation before the emotional roller coaster hits. Groups such as these offer children a place to air their feelings when times get tough.

Many parents decide not to risk telling the school until they are ready to tell the children, in case the news leaks. However, teachers and school personnel often see changes in behavior and academic performance

before the children, or they, are told. If the children are reacting negatively to the emotional climate at home, uninformed teachers may
misinterpret the child's change in behavior or slipping academic performance and draw unfair conclusions. An adversarial relationship may
result at just the wrong time: when the child needs understanding,
rather than pushing. If teachers are kept in the dark as to the home situation, a poor grade or a call to conference with the teacher may be the
first warning the parents get that, while they have been keeping their
impending separation secret, their child's academic and social well-
being has been compromised. Parents, children, and teachers can be
caught in an uncomfortable situation; too late the parents realize they
have unwittingly created a problem by not keeping the school informed.

Once you have separated, it is important to communicate to the
school that, as parents, you both want to stay involved. The school
needs to duplicate all report cards, school notices, calendars, etc., and
send one to each of you, as well as make arrangements for separate
teacher conferences if necessary. Be prepared to make these requests
more than once, in person and in writing—and keep making them at
the beginning of each year so you both stay in the loop.

Day Care

Another consideration is when to make arrangements with day-care or
after-school care staff. Especially if both parents have differing work
hours or the economics of divorce force acceptance of new career
responsibilities, changes in day care have to be made and can't be left
to the last minute—there usually isn't flexibility on the part of the
provider. The current provider may not have long enough hours, or
allow pickups after 6:00 P.M., or have any way of accommodating sick
children if you can't come get them in the middle of the day. Sometimes each parent needs different drop-off and pickup times, and
providers won't accommodate that, or they may insist on charging for a
full day even if one of you can get the kids at lunchtime twice a week.
Of course, negotiating ahead opens the possibility that something will
get said to the child or a conversation with another parent will be overheard (remember the gossip mill is irresistible), so be careful to make
sure the provider knows when your child will be told and understands
the importance of keeping the information confidential.

The Workplace

What and when to tell people at work is another complicated decision. No one wants to jeopardize their job prospects while so many life changes are pending. Making people aware of family conflicts can appear to put a promotion out of reach just when your self-esteem and your wallet really need it. In competitive environments, it's natural to be concerned that fellow workers might take advantage of the demands made on you by your personal troubles. Both men and women may find themselves inappropriately propositioned and potentially compromised. On the other hand, many coworkers have gone through the experience of a divorce, and few will be so spiteful as to wish a hard time on you or your kids. Often people will help out when you need personal time for yourself or some unexpected child crisis arises. Even if you have to keep the whole thing secret for a long time, it's wise to find out what types of flexibility your company allows in terms of working at home, altering your work hours, etc. Since such specifics have had no previous relevance, many people are unaware of company policies that may turn out to be invaluable.

Places of Worship

Many families are actively involved in religious institutions, which can be called upon for spiritual guidance during times of stress. Perhaps someone you have contact with may offer to be a mediator between you and your spouse and help avoid a divorce. Even if it is difficult to approach your religious institution because it does not condone divorce, or to face the religious community's disapproval of your behavior, it is likely that individual members of the religious community will reach out to be a source of comfort and friendship to you and your kids.

When the Kids Find Out from Someone Else

Should you get caught up in the predicament of having your kids learn about the divorce from someone other than you, tell the truth right away. Clearly Jenny is feeling humiliated and angry at the indignity of being "the last to know." She already feels betrayed. Her parents have an uphill battle to recover her trust; any further deception will make it all but impossible. If you do not know what the future will bring, you should tell them that. Children will tolerate uncertainty; they will not forget lies. If possible, both parents should be present to talk with the children, since both have been complicit in the deception. Despite the sincerity of your protestations and apologies to your children, the climate in your house is likely to be quite chilly for a while. Finding out about the divorce from others is always hurtful and confusing, and can set the stage for a lifetime of distrust.

General Guidelines

Deciding whom to tell is difficult. You will want to keep the number to an absolute minimum until you find the right time to tell your children. Please keep the following guidelines in mind when you make your decisions:

- Gossip is irresistible. Once adults hear, they will inevitably talk to their friends about "the news." Children are no different. They only need to overhear a careless word and they will spread it. Sooner or later, it will circulate to your child.
- Carefully judge which family members to inform. Allegiances and affection don't always follow bloodlines.
- Without disclosing your personal reasons, it is possible to arrange more social contacts for your children with their peers and other adults who care about them or will take an interest in them, thereby broadening the kids' support network for the days ahead when they will really need it.
- Check your school's resources for ways the staff can work with you to help prepare the kids. Teachers, when informed in a timely manner, have less chance of misinterpreting new behaviors and can be a stabilizing influence.
- No matter how careful you are, once the decision to separate or divorce has been made, it's highly unlikely you can keep it secret from the kids for more than four to six weeks.

Reassuring the Children

3

In which Kim, age twelve, isn't convinced that
everything is going to be OK.

Child's Point of View:
Is Everything Really Oĸ?

I wish I had someone else to talk to besides my diary, but I can't even tell my friends what's going on, because I don't know. Every time I ask Mom, she just tells me things will be oĸ. I used to believe it, but now I'm not so sure. I know Mom thinks telling us not to worry makes me and Jonathan worry less, but she's wrong. Even though he's only six, Jonathan came into my room tonight to ask if *I* thought we were oĸ. I laughed and said, "Sure." He smiled and went back to bed. Now I feel I might have told him a lie.

I'd ask Dad—if he was ever around. Mom says he's working harder these days, but I don't think that's the whole story. I'm not sure they even sleep in the same bedroom anymore, and they never go to church together, which is real strange. Most of the time, Mom seems to be off in another world thinking about something other than what she's doing. I feel like most of the time I'm only getting half the story, and I don't know what to believe anymore. I'm almost ready to bring up the "D" word, but I know that I'll get told, "I don't want you to worry like that," or, "Dad and I will take care of everything, honey."

But everyone seems so tense. Even Jonathan, who used to be kind of fun most of the time, just sucks his thumb a lot more and sits in front of the TV. We'd all do things together and he would laugh and seem like the happiest kid in the world. Now that doesn't happen much.

It gets to me. I'm sort of floating with this vague sick-to-my-stomach feeling. Today I asked Mom what was happening, but, although she answered all the questions, I don't feel any better. I wish just being told everything is oĸ would be enough, but I still have the feeling something really awful is going to happen.

Parent's Point of View:
I Just Want to Shield the Kids

It's been about six weeks since we decided to get divorced. But that decision has generated endless additional decisions to be made.

It's pretty clear that money is going to be very tight. Too tight. John says that I could sell the house and the equity would give me a nice cushion, or else I could go back to work full-time. But how could I take time off to get Jonathan to all the physical therapy appointments he needs? I'm not sure what's best for the kids. I'm worried about making too many changes too fast.

The problem is no decision seems to be right, because every decision is based on things we don't know yet. How can John decide where he will live before we've decided whether I am going to move too? His budget depends on how much money the kids will need every month, and that determines his work schedule, so it's tough to figure out how often and for how long he will see the kids. What exactly should we tell them?

And I can't stop obsessing about how unfair all this is. I oscillate between being angry, disappointed, bitter, scared, and overwhelmed. These emotions interfere with everything, but I feel as if I should at least be able to protect the kids from some of this chaos.

Like yesterday. I had no idea how much to tell Kim when she wanted to know what was going on. She had noticed John and I didn't go to church again and asked why not. I couldn't tell her that it's because the church won't sanction divorce, so I made something up. Then she wanted to know why her father was away all the time. I told her he was working extra hard. Then she asked why I seemed like I was so spacey these days—forgetting her dental appointment and not listening to her. She was concerned that Jonathan might be getting sicker or that she'd annoyed me. I told her not to be such a worrier and tried to distract her by watching her favorite TV show with her. It didn't work. She stopped asking questions, but the last thing she said when she went up to her room was, "Are you *sure* it's going to be OK, Mommy?"

I felt like saying, "Hell, no. It's not OK." But I nodded reassuringly and tried to grin. If it hadn't been so late, I might have told her the whole story. Told her I was sure we were getting a divorce. Asked what she thought—say about moving or what she'd do if she had to choose between gymnastics and piano lessons. But although I feel guilty about not giving her a say in what's happening, it's not fair to make her a friend and confidant in this.

Right now the kids and I are caught in a nightmare. I keep hoping I'll wake up and it will all be a dream, but unfortunately it isn't.

Making Sense of It All

During times of stress and turmoil, parents want to be able to say something to make the children feel safe and secure. This need is especially pressing during periods of heightened uncertainty, such as when a parent is planning to leave the family home. Words can indeed soothe children, especially younger ones, but their effect cannot last unless subsequent actions and events validate what has been said. When the actions don't, well-intentioned statements become empty promises that lead to distrust and suspicion, even for kindergarten-age kids. Children are ruthlessly logical at these times. They can see through inconsistencies. After all, if you could really "take care of everything" or "make everything all right," then surely there wouldn't be any divorce. So what validity do these statements have? Offering superficially comforting phrases just raises their anxiety.

Moreover, the distrust is magnified if the affect that accompanies the words does not make them convincing. Parents are playing to a tough audience, as children are excellent readers of body language and easily spot the discrepancies between what you say and how you say it. Significant acting talent is required to get away with statements such as "Everything will be OK," when your life is in shambles because of a divorce (especially if you don't want one), the level of adult hatred is intolerable, or your spouse is leaving for unknown reasons or adultery. Telling the grade-schooler or the adolescent "don't worry" is fruitless when you've let them know you can't stop yawning at dinner because you're awake "thinking about things" most of the night.

Some people maintain they can put up a good front for the kids. Perhaps you can, on occasion. But don't forget the telephone conversations your children overhear, the background noise of long discussions well into the night when neither parent can agree with the other, and the constant anxiety and tension which make tempers flare at the slightest provocation. Children who are living with all that, day in and day out, watch and listen intently and pay more attention to actions than a few words, no matter how encouraging those words might be.

Unfortunately, when blanket reassurances fail to work, it is tempting to explain what is happening by putting the blame on the other parent. Opting for such a destructive strategy gives the clear message to your children that they, too, need to take sides. This is a disconcerting position to be put in, since they may well feel allegiance with the leaving parent while simultaneously feeling afraid of alienating the remaining parent on whom they depend. Children well understand the significance of taking sides. They make hard social choices every day in a world where being on the winning side seems critically important. Often they live with the consequences of a "bad" decision. So, as their family splits apart, feeling pressure to take sides and deciding which side to take increases anxiety, guilt, and stress.

When everything is not OK for you or the children, acknowledging the uncertainty which has everyone on edge is a better tactic than bland words or angry accusations. Denying their rightful concerns by frequent reiterations of "don't worry" and "everything will be OK" provides little solace when the day-to-day atmosphere of tension doesn't change. Every parent wants to believe that words like "I'll always be here for you" will relieve their children's anxiety, but the kids are not reassured if the parent is no longer "there" in the full sense of the word.

The clear goal is to end the uncertainty as soon as possible, since that lessens the need to provide empty reassurances to the children. Don't fool yourself, however, into believing that actually composing the provisions and then coming to accept the inevitable compromises in any settlement agreement is anything other than a daunting task. The emotional and practical unknowns make everything seem ambiguous; the future is blurry and feels more threatening than usual. At any given moment, personal issues are often paramount, and it is difficult to answer any question without getting mired in guilt and self-blame, or anger and denigration of the other parent. In the midst of all this confusion, many parents come to realize for the first time how different their self-interest may be from that of their children. Each adult faces many choices about how to put his or her individual life back together again. Each must decide how to combine a new single-parent role with a new social and romantic existence, while trying to develop a career that may have added importance because of the economic restrictions imposed by just about every divorce.

It is when adults need to make personal choices that are not in line with their children's preferences that the conflict over what to say intensifies. Reassurance is now not the sole appropriate response—it may, in fact, serve only to silence questions and concerns. It is important to explain to your children what you are doing and why. For example, if economic necessity dictates going back to full-time work, tell them that. Talking with them about the advantages of having more money (or more independence) and what are the possible day-care/babysitting arrangements is preferable to deceiving them right up to the last minute. They'll find out what you've done, and the cost, in terms of distrust, simply isn't worth it. Letting them have input into the situation and giving them choices among the available options will decrease their resentment.

It is important to be up-front with your children about where other significant relationships fit in your life so that you can minimize the children's fears of being displaced.

If you are involved in a relationship that is not likely to be ongoing, minimize the competition by limiting phone calls and seeing the other person when the kids are with the other parent (see Chapter 12). If a significant romantic relationship is drawing on your attention, explain to the kids that you love to be with them but need adult company too, just as they need time to spend with their friends. The conflicting demands need to be openly acknowledged and your children's displeasure addressed, hopefully by spending more time with them. This is preferable to trying to coerce children into seeing the world your way or telling them that they're overreacting when they complain they have to share you with someone else. Insisting on your point of view burdens the children with the feeling that they are obliged to support you emotionally, rather than vice versa.

If they are told the truth, children handle uncertainty and unpredictability better than adults give them credit for. If you do not know the answers to their questions, say so. Even the best-intentioned deceit does not play out well over time. In the midst of divorce, children long to be able to trust what you say. If you have had to tell them you are separating, before the details have been worked out, it is better to explain you don't yet know where you'll be living, that you don't know how much time they'll be with you and how much time will be spent with the other parent, than to gloss over their concerns. While initially awkward, these conversations present an opportunity to invite the children to say what *they* want. Including them in the process is much better than keeping them guessing from the outside, constantly wondering whether you're telling the truth or whether you really care what they think or feel.

General Guidelines

Especially when the future is uncertain:

- Children need to voice their concerns. Being told "not to worry" or "someone will always take care of you" can stifle their willingness to share their viewpoints, leaving them feeling vulnerable, rather than seeing they have some control over their lives.
- Limit reassurance to words that can match your actions and your ability to carry through with your promises.
- Kids know when you are worried; they see the changes in your behavior. Talking about your concerns makes it easier for them to talk about their feelings.
- Being a good parent does not mean you must have all the answers. Tell the truth. Fabrication, no matter how well-intentioned or how good the words sound at the moment, always leads to distrust and recrimination.
- Try to include the children in the process of building a new life. Helping them understand the dilemmas does not require making them confidants. When there are choices, letting them have a voice in certain decisions, such as where to live, gives them a sense that things really are being worked out, even when there are no simple black-and-white answers
- Don't underestimate the degree to which children think about the implications of what is happening. They worry about their own future and they worry about how each parent will manage without the other.

Remember that even long after the divorce decree has been granted, children who have come to trust in your truthfulness are more likely to want to work with you than against you.

Telling the Children

In which fifteen-year-old Sandy tells what it's like to hear only part of the truth when her parents reveal their decision to divorce

Child's Point of View:
Why Won't They Be Straight with Us?

I knew they'd do it on a weekend, but why right before the Junior
Prom and just before school ends? Couldn't they have waited just a little longer? It's not like this was earth-shattering news. Yeah, sure I
cried, and Robert blocked it all out, and Katie sat there like a statue. I
wonder what they expected, especially since Robert and I both know
each of them has had an affair in the last year—maybe still going on—
but they didn't see fit to tell us that! I kept hoping someone would
trust us enough to be straight, so I kept asking, "Why?" Dad said they
were unhappy, but that's not an incurable disease. And how many
times do the teachers in the church say to forgive and compromise
when you can't get along with someone? So "unhappy" doesn't cut it
and neither do the affairs—watching TV, it seems everyone does it
these days. I wish I'd had the nerve to tell them we know about their
"special friends."

Maybe it would be easier to accept this if we could see what was
coming next, but they seemed to be in such a rush to tell us, that
there were very few answers. It's funny because I got the impression they'd decided to do this a while ago, yet they still don't have
much figured out. It's scary to think that as of tomorrow morning,
unless he's in the office, I won't know where Dad is. I can't believe
he'll continue to sleep here. I hope he doesn't move in with another
woman. I know he said we'd see him, but where and when and how
aren't clear. Just like how they don't seem to know who will pay
for my gymnastics next year—even though they both say they want
me to do it. Where will we spend Christmas? What about birthdays? For that matter, it would be nice if they'd at least asked
where we want to live, or how often each of us might want to be
able to see Dad.

This is rotten. I don't want to feel angry, but I do. And I don't want
to cry again tomorrow morning when Dad leaves, but I will because he
won't just be leaving for work. It helps that Mom thinks this is for the
best, but maybe she'd just rather be free to be with someone else too.
Wonder when we'll get to meet these other mystery people we aren't
supposed to know about.

Parent's Point of View: How Do We Go On from Here?

I worried that this was going to be the most difficult thing I ever did, and I was right. Problem is it's only Friday night . . . and I suspect the weekend will be *long*. Actually it's almost Saturday morning and Sandy is asleep on the sofa opposite me. I don't dare disturb her, because she'll start crying again, but I don't want her to wake up alone either. It's amazing how I convinced myself the kids would understand and somehow see this was best for everyone. I practiced what I was going to say, maybe too much, since it may have sounded rehearsed to them. But there was Robert with his hands over his ears, Sandy crying, and Katie just staring at me as if she was drugged. I started out OK. Then as I talked, the enormity of what I was doing hit me.

I don't think I really said much of what I thought I should. I certainly didn't tell them about falling in love with someone else. I tried hugging them, but it didn't seem to do much good. While I don't know exactly where I'll live two weeks from now, I made it clear I wasn't going to be far away and we'll still see each other a lot—as soon as the schedule gets worked out. All three nodded yes when I asked if life wouldn't be better for them without their parents fighting all the time. But I didn't have a real good answer when Katie so plaintively asked why that meant I had to leave. If I told them the truth about loving Kathy, I feared it would sound like I love her more than them, and that's just not true.

So we watched some television. It might have been different if their mother had said more, rather than just agreeing a separation was necessary. But I do understand how uncomfortable this is for her, and at least she didn't say anything negative.

The question is where do I begin tomorrow? Should I try to make this weekend fun? I mean, why do I keep feeling like it's our last weekend together when I know it's not? Should I make plans for next weekend with them? It's not easy to say you're moving out, but then not be moving right that day. Both Ali and I wanted to let them know we are separating so we wouldn't have to go on pretending everything is fine. On the other hand, we haven't told them the whole story, so we are still guilty of being less than honest about why a divorce is inevitable now.

Making Sense of It All

Telling the kids you intend to get a divorce is one of the scariest, most arduous tasks you'll ever face; in fact, it's so daunting some parents avoid it altogether—they either leave abruptly or never follow through on the decision. Others take the "spur of the moment" approach, hoping to lessen the anxiety, their own and the children's, by minimizing the significance of the event. The majority of parents, however, understand the value of carefully considering the timing, as well as the words they use and how they say them.

Timing

For some couples, the end may be sudden and unplanned; one parent just walks out on the other, so the children are deprived of any opportunity to sit down with both parents and talk. In this situation there will need to be many explanations and reassurances when the emotional heat of the moment passes. If physical violence has been involved, it is unlikely that the traumatic events the children have witnessed or come to learn of will ever be forgiven or forgotten.

Hopefully, you will have the luxury of the challenge of *deciding* when to tell the kids. Remember, your hesitation to face them should be a catalyst to do it well, and the delay in getting up your nerve is beneficial, since you need to know certain vital facts before you sit down with them. At minimum, decide where they'll be living, where each parent will reside, and the specific ways and means (see Chapter 13) they can use to contact each parent. Having a tentative schedule of when you'll be seeing the kids over the next few months allays their concerns about the future. Being open to the modifications your children suggest gives them a feeling of having some control and indicates you're listening to their needs, not just paying attention to your own.

Finalizing plans so you have concrete information to share with the children often takes several weeks from the time the decision to separate has been made. Long delays create difficulties, since the children often observe a dramatic change in how their parents are acting. If you are markedly friendlier to each other in this interim period, telling the children you want to divorce may make little sense. During this time, parents often seek to compensate for their guilt by playing the "good guy" and easing up on discipline; letting such permissiveness go on too long will not make the adjustment to the divorce any easier. Moreover, the longer you delay, the more likely the children will "discover" your secret by overhearing a conversation or some other chance event. That can be a catastrophe (see Chapter 2).

Of course, once they've been told, many children seek to do their best to keep their parents together. The manipulation and the emotional pressure can be anguishing. So while the thought of living apart from your children may make the divorce seem hardly worthwhile, don't linger with both parents living in the same house once you've announced the separation. If you tell the children on a weekend, everything should be in place for you to begin living apart during the following week.

What to Say

Unfortunately, thinking about what to say and finding exactly the right words can be an effort which takes a lifetime. Going over it in your mind is important, but most parents find they're more comfortable if they just get the framework set and don't try to memorize every word. If your nerves won't handle that approach, perhaps write a few notes or a couple of key phrases, but don't make it sound like you're reading an official proclamation. This is, after all, a very personal moment.

The single most important element is the truth. That doesn't necessarily mean disclosing everything—if for no other reason than you will have to limit how much you say to accommodate the limited attention spans of your children. In the few minutes you've got, let them know:

- Why you are separating.
- Are you definitely getting a divorce, legally separating, or temporarily living apart? If it's either of the latter two, it's reassuring to the children to be told how you intend to work it out, and how long you think it might take before you can be more definite about what will happen to the marriage.
- What is the immediate impact on their lives? Will they stay in the same house? Which parent will live with them?
- When, how, and where will they see the parent who is moving out? How will they stay in contact?

This may be all the kids can take initially. It's common, however, regardless of the ages of the children, for the conversation to cover the substance of what happened to the relationship between Mom and Dad. Emotionally charged as the talk is likely to be, there may be tears and stony silence, but rarely anger . . . just yet. Sometimes the children's distress, or your own, may cause you to leave things unsaid, but there will be many more opportunities to fill in the blanks.

It is tempting to reassure your children that, despite the fact that as adults you have lost the love between you, you will never stop loving them. Do not be surprised if these types of statements just increase the children's distress. This frequently happens when children, following the adult quarrels of the night before, have been witness to many mornings-after filled with reassurances of "I love you, honey," only to see the quarrels resume again. Therefore, words such as "I'll love you forever" or "I'll always be here for you" are not likely to be consoling. Giving the kids a believable reason for what is happening is much more comforting, e.g., "We're tired of fighting and all our attempts to stop just don't seem to work" or "I feel lonely all the time" are much more constructive than "We just don't like each other" or "We just don't get along" (see Chapter 3).

Most adults abhor public speaking and they certainly don't like to have their performances critiqued. Unfortunately, what children often remember is not just what you said, but how you said it. They make their judgments and base their emotional reactions as much on the nonverbal cues and the subtleties of voice inflection, as on the content of the verbal statements. If you're pacing around the room and can't look them in the eye because you're so nervous, tell them honestly how you feel. You will be contending with many conflicting emotions that will affect your behavior, and it is better to explain that to your children than have them draw some very erroneous conclusions.

Nobody ever feels they do a perfect job. The children may interrupt, your spouse may interrupt. You may not end up saying what you planned, but do not lie. If you're tempted to concoct a story on the fly, if you veer off the truth in an effort to make yourself look better in their eyes, children will see through it for the elaborate scam it is. After all, it's just like the behavior of the child who adamantly says, "I didn't do it!" when you, as his parents, know he did. Children are masters at deceit; they'll know a performance when they see one.

So here are four more guidelines:

- Be succinct, simple, and clear, but be honest about your emotions because they affect how you say the words.
- Avoid blanket reassurances about the future.
- Give them a believable reason for what happened in the relationship, or why you personally made this decision.
- Stick to the truth and don't embroider in order to look like the "good guy."

Many of you may question the wisdom of these eight guidelines, especially if, as in the diaries, one or both of you are having, or have had, an affair. While this certainly increases the difficulty of talking with the children, we would argue that trying to hide an affair from them increases the risk of distrust and emotional estrangement in the long term as the children will inevitably find out the truth. At the time of telling the kids about the decision to separate, the affairs should be acknowledged. Thankfully, they are not likely to become the central point of discussion; most children will be far more concerned with what will happen to *their* lives in the future—when they will next see the parent who is leaving, whether they will have to move house, etc.,—rather than with what happened in *your* lives in the past. With younger children, the issue of infidelity, once raised, may not resurface for a long time, as it is a concept they will find hard to grasp; with kids over ten, as sex is already on their minds, the issue will most likely come up soon and require discussion in the conversations which follow the initial announcement of the separation.

In most families in which extramarital involvement has occurred prior to the separation, one of three scenarios has taken place at the time of telling the children:

1. One parent has had an affair, now over, from which the marriage could not recover;
2. Both parents have had extramarital relationships;
3. A current entanglement becomes the "reason" for the separation.

In the case of a long-dead affair, both parents would be well served to concentrate on cataloging the other reasons why they have been unable to make the marriage relationship work and the planning they have done for the future, rather than dwelling on the whys and wherefores of the extramarital relationship. However, they should not lie or obfuscate. The kids will probably not want to dwell on "past history" anyway, so there is little to be lost by acknowledging the moral lapse and moving on. At least, the risk the child will discover the truth at a later date and feel betrayed is avoided.

When both parents have had liaisons, they often collude not to raise the subject. This is a risky decision. During the process of reaching a settlement or when new relationships become part of either parent's life, the past has a way of resurfacing. When it becomes clear their parents have been less than truthful, the children's trust will decrease and emotional distance will increase dramatically. Confessing at the outset that both parents have had affairs evens the playing field and ensures that neither gets cast in the children's minds as the "victim." It also signals to the children that their parents are prepared to be honest and forthright with them, even when there is tough news to share.

The parent who is leaving for a "current" affair usually feels especially vulnerable mentioning the subject, because it leads to him or her being cast as the "bad guy," and raises fears in the kids that they too will be displaced by this intruder, i.e., "If it happened to Mom/Dad, it can happen to me." Failing to mention the outside relationship, however, will only heighten the sense of betrayal when the affair is eventually revealed, especially if that happens in an angry outburst by the other parent. So confess the affair when you tell the kids you are moving out, and be prepared to spend time answering the questions generated, e.g., "How could you do this to Mom/Dad?" "Do you love him/her more than us?" "Why is she/he better?" "When do we meet the mystery person?"

It may be painful for your spouse to listen to your answers. Especially if the older kids are asking probing or sexually oriented questions, you can minimize friction with the other parent by answering these questions alone. Try to reduce the backlash from the children by avoiding direct comparisons of your lover with their betrayed parent. Focusing on what you've learned about yourself and what you feel, rather than comparing the attributes of one person with another, puts less pressure on the kids to defend the parent who is being left and may save you embarrassment if this relationship does not endure (more than 80 percent do fail when they are suddenly "for real" and no longer "an affair").

Of course, the responsible course of action, from your spouse and children's points of view, is to end the affair. Ending the affair frees you up to reflect on the priorities in your life and where your children fit in. It also avoids engendering acts of hostile retribution that occur when a spouse is abandoned or "traded in" for someone else (see Chapter 12). If you can keep focused on helping the children through this precarious time, you will, by putting their needs above your own, earn their trust and maybe forgiveness. If you are unwilling to give up the affair, you need to ensure the children do not need to compete with him or her for your attention and love (see Chapter 12).

Even if you have been faithful in your marriage and are truly the "wronged" party, it does not release you from the responsibility to help the children through these explanations. While you may voice your feelings of anger, betrayal, resentment, and loneliness, that does not give you the latitude to indulge in character assassination, even if you make it part of a lesson to your children about the importance of honesty and morality in their lives. Rest assured your children will come to recognize the irresponsibility, emotional shallowness, etc., of the other parent, if that is the case, without your prompting. In the long run, they will be grateful to you for letting them come to their own conclusions in their own time, rather than making them side with you.

Who Speaks and Where

Whatever your personal reasons, we have found the best way to tell the children that you are separating is for both parents to do it together. This keeps the conversation focused and minimizes acting out, by the adults or the children. Presenting them with a joint decision tends to minimize their own feelings of being at fault and allows both parents to serve as comforters. This approach requires fairly congruent versions of the truth, so make sure you and your spouse agree what is to be said. At least, a joint session minimizes the temptation to get into conflicts about who is the "good guy" and who is the "bad guy." Our experience has shown that a joint session does not change the number or nature of the questions asked.

Given the likelihood that tears will be shed and emotions exposed, most families choose to tell the children at home. Who should begin is problematic. If the person initiating the divorce is also the person who will be moving to a new location, it usually goes smoother if that person begins. Being first may feel like asking to take more of the blame, but that's where what you say, how you say it, and the future planning you've done become so important.

The Sequence

This initial conversation is often quite short. Many children don't want to hear it all. Even carefully crafted words seem inadequate, and either tears intervene or the silence from the listeners becomes too much to bear. We'd therefore suggest approaching this initial conversation with the understanding that multiple subsequent conversations will be necessary. The weekend is the most likely time to be able to stay available for questions and concerns. Beginning the conversations on Friday night can lead to a tumultuous evening and a sleepless night for everyone. We suggest waiting for Saturday morning, though we know you may lie awake in anticipation.

Following the initial announcement, everyone will probably need a break; generally no more than an hour. How you then spend your time is determined by the best way(s) to fill in the gaps for the children. Even when the kids are very close in age (hence, at the same cognitive level), each child goes through an individual process because of the differences in emotional reactions. Often, the parent who is leaving will spend the rest of Saturday morning with all the kids, trying to answer the general questions. Hopefully, that parent will be prepared to give the same answer many times over about how to be reached and the new living arrangements. Each child may need the same facts phrased in a slightly different way.

Lunchtime then forces another break, and during the afternoon parents can spend time talking with each child individually. While parents may be able to do the morning together, it is often emotionally impossible to continue as a group throughout the afternoon, and many children are freer to ask questions when talking with a single parent. Both parents need to be flexible. They must try to remain available for any child as there is likely to be some back-and-forth as kids look for hopeful signs that this decision can be reversed or test to see whether each parent is saying the same thing. The temptation to have Saturday night together for "old times' sake" may be strong, but fireworks are as likely as the pleasant remembrances of happier times.

Actually, that closeness more often comes on Sunday. The parent who is leaving may take all the kids out on an activity (although no one should be coerced into going) and can then spend the latter part of the afternoon talking with individuals, especially if one child is having more problems adjusting. At the end of the day, everyone typically wants to have a last meal together. Unfortunately, often the parent who is leaving begins to feel like an outsider and retreats to pack or make other arrangements. Meanwhile, the children and the residential parent try to figure out the days ahead, and the kids often get a more complete rendition of that person's side of things.

In the days after one parent moves out, contact is critical. Everyone is lonely. Some children withdraw, and at least making the attempt to call or see them in some neutral spot is well worthwhile—but often, going back to the house just triggers more tears and kindles fantasies that won't be fulfilled. Certainly make definite plans to do something with the children no later than the next weekend, remembering that if the visit is too short it can be frustrating, especially if two or more kids are seeking attention, explanations, and clarification of future plans.

General Guidelines

- Telling the kids about your decision may be the most important performance in your life. Take the time to think about it and make the necessary preparations to answer their questions about living arrangements; continuing contact; and when they're going to next see, and how often thereafter they'll spend time with, the parent who is leaving.
- Ideally, both parents should tell the kids together.
- Tell the truth and nothing but the truth. That doesn't mean that everything has to be disclosed, but don't make statements that have to be retracted later on.
- Give the kids a reason for the divorce that makes sense to them as kids. A statement like "We want to stop fighting, and we haven't been able to do that despite all our efforts" is much better than "We can't get along anymore."
- Extramarital affairs should not be hidden, nor should they be the focus when telling the children of the decision to separate.

- Expect the process to take two days, and even then, it won't be over. Stay flexible, keeping both parents available and letting the kids talk with whom they want, rather than setting a schedule.
- Let the children visit where the departing parent will be living; choose new bed linens/comforters; bring a few clothes or toys over; or, at the very least, see its location.
- Say good-bye when you leave; don't just disappear. Fix a date for the next time you'll get together, and make sure everyone has all the specifics, e.g., E-mail addresses, phone numbers, fax number, contact addresses.

Buying Presents,
Buying Love

In which Patty, age thirteen, wonders
whether Dad thinks he can buy her love
with a new bicycle

Child's Point of View:
Gifts Don't Make Everything Oᴋ

After your parents get divorced, you never know what your weekends will be like. Two weeks ago Dad decided not to come get us because—well, I'm really not sure—though I guess he had his reasons. Then this Wednesday he called after a long silence. He used to call a lot, but hardly ever now, so I was surprised. He said he wanted to make sure we were coming this weekend . . . as though it's us who cancel weekends! I couldn't resist asking him if he was sure *he* was going to be there.

So, Friday he picked us up. He was in a great mood. Bought us ice cream, rented a video, even spent some time reading with Rick. Friday I went to bed right after I finished my homework, because he said Saturday was going to be a big day, but he didn't say why. Saturday morning he asked me to put some laundry in the machine in the basement, which is the kind of thing I don't like to do. But when I went down, padlocked in the rack next to the washer was a brand-new bike for me. He had a big sign on it—"For Patty, my best girl."

It's an awesome bike, exactly the one I wanted since last Christmas. I went running back upstairs all excited, and he told me he'd give me the lock combo if I forgave him. I said sure, but now, thinking about it, I'm not sure what I forgave him for. Leaving us? . . . Not coming the last weekend? . . . Not calling much anymore? I tried not to think about it at the time, but now I feel like I'm in some kind of conspiracy with him against Mom.

We rode all Saturday and Sunday. I had fun, except I couldn't help thinking about all the times we went biking as a family. I wanted to take the bike home, but I wasn't sure if I could. Then Sunday at dinner, right before I was going to ask him, Dad told me how much it cost, reminding me I should take extra good care of it. Now I don't want to risk taking it home, and I'm almost afraid to ride it.

Mom seemed sort of angry about me getting it at all, and then said I should bring it home and ride it to school every day. After all, she pointed out, it's mine now . . . isn't it? Or is it?

Parent's Point of View:
I Resent the Extravagant Gifts

Sometimes when I ask the kids what they did at school that day or during the weekend at Steven's, I get "Nothing . . . ," as in "It was OK." Other times it's "Nothing . . . ," as in "Don't ask." Telling the difference is the hard part! I got a "Nothing . . . ," last night when I asked Patty what they did at her father's this weekend and a similar "Don't ask . . . ," response from her brother.

Then tonight, I walked into Patty's room with some clothes, and she hurriedly tried to put away a couple of photos she obviously didn't want me to see. I asked if I could look and she handed them over reluctantly. I immediately understood why! They were from this weekend, and there she was riding a brand-new bike with her dad: one of those mountain bikes with shock absorbers. She was embarrassed when I inquired about it. She said she hadn't asked for it, quickly adding she wished her father had spent less money and gotten something for Rick too.

Trying to stay cool, I told her it looked awesome, but I was pretty angry. She and I went to look at bikes last Christmas. It was heartbreaking when I had to tell her I couldn't afford that one, even though it was her dream bike. I'd actually been hoping Steven and I could split the cost for her birthday next month. The more I think about it, the more I really resent that he bought it without telling me. Biking was one of the few things we used to do together before the divorce. At bedtime Patty asked me if I was OK, because I'd been sort of quiet all evening. She said she still felt funny about accepting the present so enthusiastically, because, she said, "Dad's acting as though this makes everything OK, but, although I'm grateful, I still want to tell him it isn't."

I asked her if she was going to bring the bike home and use it to get back and forth to school. She hesitated, shook her head, and said she was worried that the more she used it, the more it would make Dad think she could be bought off with expensive gifts. Then she got all teary. She was upset because it cost almost as much as one of the support checks she knows we haven't gotten this month.

I wonder if Steven realizes how ambivalent all this makes her feel? This is the third time he's splurged on an extravagant gift for her. The last time it was those velvet pants. All he ever gets Rick are more action figures. I told her to go to her Dad's apartment tomorrow after school and bring the bike home. Patty hesitated, clearly uncertain she wanted to do that. Dad would be mad if she didn't take care of it, or worse, if it got stolen. I assured her it was safer in our garage than the basement of his apartment building, but she looked anxious. I have a feeling it won't appear here any time soon!

Making Sense of It All

Bringing a present home from a business trip, buying flowers as a peace offering after a disagreement, splurging on a birthday present for a loved one, offering a gift to the host and hostess at a party—these are all ways adults try to communicate their feelings for each other. Because adults understand the conventions, the giving and receiving are seldom misinterpreted. The hostess is unlikely to see the plant as a love offering; the brother unlikely to see his birthday present as a bribe. However, children with divorced parents are prone to wonder about the purpose of gift giving, especially if it is unexpected and "undeserved." This does not mean they will not be happy with the gift, but there may be some ambivalence attached.

Being bought presents by their parents is a normal part of every child's experience. What parent hasn't purchased an extravagant present right before Hanukkah, Christmas, or a birthday? Maybe to assuage feelings of guilt: "I've been working too much lately," or "I've been too caught up in my own issues." Maybe to highlight how proud they are of their kid's achievements: "She deserves the reward for a great report card." Or maybe to make up for times when they couldn't or wouldn't buy yet another toy, game, or book. Parents on business trips often bring back special gifts as a way to say, "See, I still love you," and to hopefully mute some of the anger and distance that follows a long absence. As gift buying has so much significance, and gift receiving is so exciting for children, it's easy to see how divorced parents, trying to overcome the lack of contact or wanting desperately to make up for a missed weekend, get tempted and often give in to buying expensive gifts for their children. This is more likely if the parent has limited time with the children, or if that parent doesn't think the custody or visitation arrangement is fair.

Despite appearances, getting a gift is not always a positive experience for kids. So what can the problem be? The parent wants to give;

the child wants to receive. It seems simple, but it's not. Children are experts at looking for the motive you have in buying them a gift, and they care about the motive as much as an adult would. They are naturally suspicious if a present appears out of the blue. We have found that children do not want gifts as substitutes for time together; so if this is how gifts are used, it will disturb them. The kids do not want gifts without an apology if used as a way to assuage your guilt; a gift produces less conflict if presented with an admission from you that you feel bad about whatever it is you may have done. They do not want gifts that will upset the other parent—the bike Mom was going to get them, the skis Dad has been saving up for. They do not want too many gifts or too frequent gifts—it makes them think something is wrong or something bad is going to happen. They do not want gifts they cannot keep—the bicycle that has to stay at Dad's in case they lose it at school, the jacket that has to stay at Mom's because it's "too good" for Dad's weekends. Most of all, they do not want to feel bought off. They want you to earn their trust and love with your time and honesty and affection, not with money you may or may not have available to spend on them.

So beware of the subtle, and not so subtle, messages that affection can be bought with the right present. Some come from consumer magazines and television advertising, others from your kids. Do not fall into the trap of thinking that saying "No" to your children's material wants will cost you their love. We have seen necessities for the adult get sacrificed, prudent investments for future education be forgone—all with the high expectations of being able to purchase loving parent-child relationships. The tendency to allow your children to manipulate you into buying things as proof that you love them, or that you are as generous as the other parent, is one to be strongly resisted. Otherwise, there is likely to be an argument every time an outing takes you into a store. Though raising a child is expensive, love doesn't come with a price tag.

Beware of competing with your spouse and trying to prove you're the best parent. Even after the divorce decree, the competition tends to continue: the parent who has more time with the children wants to prove the rightness of that decision; the other seeks to prove to the ultimate judges, the children, that she or he is really "the best."

Considering their level of sophistication, it might seem that adolescents would quickly see through the ingratiating ploy of gift giving and resent it more than their younger siblings. In reality, adolescents may be happier with gifts as a substitute for time than the four-year-old or the seven-year-old who often craves contact with parents above all else.

The irony is that, as the gift giver, you may not be shown the ambivalence engendered by your excessive use of gift giving. In fact, the other parent may be the only one who sees the fallout.

General Guidelines

We all give gifts. Some reasons for doing so are better than others. Try to remember the following so the gifts can be treasured:

- Children pay a cost that is too high to bear when gifts replace parental time and attention.
- If your children prefer your gifts to your time, then the relationship is in big trouble.
- Minutes mean more than dollars. "We don't have enough time together," is said just as often by kids as by adults.
- If you leave the price tag on or you make a point of what the gift cost, it's not really a gift—it's a notice of debt or obligation.
- Gifts are fine, but a definite luxury when finances are tight for either parent. Don't put your child in a bind by having a gift cost a support payment or somehow seriously hurt the financial status of the other parent.
- If you spend money on the kids and expect an emotional payback proportional to the dollars invested, spare the children your disappointment when their reactions don't fulfill your expectations.
- If you have more than one child, the gifts need to be comparable in value to each child. That does not mean they have to cost the same. But if one child's price tag is always greater than the other's, the message of favoritism will be clear.
- Don't spoil birthdays or holidays by competing with the other parent or putting the other parent in a position of resenting your gift. Such acts ruin the celebrations for the children. If you are escalating into one-upmanship, call a truce before the losses get to be too great.

Children Blaming Themselves for the Divorce

In which ten-year-old Albert feels guilty
about precipitating Dad's departure

Child's Point of View:
If Only I Had Been Good . . .

I wish I hadn't stayed up to watch the ball game last night! Mom had said, before she went to the PTA meeting, that I needed to be in bed by nine. I didn't argue with her, as she never gives in on a school night, but I knew I could get Dad to agree with me once she'd gone. So when he settled down in front of the TV with his beer, I offered to make some popcorn . . . and how could he send me to bed when I asked if I could share it with him? It was a great game and neither of us noticed the time. So when Mom walked in at 10:30 P.M., during the eighth inning, I was still curled up on the sofa with Dad.

She went ballistic, yelling at me that I should have done what she said and that she refused to be late for work again if I overslept and missed the bus. I told her that Dad had said I could stay up with him, but that only seemed to make her madder. Dad nudged me to stop arguing and go to bed. There was no way I could sleep! I could hear Mom ranting on about Dad having no control over me and never setting limits and how much extra work she had to do. Then I heard a crash and the door slam. I fell asleep, but this morning nobody got me up for school, and when I went into the kitchen to get breakfast, Mom had her serious voice on and said she needed to tell me something.

I knew before she said it. Dad's not going to live here anymore. I asked when I would see him, and she just said he was coming to pack his stuff tonight. I meant, like, when would I see him after that, but I didn't dare ask. I said I'd go to bed early every night for the rest of the week . . . but she said that wouldn't change anything. I said I was sorry, but she said it wasn't about my behavior last night, it was about Dad's. Deep inside I know it was my fault. I got him into trouble. I mean, if I'd been in bed, Mom wouldn't have got mad and Dad would still be here. I'd be good forever if she'd just let him come back.

Parent's Point of View:
That Was the Last Straw

I'm glad it came to a head last night. There's just so much I can take. I have to do everything myself: keep everyone happy at work, keep everyone happy at home, but nobody thinks it's their job to keep me happy.

Last night I didn't want to go to the PTA meeting either, but they were deciding on the future of the music program and I knew it would get cut if nobody turned up to defend it. I wanted Paul to come with me, but he decided to "baby-sit," which actually meant watch the game on TV. That really ticked me off! He's the first to complain when I don't feel like doing what *he* wants, such as going out for his idea of a romantic dinner—at Taco Bell! He's always complaining we never do anything together and we don't share common interests. I would think that education is a good example of an interest we could share, but obviously baseball is more important.

I suppose I could just pursue my own friends (whom he doesn't like) and hobbies (which he despises), but then if I leave him alone with Albert for long, I find he's let him stay up late or gobble junk food, or agreed to take him to some violent movie I think is inappropriate. Last week he bought him one of those shoot-'em-up computer games, which Albert says he much prefers to the "boring educational games" I bought him. Last night there was popcorn all over the sofa and floor, and who do you think is going to have to clean that up? Living with Paul is just a lot of work and I get nothing back. No thanks, no affection, no help with Albert . . . , nothing.

I've been telling Paul for a year now that if things don't improve, he's going to have to find somewhere else to live. He's always shrugged it off in the past. Won't even contemplate marital therapy. Well, his shrugging days are over. I called an attorney this morning, and I'm filing for divorce. Albert looked upset when I told him Dad was moving, but I told Albert it wasn't his fault.

Making Sense of It All

Many children hold themselves responsible when their parents get divorced. Albert feels directly involved in what's happening. As a result, when told his dad is moving out, he looks to the last episode of parental disagreement about his behavior and thinks that he may have precipitated the family crisis—hence his promises to be good from now on. Although assured that the single incident described was not the cause of Dad's leaving, as time goes on he is likely to start wondering whether his role in precipitating arguments between his parents may have played a major part in the unraveling of the marriage.

Time and Money

Children hear their parents' wry jokes about the "good old days" before they had kids, and naturally assume that they have produced the "bad days." Many parents may be working toward common goals in trying to fulfill career, community, and parenting obligations. Unfortunately, time and energy for the marriage relationship itself may get sacrificed in order to meet all the other demands. If children hear constant complaining and arguing about who does what for them, they can and often do conclude that the "bad things" wouldn't have happened if they were not in the picture.

Occasionally, in fits of irritation, parents say some damning things in the kids' presence: comments they regret, like, "Sometimes I wish I never had kids, . . ." or, "If it wasn't for the kids I'd be out of here. . . ." More often, however, it is the atmosphere after adult arguments, or statements overheard when adults think the kids are fast asleep, that convince children that they are significantly at fault when their parents divorce. Parents argue over many things, but because trips and new adventures are so important to kids, disagreements about vacations or weekend activities often make a lasting impression. Commonly, one parent wants to share a dream vacation alone with their spouse, while the other parent, tempted to agree, notes they then can't afford to go to Disney World or Six Flags during the school break as promised.

If it isn't vacations that start arguments, then the subject is likely to be money or the shortage of it. With the good intentions of showing affection and teaching economic reality as well, how many times do parents make a point of saying, "I'm spending this on your clothes, rather than buying something new for myself"? Years later, when the pressures of a second job or too many hours of overtime take their toll on the marriage, children are forced to wonder whether all the presents, clothes, treats, etc., that they demanded caused many of the economic and relationship tensions. Gift buying and lack of discipline often create parental friction in the early years, and these issues continue to be the flash points for marital disagreements.

As children get older, their schoolwork and outside interests may become the major source of tension, as they consume parents' time and energy. Kids often hear parents' humorous remarks, accompanied by forced laughter, about "ships passing in the night." They're aware of the change to anger, distance, and disappointment when these remarks become complaints; the lack of family time becomes grounds for unhappiness, as one parent is running one way to pick up one kid, and the other is carpooling elsewhere to accommodate sports competitions or extracurricular activities. It's hard to make the logistics work. Every parent holds on to the fantasy that they still have the energy they had fifteen years ago, reassuring each other they'll plan time together after all the kids go to sleep . . . except the kids have the stamina now and they may be the last ones to turn out the lights! For children who have been very insistent on the absolute necessity of pursuing all their activities, parental arguments and hostility over time no longer spent together may convince kids they are to blame: "My activities and interests meant my parents never saw each other, and now they want to split up."

Fault, or Fantasies of Power?

People of all ages seek to make sense out of events they do not understand. For young children, it may be by deciding they caused the events; for adolescents or adults, it may be by deciding that as it *couldn't* be their own fault, it must be someone else's. In our complex world, especially in the realm of human interactions, everyone tends to look for simplistic answers. Egocentrism and the desire for simple answers shape every child's reactions to divorce, but there is still more to children's assertions of fault that parents would do well to understand and acknowledge. Guilt and feeling at fault most likely occur in situations in which people believe they had, or still have, the power to change the outcome.

Children cling to the hope that they can bring their parents together, and hence reinforce their feelings of guilt and responsibility. Many experiences in life make children rightly conclude they really do have the power to make their parents happy. During the separation, and often for years after the divorce, children repeatedly hear how much they mean to their parents, how much joy they bring, and how empty life would be without them. All parents say these things, often hundreds of times, before the separation, but during and after divorce these remarks take on added meaning. One common result is kids devote not only a large amount of time to fantasizing about bringing their parents back together, but also a large amount of energy trying to decrease the tension. Even four-year-olds will say, "I'll be good if they don't fight anymore," or, like Albert, be willing to go to great lengths, such as going to bed early.

As individual couples move closer to the decision to split up, they, consciously or unconsciously, try to avoid upsetting their children. If parents can't make sense of their own lives and the process they are going through, they rarely talk or behave with their children in ways which leave the kids feeling "not at fault." All too often, discipline lapses, and so the kids manipulate situations to their advantage and drive even bigger wedges between their parents; kisses multiply as parents look for affection in return for giving it; and poor behavior, which was never allowable before, is frequently ignored. These parental behaviors do not decrease a child's perception of being at fault; indeed they increase a child's sense of power, which may then paradoxically increase the guilt feelings and fuel the child's anxiety to fix the broken family.

Other Effects of Feeling at Fault

No one likes to feel at fault for breaking up a marriage, so many children develop somatic complaints, become unusually compliant, act out by throwing tantrums, threaten to run away, or show major changes in behavior style, e.g., become either unusually apathetic or unusually aggressive. Guilt commonly leads to feelings of not being good enough, especially when one parent takes on a much less involved role in the child's life. The child is left wondering, "What did I do that caused Mom/Dad not to want to spend time with me?" Feelings of rejection can easily be created by a visitation schedule that defines a lesser or distant role for one parent. Rather than bringing closure, a settlement (establishing this type of visitation schedule) can cause a loss of security and self-esteem for those children who blame themselves. Losing access to one parent makes children feel helpless and is experienced as punitive.

Helping Kids Talk It Out

Merely understanding your children's interpretations of what is going on is not sufficient: their understanding of their role needs to be discussed. Simply telling your children they are not at fault, as Albert's mother does, says to them that their parent is not listening or does not understand. Reassurance may be called for as the last step, but it should not be the first. Hopefully, talking about the realities of your marital relationship will enable your children to hear very directly that the adults in their lives are responsible for their own decisions. It can be illuminating, at the very least, to encourage your children to talk about exactly what they have heard and how they believe their actions might have caused the marital rift. Equally important are your children's perceptions about what can be done to "fix things up." As a parent, you may be tempted to quickly terminate these conversations if your children insist they heard you say things you never said, or quote statements out of context and come to false conclusions. Nevertheless, it is important to hear them out. It can be one of the best learning and teaching opportunities in the whole divorce experience. It gives you a chance to understand what your children are thinking and to offer your own point of view, without necessarily contradicting or undermining that of your children (see the following examples). Hopefully, the more parents and children talk, the less the children are likely to feel at fault.

Fault is a difficult issue and your own perceptions of who is, or was, to blame for the breakup of your marriage may change over time. Early on in the breakup, life itself may be confusing, and most adults alternate between blaming themselves and blaming the other parent, though neither is constructive. The following are some exchanges that demonstrate how to stay focused on making sure your child doesn't trap himself in this circle of blame while trying to discover who is the "bad guy": me, Dad, or Mom?

A "shutdown" response will rapidly terminate the conversation but not reassure your child. The "talk-it-out" response leaves room for your child to understand better and return to the subject at a later date.

Child: "I always make Daddy angry. . . . Isn't that why he left?"
Parent, (shutdown response): "That's not why Daddy left."
Parent, (talk-it-out response): "Yeah, sometimes you did make Daddy angry. And we made you angry. But that is part of living with someone. You also made us each very happy, and you still do. What happened was that Dad and I never got beyond being angry with each other. We were never able to resolve things between ourselves. You did a lot better than we did. When we told you we were angry

because you got home late, you actually started to get home on time. So you didn't make Dad leave. Dad was angry about many things, and that was part of why he left. I'm not sure he or I understand it all, but we'll keep trying to explain it to you, because neither one of us believes that you caused this."

Child: "I feel like I caused you and Mom to split up."

Parent, (shutdown response): "That's just not true. You shouldn't feel like it's your fault."

Parent, (talk-it-out response): "I understand you do feel guilty. But I know you aren't. I don't blame you and neither does your mom. Is there something we said or either of us did that makes you think or feel you caused our problem?"

Child: "If I wasn't here, then you never would have argued all the time and you'd still be together."

Parent, (shutdown response): "I don't want you to talk that way. You shouldn't have those feelings."

Parent, (talk-it-out response): "You're right that we argued about you. But don't you remember that Mom and I argued about what food to cook, what plants to buy for the garden, which car to use? For a long time it was just a way of having our own say; but then we found out there was little that we did share in common—and we both want to live with someone with whom we can share a lot. Sometimes what you did or said was a problem for us, but it wasn't the problem between me and your mom. We both still want to share lots of things with you, have good times with you, but we don't seem to be able to do that with each other anymore. It makes us both sad that we can't. But that's what caused the divorce, not anything you did."

Child: "I think I caused the divorce because you and Dad never have any time together. When Dad wasn't traveling and he was home, you spent all your time with me."

Parent, (shutdown response): "That's not true."

Parent, (talk-it-out response): "We did spend a lot of time with you. But that's because your Dad and I both wanted to do that. We could have, we should have, made other decisions so we would have had more time together. But there was no way for you to know that, or to help us see we should have been behaving differently. I'm sure if we had it to do over again, we'd still spend just as much time with you. I'm not sure I understand everything that happened between your dad and me, but I'll explain what I can. Hopefully, it will help you see that you didn't cause us to separate, although I can see how you might think that."

General Guidelines

- Children need the opportunity to talk about why they feel at fault and how they think they caused the divorce. Inviting these conversations won't create a problem, since the guilt feelings are already there. Parents should help their children understand that adults are responsible for their own actions and decisions.
- If your children feel at fault, willingly give them the time to talk, and listen carefully. Encourage them to be very specific about what "I (the child) did" to cause the divorce and what "I (the child) might do" to fix it or stop it from happening. Hearing them describe it in their own words, and then responding, is more constructive than blanket reassurance.
- When children feel at fault, they will also feel responsible for righting the wrong. Just as they didn't cause the divorce, children need a clear statement from each parent that they can't prevent it or reverse it.
- Seeking to make Mom or Dad happy gives the children a sense of control and purpose. Schedules that severely restrict time with one parent limit the children's ability to feel like "I'm playing a positive role" with both parents, and may feel like a punishment.
- Telling children "it's too complex to explain" or "you would never understand the reasons for the divorce" may be transiently reassuring, but it still leaves them wondering whether they have the power to change their parents' plans.
- Children feel better when they've constructed an explanation that makes sense to them. Don't take that away, but offer the whole picture, e.g., "Yes, we argued about you, but you didn't cause the breakup. . . ."

Short Visits 7

In which Mary, age eleven, complains about
the visitation schedule

Child's Point of View:
Why Such an Awful Schedule?

I don't get it. How come my parents have put together the most ridiculous schedule of visits with Dad? I mean, who decided that it was a good idea for him to come on Thursdays and take me to school? First of all, I'm grumpy in the morning. Second, it doesn't give me enough time to actually tell him anything, even if I wanted to (which I usually don't at 7:30 A.M.). And third, it seems to put Mom into a really bad mood, so I can't talk to her either.

This morning was a great example. Mom had been out last night and slept through the alarm; so by the time she got me up, it was already late. I woke up to all this "Hurry up! Your Dad will be here in twenty minutes." That was followed by lots of mutterings about how ridiculous he is to insist on picking us up on Thursdays and how inconvenient it is to have to get us ready so early. Anyway, I managed to get dressed in time and could see Dad waiting in the driveway for me, but I couldn't find my homework and hadn't had breakfast. I asked Mom if she could go and tell Dad I'd be out in a few minutes. Well, that was a mistake! I got the "I don't want to talk to your father any more than I have to" routine, and so by the time I got outside, she was mad with me, he was mad with me, and I was just mad. "Why do you have to come pick me up on Thursdays when I don't like it?" I asked. "It's the rules," he said, shaking his head, making it clear there was no way to change those rules. Then he added, "And you know who made the rules? . . . Mommy." There was a horrible silence, until my brother David started crying. Apart from his sniffling, everybody shut up all the way to school. I don't get it. Who *does* make the rules?

If I knew, then maybe I'd know who to talk to. My parents keep telling me to use words to say what I think. They say I should always "speak my mind." So why don't they give me a chance to do it now, when I really have something to say?

Parent's Point of View:
It's the System's Fault

Sometimes I wonder why I ever agreed to this temporary visitation schedule. I feel locked into it now, but it clearly doesn't work well. It all happened so fast. One minute we were arguing over how many days a week Ron would get to see Mary and David, and I was getting all upset because what he wanted didn't fit in with my work schedule. The next thing I remember is sitting with a court officer who just seemed bent on getting an agreement on paper so she could get us out of there without taking up the judge's time. Even my attorney seemed to be telling me that what Ron wanted was reasonable and perhaps I should just stop objecting to everything. But I really couldn't work out what to object to and what to let go.

Then the two attorneys conferred and came up with what sounded like a workable plan. I was so tired of all the arguing that I told myself it would be fine. I know now I shouldn't have agreed without thinking it through, but I felt pressured to "cooperate," rather than let the judge decide. My lawyer said she considered the proposed plan acceptable, as apparently it's pretty standard. I really wish I had talked to my divorced friends before going to court—I could have been more prepared.

The kids are now stuck with a whole series of short visits with Ron that completely mess up the continuity of the week. They complain that by the time he picks them up on Tuesdays, there is no time to do anything except gobble down a meal before being brought back home. At that point, they are too tired to do homework and it's as much as I can do to keep David awake for his bedtime story. And Thursday mornings, when Ron comes to bring them to school, it's even worse! I mean, what's the point? You can't get quality time on a car ride! And I'm rushing around trying to get them up and fed while I can see Ron fuming in the car when they're a minute late. This morning was a typical Thursday. By the time they left, I was mad, Mary was sulking, and David was on the brink of tears. This can't be right.

Especially on weekends, the kids end up blaming me for making them go with Ron when they don't want to, but it's the system that is really screwed up. It expects separating parents to know what is the best way of allocating time with their kids. Now, with hindsight, I see it's not just a matter of dividing up the week into a number of hours, but someone needs to look at what you can *do* with those hours and whether it works from the kids' points of view. I agreed to this schedule because I thought the lawyers would know what's workable, but obviously they either didn't know, or, they didn't care.

If I want to change this temporary order, I'll have to go back to court, and that's more money and time I don't have. The scary thing is that it seems like the temporary order always gets to be pretty permanent. That's what my friends tell me now. I wish I had known all of this earlier, but I was such a wreck then—worrying about how I was going to make ends meet.

Maybe I should talk to Mary and David about it. If they want to change, then maybe it would be worth the effort. David probably won't say anything, but I bet Mary has plenty to say. I wonder if the court would listen to her, now that we've tried this. They sure didn't give her a chance to say anything the last time. When I asked why she couldn't be asked what she wanted, I was told, "That's not how it's done." After having to live through this schedule fiasco, I think the court should rethink how it *is* done.

Making Sense of It All

We have found that it is rare for the visitation schedule set during the early phase of a separation to continue to be satisfactory to everyone in the family as time goes on, especially if the schedule includes several short visits per week. Short visits are usually very unrewarding for parents and children. Parents come to realize the problems with the schedule they have agreed to, but often the desire to amend it is tempered by a natural reluctance to go back into court and a failure to recognize that short visits are often the cause of the difficulties; not that the kids don't want to spend time with the visiting parent.

The original schedule you try when you first split up quickly becomes outdated. Thankfully, your life will change, usually for the better, as the chaos that dominates the early months settles and you make time to reassess the visitation schedule and whose needs it satisfies. Many of you will come to the conclusion it satisfies no one. "How could I have agreed to that?" you may ask yourself, or, "How could my attorney have let me agree to something so impractical?" The truth is that court officers and attorneys often do not, nor can they be expected to, have an adequate appreciation of all the emotional needs of family members, especially children, at the different stages of separation and divorce; so it's no wonder the court falls back on formulas or past precedents. The formulaic approach is certainly to the advantage of the courts, as it facilitates getting a fast agreement and helps to prevent a backlog of cases waiting to go in front of the judge; but remember it may not be to *your* advantage, and you are the one who has to live with it. It's much better for the kids, and eventually for *both* parents, to avoid this trap by opting for an initial trial period of at least a few months, perhaps as long as a year. Then if your agreement contains plain language about ways that the schedule can be revised, you all can profit from lessons learned.

Regrettably, if you have been unable to agree, some of you may be facing a court hearing to determine the visitation schedule. You'll be happier later if you try not to work against the system, nor let it determine your fate:

- Going to court is a traumatic experience for most people. You are likely to be anxious and overawed and to have a tendency to agree to suggestions in an attempt to look helpful. Before you face the court system, try to talk with friends who have been through the process themselves and get their advice, or, better still, take a friend with you. Although we know it is tempting to try to keep all the divorce issues private, friends, if asked, are generally willing to offer insights based on their own experiences.

- In the court environment, upset parents are vulnerable to being steamrollered into an agreement that not only may not work well in the short term, but, worse, can become the basis for the permanent custody arrangement.

- Have your attorney make a proposal for a nonprejudicial trial period of different visitation schedules over the next six to twelve months. After that time, an initial schedule can be agreed upon.

- Don't acquiesce to a schedule of visitation that you cannot honor given your work schedule. Better to accept a little less time with the children than repeatedly fail to meet the agreement or have to hire baby-sitters to fill in for you.

- Make sure your attorney understands what is important to you so he or she doesn't trade time and days as though they were all of equal value, i.e., Friday nights may have a religious significance or Monday nights may be your night for a class or hobby.

- Resist the temptation to agree to a proposal just to save a few dollars in legal fees or to escape the courtroom as quickly as possible.

Before accepting any new or revised proposal at a court hearing, think it through with a friend, with your attorney, or by yourself. If you need time, take it—a lot is at stake. Remember that it is you who have to live with the agreement—not the court and not your attorney.

If you think through the issues, you are much less likely to end up with a schedule that places an unnecessary burden on both parents and children, such as the one described in these diaries. It is most families' experience that short visits don't go smoothly, especially when time is pressured (having to get to school on time) or parent-to-parent handovers are involved and the children are affected by the tensions between parents (see Chapter 9). If you are the residential parent, it is hard to work around frequent transitions. If you are the nonresidential parent, you will be faced with the daunting task of creating quality time with your children in so short a period that it barely allows them to adjust to the change in parent, let alone relax and enjoy themselves. Children tell us they often just feel like pawns in their parents' game. While the total time allotment may be fair, when it is chopped up into short visits the structure makes the time frustrating for everyone concerned.

Mary highlights a common situation that inevitably ruins someone's mood at handover time. She is already ambivalent about going with Dad; an ambivalence her mother reinforces by implying it's her father's fault the schedule doesn't work. By keeping her ex-spouse waiting without an explanation, she virtually guarantees that he will be in a bad mood too. Poor Mary! Mirroring all the anger around her, she just lashes out at Dad, who promptly lashes out at Mom, leaving Mary lost in the middle.

General Guidelines

Careful thought should be given to even the temporary schedule. It is common to find that arrangements that on face value seem fair do not work well.

- Dividing time with your children is not just a matter of allocating hours. It is important to ensure that whatever time is available to each parent is allocated in emotionally rewarding blocks of time.
- For most parent-child relationships, a tolerable schedule means a minimum of forty-eight hours on a weekend or overnight on weekdays. The shorter the duration, especially less than three hours, the higher the likelihood of emotional frustration and acting out.

- If you are finding the agreed interim schedule tough, share that feeling with your child, rather than assume you are alone in that feeling.
- If time is tight or the visit is short, try to agree on optimizing the logistics; for example, calling before you leave to pick up the children so they can be ready when you get there, or picking them up at the end of school.
- Try not to blame the other parent for inadequacies in the time allocations. This forces the children to take sides and invites them to start thinking with whom they would rather be.
- Review the proposed schedule with your children before signing any final agreements.
- In the final settlement, always incorporate a right to review the schedule after six months or a year. This should be automatic and can be done by letter or through a mediator. If either parent is unwilling to discuss a revision, a further court appearance should be required.
- Being a single parent demands that you understand that your own interests and the children's are not always in sync. Expect that emotional and logistic conflicts will inevitably arise. Blame and guilt, although normal, will not solve the problems. The passage of time and the ability to be flexible in the face of rapid changes in your and your children's lives will lead to constructive resolution.

Rest assured that it is possible to come up with a schedule that meets everyone's needs so that time together is enjoyable. Look back at what has and has not worked so far, and you'll probably see that the visits that are less than overnight and shorter than two nights on weekends are the ones that cause problems. If you're the parent who has to manage those short visits, it's no wonder that you feel like you can't connect with your kids.

When the schedule causes conflicts or acting out, it is tempting for one parent to say the answer is to shorten the visits even further or eliminate them, but that is rarely what the kids or other parent wants. Both of you may be hesitant to experiment, for fear of making another mistake, so in Chapter 8 we offer a few models other than the typical short-visit structure where one parent sees the children for part of every other weekend and one night a week. Sometimes, more creative schedules are better suited to a family's needs.

Creating a Schedule

8

In which Ellen, age twelve, can't anticipate
what visitation schedule would work
best for her

Child's Point of View:
How Would I Know What It's Like to
Live in Two Places?

I talked to Betty last night about what it was like after her parents split up. I didn't really want to know all the stuff about feeling sad and embarrassed; what I really wanted to know was how it's possible to live in two separate places and feel at home in each, when neither has everything you want—like two parents! My parents keep asking me what I want them to arrange, but how do I know what it will be like when Dad has actually gone? Anyway, they don't seem to know where he's going to live, or whether I can have a computer in both places, or whether he'll be able to get home early enough to help with homework; so how do I know whether I want to go to his place on weeknights or just stick to weekends? Betty said she heard of a girl in ninth grade who spends one whole month with one parent, then switches. I don't know if I want to be away from Mom that much, but at least I wouldn't be living out of my suitcase and book bag!

I wish I could just decide week by week what should happen, but both Mom and Dad say they need to plan around a fixed schedule. That's great for them, but my schedule isn't fixed at all! Every season I play a different sport, and next semester I want to be in the middle-school play, which means I can't catch the bus home. Mom can't drive, since she isn't free, and Dad isn't going to want to pick me up just to bring me home, so how's that going to work? Not that the word "home" means much now. Oh, this is so complicated!

Parent's Point of View:
How Do We Accommodate Everyone?

Trying to devise a schedule feels like physically dividing your children. It has to be the worst part of the divorce, but I've said that before about almost everything! This feels so permanent and so immutable, even though Barry and I agree we'll change it if it doesn't work, but doesn't work for whom? What works for me may not work for him, and I keep asking Ellen what she wants and she just either cries or says she doesn't know. I can't ask Natalie what she wants, because she barely understands what's going on.

I want a schedule in which I can see them every day; Barry says he wants to see them every day too. I know that will be confusing for the kids, but I can't bear the thought of being here without them for days on end. I can't help thinking that as Barry's the one who is leaving us, not seeing the kids as much as he wants is the price he should pay. He says that's not fair. My attorney says that "fair" is defined by what you can get your spouse to agree to! So far, all my attorney has done for me is tell me that every other weekend and one evening a week is standard father visitation time, and that I shouldn't agree unconditionally to anything Barry wants. Barry has already said "the standard agreement" is unacceptable, so what's next? My mother keeps saying that I shouldn't fight for the maximum time, as I will need some time for myself, because looking after the kids without a man around is exhausting. She should know; she did it for fifteen years! I don't know who to listen to, or even how to bear thinking about it without becoming really angry or really upset, but I know it has to be done.

Making Sense of It All

Visitation schedules are often the source of profound dissatisfaction for adults and children, but they are necessary to provide the structure needed for everyone to plan their own lives. Parents can alter their work commitments to make the most of their time with the children; similarly kids, knowing when transitions will occur, can tell their friends where they will be, and be better able to plan what they want to do with the available time.

To successfully devise a good framework for the schedule, you must be realistic and take into account your own needs and limitations, rather than try to fulfill your fantasies of being the "ideal parent." Similarly, don't get trapped by relying on court precedent or compliantly acceding to an attorney's advice. However much you wish you could, if you can't get out of work early, don't agree to pick up the kids at five o'clock on your evening. If you suspect there will be times you'll need a break from being the "one and only full-time parent," don't make demands to have the children sleep in their own bed at your house every night of the week. Most important, ensure the basic visitation framework provides your children sufficient time with each parent to accommodate and protect their need and, in our belief, their right, to maintain healthy relationships with you both.

That adequate allocation of time, unfortunately, rarely happens if you rely on court precedent or blindly follow an attorney's advice. If you find it hard to reach any sort of agreement alone, a divorce mediator will usually help you to resolve the issues with the least confrontation.

How to Start

First lay out your personal and work obligations on a weekly or monthly calendar, and then decide what time you want and can manage with the children. When you have both done this and each of you thinks your request is fair and equitable, check to see if it is agreeable to the other. If yes, then proceed to more detail. If no, then try switching so that what was time with father is now time with mother and vice versa. If this is also unacceptable, then probably one parent doesn't really have enough time to maintain a strong parent-child relationship.

Second, give some thought to the two big issues that have the potential to derail your plans: transitions from the care of one parent to the other and the frustration of short visits. In our experience, especially in the early stages, how often and under what circumstances the children move from one parent to the other is a key decision. In practice, the more frequently these handovers occur, the more child behavior problems are likely to challenge you, e.g., screaming sessions in the driveway, your dinner visit spent with a sullen withdrawn child. In theory it may seem ideal for the kids to have a quick dinner with Mom or an ice cream two or three times a week. Indeed it was, or would have been, when Mom was living at home, but it isn't always a workable plan when you are living apart, because it involves multiple handovers and short visits. A schedule that minimizes the number of transitions and in which handovers are set up at neutral locations without parent-to-parent exchanges, is usually the most successful (see Chapter 9 and Chapter 10).

Third, once these criteria are met, then it's time to look at ways to make the schedule satisfactory for your children, including what activities each of you will be responsible for and ways to accommodate the ongoing need for schedule changes as your children get older.

Find Out What Works with a Trial Schedule

Because living apart is a unique experience and the children face many challenges adjusting to the new lifestyle, parents would be well served to look at the first months as a trial period. (During the initial separation, parents would be advised to put in writing that this is a trial, so as not to prejudice a final ruling on custody or visitation.)

Basic Considerations

It often takes months for older children to begin to understand their own reactions to their parents' decisions and have some inkling of the choices that are best for them. During this transition time, they may want rules and schedules one moment, and then complete latitude the next. Younger children face different problems. They must adapt to spending substantial time away from the person who has been their primary caregiver, usually their mother. For a one-year-old, a substantial time may be measured in hours; for the kindergartner, in parts of a day; and for the second grader, an overnight away from Mom can be a difficult experience. Unavoidably, the disruption and loneliness of the separation or divorce make parents and children more reluctant to be away from each other. This time away may need to be gradually increased, rather than instituted from the start. Negative behavior toward the nonresidential parent, usually the father, is hard to tolerate, but it needs to be understood in the context of the divorce. Oftentimes it is a reflection of the child's anger about the change in his or her life, rather than a reflection of the feelings about that individual parent. If the children seem angry with the departed parent and reluctant to participate in activities with him or her, it is still the residential parent's responsibility to encourage contact and help increase their confidence, rather than limit the time spent with the nonresidential parent.

Especially where young infants are involved, e.g., ones who are breast-fed and now will be bottle-fed when they are with their fathers, or children who have only limited experience with play groups or day care, a progressively evolving timetable can be used to ease the adjustment. For infants, this may mean starting with eight or twelve hours for each visit; for older children, twenty-four hours or whatever block of time can be committed so the father is there the whole time. As the parent and child get more comfortable with each other, and as the less-experienced parent gets more comfortable with the nitty-gritty of cooking, bathing, and bedtime routines, the time can be increased. After a few weeks it will usually be obvious how much time that parent can manage and what amount of time is sufficient for the children, though the two may not match exactly.

With older kids, trying some variations on this theme is beneficial and sets the foundation for an ongoing conversation about what they want and expect in their lives, as well as what the parent is able to accommodate in terms of the schedule. Children are understandably hesitant to voice their need to spend their time in ways that might meet with one parent's disapproval. By emphasizing that the goal is to experiment and find everyone's comfort zone, "mistakes" are less likely to have long-term effects, and everyone is freer to try new arrangements. It's helpful for parents to acknowledge that there will have to be compromises for everyone. This process of accommodation may be a new family activity that's difficult to learn during the separation and divorce.

Any constructive dialogue can be hindered by continuing parental hostility, since hostility limits any willingness to listen to each other's point of view or consider differing opinions about the children's needs. Hostility also lessens receptivity to children's requests for more time with one parent or for activities that limit parental time, including after-school activities, classes, or just hanging out with peers. Parents have to be careful not to "unconsciously" rig the schedule to annoy their spouse or keep their kids with them more, and then "find" that ballet class just doesn't fit or soccer practice is impossible. However, with a degree of cooperation from and consultation with the kids, the particulars of the schedule will work out. Remember that the adults can't make all the scheduling decisions on their own—if they do, the compromises of work schedules, financial support, car-pool schedules, weekend arrangements, etc., will likely be for naught.

All schedules, however, eventually warrant revision, because children's interests and activities change, and parents' social and work commitments alter. Even a satisfactory schedule requires some flexibility to respond to immediate crises or the acute needs of an individual child. We would advise that every separation or divorce agreement should provide a simple mechanism for changing the schedule, or else, as happens in too many families, the schedule becomes a straitjacket resented by the children and one or both parents.

Specific Considerations with Multiple Children

Organizing one child's schedule is hard enough; with multiple children, the task can seem overwhelming. Even when you figure out how one child can get to karate and soccer while the other has a music lesson, there are three specific facets of a schedule to consider:

1. Individual activities—It's always more convenient to move the kids as a group, but, when given permission to voice their own wants, even young children (four to six years of age) will ask for time to do things the others do not like to do. The number of hours in the week may limit the possibilities, but the number of hours in the month probably will provide occasional opportunities for individual activities with each parent.

2. Time alone—Many parents come to cherish the times with just one child, even though they may be giving up time with the other(s). Younger children often seem to get this time alone because they appear more needy, but it is equally important to safeguard the older child's private time with the parent too. In large families this can be tough to manage, but as the years go on it becomes critical.

3. Spontaneity—What any schedule lacks is spontaneity. While everyone generally wants more time together, kids find it difficult to accept that there are occasions when it's not acceptable to breeze in on Mom or Dad, even if they live close by. Giving the kids the chance early on to voice their opinions about the schedule lets the adults do the same, and provides parents the chance to make any restrictions seem like joint compromises, rather than edicts that will be resisted and fought against.

Parent Dialogues: No Winners, No Losers

A major benefit of a trial period is that it helps parents begin the process of learning to talk amicably with each other about their kids, even though their relationship is less than friendly. It is a skill worth learning early, as this dialogue will need to continue for many years to come. As time heals wounds, hopefully the process will get easier. Sadly, most families do not get to conclude the initial negotiations in a way that protects the children's best interests. The legal process of granting "visiting rights" as part of the initial decree makes the arrangement seem unchangeable. This is reinforced if there is a failure to incorporate a comfortable, functional mechanism for altering the time allocations or financial support as the children get older and change their interests and activities. Even worse, the parent awarded custody in a contested situation may perceive himself or herself as the "winner" and see any later requests for modification as a challenge to that winner's status.

Of course, rating divorce decisions in terms of winners and losers leads to conflict. It's tough, really nigh on impossible, to come up with the perfect plan the first time, even though the stakes seem so high. When emotions are intense, personal needs take precedence over the creativity and willingness to compromise that are necessary to build a schedule that works reasonably well. So our advice is to make sure you benefit from a period of questioning and consideration. Take time to talk with others, even though it's tempting to keep all divorce issues private. And don't forget to find a way to build in change, because it's bound to come.

We realize that many parents are reluctant to even consider the idea of change, because of the potential legal ramifications. Too many, primarily fathers, have been caught in the following predicament: the financial demands of meeting the cost of supporting two households result in more work hours. This limits their "free time," so they may be absent, working at home, or continually doing chores when the kids are with them. In response, the kids don't want to come or demand the freedom to be able to go home to Mom's. Many fathers would like to be responsive, but they face a tough choice. Trying to change the level of support so they can cut back on work is unlikely to be acceptable, nor may it be economically feasible for the mother, but fathers quite justifiably fear that any agreement to spend less time with the children, even in the short term, will be used against them in court. If you are in this situation and you need to alter the arrangement temporarily while you sort out your life, ask the other parent to co-sign your written statement that acknowledges why you're altering the schedule and what schedule of responsibility you are working toward.

General Guidelines

If you're beginning this process, keep the following general guidelines in mind:

- Your children need and have the right to sufficient time with each parent to maintain a meaningful parent-child relationship.

- For most parent-child relationships, the minimum satisfactory time period together is forty-eight hours on weekends or overnight on weekdays. The shorter the duration, especially less than three hours, the higher the likelihood of emotional frustration and acting out.
- How do you determine whether the division of time is in the best interests of the children? If they cannot develop and maintain meaningful relationships with each parent in the time available, then it is not.
- How do you determine whether the division of time with the kids is fair? Put yourself in the other parent's shoes: if *you* wouldn't accept the time your spouse has with the kids, then it is not.
- Try to negotiate a trial period where each spouse acknowledges in writing that there may be "mistakes," but that the learning process will benefit everyone and lead to change.
- Parent-to-parent handovers create tension, especially for children who have separation problems, and offer possibilities for manipulation by all age groups.
- Try to make handovers at neutral locations with only one parent present at any given time. Don't assume the children have to be picked up from "home"—meeting them or dropping them off at school, a friend's house, or the library works well.
- Be creative about transitions. It may allow an opportunity for a single child to talk with a parent. For instance, the adolescent may walk, bike, or take public transportation home while you pick up another child after soccer. The adolescent gets some "free time," and you have a chance to chat with your other child.
- Planning a schedule will go much more smoothly if the children are involved in the planning at the start.
- If the children don't raise the issue, openly discuss their having time alone with each parent. Make allowance for it, because it will be used.
- Never forget that children are individuals. If you have more than one, don't treat them like an indivisible unit just to simplify the logistics. Sometimes that means each of the kids has a slightly different regime, but you'll hear the need for that when you talk with them about their preferences.
- As choices may be necessary, get every child to make a list of current interests and what they might want to try in the next few

years. If the level of parental hostility is high, using a third person to listen to the children and then convey the information to the parents can be helpful.

- Interests, goals, and activities change. As part of formulating a schedule, encourage kids to join in devising a mechanism to make changes, e.g., some families hold an E-mail chat session, or have a democratic meeting.

Individual Adjustments

Once you've given some thought to the framework and the previous general guidelines, don't forget to add the individual adjustments that make the effort more likely to endure:

- When you have to routinely be three places at once to share in your children's activities—soccer, football, and gymnastics—set up a rotation that gets marked on the calendar. Kids can negotiate any exchanges themselves—then you won't be accused of an error in judgment or playing favorites.
- You'll want to take account of individual quirks; for instance, if your children are "slow risers" or temperamentally stubborn and resistant, then you don't want a schedule that demands you be responsible for having them up and ready in the morning at an early time.
- Schoolchildren may prefer to spend more of their time with the adult who is most helpful with homework.
- Single days are difficult for all age groups, but students especially can suffer academically from the break in routine and the absence of a familiar place to work with the necessary resources.

Suggested Models

Having considered the issues involved in constructing a schedule that allows the children time with both parents, it is important to understand that the traditional every-other-weekend-and-an-evening-a-week visitation regime is not ideal from the children's point of view. While it is unconventional, we suggest that you start with the mind-set that, if both parents are able to free up sufficient time, they should try to agree on a schedule that allows them to share time and responsibility equally. Since most schedules are based on two-week periods, this means each parent starts with seven days in each fourteen-day cycle. Regardless of legal arrangements or semantics, this means no parent is giving the child to the other. The simplest solution (model 1) involves spending one week with one parent, and then the next week with the other. Such an arrangement may not be feasible in your family because it may not fit with work and other commitments. If at the time of the separation you are unable to commit to a fifty-fifty split of time, but intend to reorganize your work life to accommodate this option, make sure your attorney knows of your plans. When you consider the options, one of the following models may work for your family.

Model 1: *Seven days with Mom (Monday afternoon to the following Monday morning) followed by seven days with Dad. Then repeat the cycle.* This variation requires the minimum number of transitions, all of which can be easily done at school or day care. While it is absolutely equitable, the biggest downside is that you don't see the kids for a week and contact can be problematic if parental hostility is significant (see Chapter 13). For the children to feel they really have two homes, each parent needs to be able to offer the children a roughly equivalent place to live, with comparable personal space, clothes, computers, books, toys, etc. It is advisable to duplicate essential possessions so they do not have to be packed up each weekend. Even so, the children may be left with the feeling they are always "on the move."

Model 2: *Nine days with one parent (Tuesday afternoon until the following Thursday morning) followed by five days with the other parent.* Oftentimes, work requirements or individual preferences (adolescents may want to spend more time with one parent) require some variation on an equal split, so a nine-day–five-day cycle is chosen. This gives each parent a complete weekend, while also providing both with weekday nights to share the burdens and joys of parental responsibilities: from homework to bedtime routines, cooking to laundry.

Model 3: *Four days with Mom (Sunday until Thursday morning), then three days with Dad, then three days with Mom, followed by four* *days with Dad. Then repeat the cycle.* When younger children don't adapt well to long absences and the parents themselves can't emotionally tolerate the separation, this schedule is attractive. It does include a transition each weekend on Saturday night or Sunday morning, and this may become inconvenient when either parent starts dating or wants to take a weekend trip with the kids. Since each individual may have a different afternoon timetable, this schedule also requires flexible day-care or after-school arrangements—pickup times may not be consistent from day to day. The weekday blocks of time without the children are long enough to meet most business and travel requirements, minimizing the need for unsettling last-minute changes (see Chapter 21).

Model 4: *Two days with Mom (Monday until Wednesday morning), Wednesday with Dad, four days with Mom, two days with Dad, then Wednesday with Mom, and finally four days with Dad. Then repeat the cycle.* This variation does not require splitting weekends. We would urge caution—carefully monitor the effects of the more numerous transitions, especially those surrounding the single day. Many dual-career parents who are cooperative use the Wednesday as a safety valve to accommodate sudden changes caused by personal or work obligations. Sometimes they may shift Wednesday for Thursday (which may or may not be agreeable with the kids); when this isn't possible, the other parent has the children for the whole week. Families with younger-age children often require flexible day-care or after-school arrangements for this option to succeed, especially if the parents live far apart.

Try one of these models or your own variation. Talk with the other parent and the kids. If you are finding the interim schedule less than satisfactory, share that feeling, rather than assume you are alone. Try not to blame the other parent for inadequacies in time allocations. This forces children to take sides, and limits the possibilities for amicably establishing a new set of "rules." Keep looking for the advantages in any option, bearing in mind that in six months, or two years, whatever schedule you create will hopefully be replaced by a new, improved model.

9 Handovers

In which fifteen-year-old Ryan tells what he
would like to happen on Friday nights when
Mom picks up the kids

Child's Point of View:
I Don't Want to Go Right Now

Why should I cooperate and live my life on their timetable? I never agreed to this schedule. Mom and Dad did, almost two years ago. I didn't like it then and I still don't, because it messes up my life. Most nights I skateboard at the park with my friends until it gets dark. But I don't even get the choice every other Friday night, because I have to go spend time with Mom. All the guys love it—makes me look like a real wuss. At least now she doesn't try to pick me up with the guys there like she used to, but she still expects me to drop everything to meet her schedule. Tonight, even though I made a special effort to leave the park early, I got yelled at because Mom had to wait while I finished packing. If Dad had really wanted me to be ready on time, he would have packed for me. But *no* . . . when I got home, Mom was sitting in her car glaring, and Dad tried to make himself look good in front of her by frowning and reminding me how my little sister had begged me to be on time. Why am I always the one who gets in trouble? Katy was the one who was late last week, and I didn't hear any lectures!

If Mom doesn't like being kept waiting, she could take Katy to dinner and then pick me up later. Instead, I get a big sermon about cooperation and responsibility. A lot my parents know about that! Now Mom's been taunting me all night with "What's wrong, darling?" If she's not careful, I'll tell her the truth—I'd rather not be here at all. I'm like any other fifteen-year-old. It's not that I don't like her, but on Friday night I'd rather board until they close the park, and then watch a game on TV with Dad.

Parent's Point of View:
These Handovers Are Too Frustrating

It's always the same every weekend. The kids are never ready when I arrive to pick them up—even though they and their father know that I have to make a special effort to get there exactly at 6:00 P.M. like we all agreed. The excuses always seem plausible, yet I constantly feel like I'm getting shortchanged. I'm always angry starting off Friday night, and that's not the way I want the weekends to begin.

Last week was typical. Katy's school bus was late, so she wasn't ready. When I pointed out to Jim they were supposed to pack the night before, he shot back that Katy had Girl Scouts on Thursdays and a big book report that had been due Friday morning, so "When was she supposed to pack?" Then tonight it was Ryan's fault, as he showed up at the same time I did and wasn't ready to go. Katy had supposedly been ready for two hours. According to Jim, she was "unbelievably anxious" that they be ready in time so as not to make me mad. She'd even asked her brother to come home extra early this afternoon. But of course he didn't.

So the argument started all over for the thousandth time. Jim hinted that the kids are late because they don't really want to come see me—which isn't true. I said that if he, as their father, would set a few rules and stick to them—or rather, make the kids stick to them—none of this would happen. I know our voices were raised and in the midst of the row, Ryan stormed out and got in the car with a big slam of the door. He hasn't said anything all night, and Katy is sulking too—I don't know whether she feels I pay all the attention to her brother, or it's another time when she is withdrawing because her father is upset.

It seems to me we ought to be able to devise some system that prevents a big portion of every weekend being consumed with the logistics of the comings and goings. The kids and I just don't have enough time together to spend Friday night feeling distant from one another. And the same thing happens Sunday afternoon—they "leave" before they actually are gone. I feel like I'm getting punished for being the "visiting parent." Sometimes I wonder if Ryan is old enough to be allowed to decide whether he wants to be the "visiting child," but I don't want to suggest that. Jim would never encourage him to come, and if Ryan stopped coming, I'd be devastated.

This whole situation seems so unfair. I'm the one who earns the money. I pay the child support. I'm just as much a parent as Jim is. Why is it such a problem just to get together with my children?

Making Sense of It All

Handovers—the physical and logistic arrangements necessary when children leave the care and responsibility of one parent for that of the other—are but one aspect of the transition process. This process has multiple emotional levels and spans a duration of time that extends well beyond the period enclosed by the actual moments of hello and good-bye (see Chapter 10). While an ideal handover arrangement does not preclude difficulties with transitions, all members of the family, including the custodial parent, benefit when the routine creates more enjoyable time together and minimizes the hesitancy surrounding reunions and the sullen anticipation of good-byes.

There is no perfect handover routine that works for all families, and even within a given family, a successful routine will need to be modified over time. A few basics, however, have served as valuable guidelines for many families, whether they were creating a handover routine for the first time or determining what revisions were necessary to make a routine more satisfactory.

Setting a Time for the Pickup

Set a pickup time that is workable for the adults. While you may want the pickup to be as early as possible and the good-bye to be as late as possible, does the scheme make sense? If you establish 5:00 P.M. on Fridays as the pickup time, it can require a mad dash through traffic, which leaves you stressed out and irritable—the kids won't care how much you want to see them, if you're always grumpy. Similarly, if 5:00 P.M. means you'll always be late, then the kids and the other parent are likely to always be angry with you. This leads to adult arguments, and the kids will probably dawdle just to teach you to stick to your commitments.

The best pickup arrangements offer the kids some flexibility. If practice is over at 4:45 P.M., expecting your kid to dash away from teammates and rush home to see you is unrealistic and unreasonable. Allowing the kids some free time to spend with friends may reduce their complaints about being cut off from friends when they're with you. Alternatively, although setting a later time for pickup on Friday nights will cut into the absolute amount of time you have together over the weekend, if your children get their homework done prior to your arrival, it may be addition by subtraction. Furthermore, especially if they are somewhere "neutral," free time in the afternoon or early evening allows the kids to have a quiet hiatus, which eases the emotional adjustments of the transition.

Determining the Return Time

Setting a return time will require some experimentation. As we will explain later in this chapter, bringing the kids back to some neutral location, usually school or day care, causes much less turmoil than a parent-to-parent handover. This option often defines the time you leave them, e.g., school starts at 8:00 A.M., so dawdling and delaying are less likely to happen. If you have to bring the children back to the home of the other parent, look at the perspectives of all the players before you make a decision as to what time that should be. If you decide that late in the evening maximizes your time together with the kids, and hence is preferable, then you are obliged to make sure their homework is done and their return is not so late that the resultant fatigue or overexcitement interferes with your children's sleep.

Finally, set a time acknowledging that there is a period when emotions are volatile and behavior is different, usually starting some time before the actual parting and extending for many hours after the exchange.

Choosing the Location

The exact way the handover is done frequently reflects the parenting style of the adults and many of their own motivations. The parent-to-parent handover of the children is likely to provoke acting out on the children's part, as well as offer opportunities for the adults to vent lingering hostilities and to press more practical issues (e.g., "You never could be anywhere on time!" or "I suppose you expect me to wash their clothes and get their homework done now!" or "Why haven't I received the support check?"). If these interactions are occurring in front of the children, we advise avoiding parent-to-parent handovers whenever possible.

This is most easily managed if you agree that the pickup or drop-off will occur at a neutral, safe location where there are adults to watch out for the kids and activities in which they can participate. For example, dropping off at school or day care works well after an overnight or weekend visit. For picking up, a church group, the day-care center, school, or a library where the kids can go and wait without the parent are ideal. Such settings often take away the pressure of choosing an exact time when traffic conditions or last-minute work hassles may delay you. Children say they like this setup. It gives them free time, a sense of control, and often an adjustment interlude that makes it easier to fit in with the arriving parent, without the hesitancy felt after an immediate parting from the other parent.

If you don't have an easily accessible location like the town library, then meet the kids at the school bus, or see if a friend (or a rotating group of friends) will commit to an occasional couple of hours of child-sitting. Sometimes even teachers who stay late to do their preparation work for the next day will watch over a child.

If you've got a really cooperative relationship with your ex-spouse, then you may be able to pick them up at that house, but be careful. The friction that often develops when you are face-to-face can push the balance to antagonism and confrontation very quickly. However, we do not advocate the solution of having your children collected from and delivered to the front step of their home, as it treats them too much like packages from UPS.

Establishing the Mechanism

Once you've established a suitable location, then you have more control over the greeting and the good-bye. In a neutral setting, greetings tend to be more enthusiastic and partings feel a little bit less like being shut out of your kids' lives. Both children and parents are more comfortable if they are not being watched by the other parent or trying to be sensitive to that parent's feelings.

If you are meeting your children at "home," the major question is who's responsible for the kids being ready on time. By default, it's usually the parent from whom the kids are departing. Most adults need a break from being the "full-time parent," so it serves the residential parent's interests to have the kids ready at the designated time. Little is gained by permitting or encouraging them to act out or stall. However, if the kids themselves are resistant to the visit for any reason, it's the unusual parent who will force them to be ready on time. A pattern of delay suggests there is an issue to be addressed. The problem is that both parents have to address it, but they are likely to interpret the ambivalent behavior of their children differently (see Chapter 29).

Some parents decide to make the kids responsible for being ready. The advantage of this arrangement is that it minimizes manipulation by the parent they are leaving, but the disadvantage is that it subjects the arriving parent to the whim of the children. We all know adolescents who simply "don't get it"—that being two hours late is not acceptable, even though they have a good excuse. Some people try to work around this by using a beeper—either the kid calls them or they call the kid. A variant on that is to use the telephone, typically letting the kid call to announce, "I'm ready, where are you?" as if you should have been psychic! Either approach can be complicated when more than one child is involved—usually one is ready and one is not, so the manipulative possibilities of playing for your favor are numerous.

You may make the kids responsible, but we still advise that you set a time and make sure you're prompt as well.

Other Considerations

While neutral locations often work the best, there are times when picking the kids up at home has a purpose. If they have moved following the divorce, children often want you to understand where and how they live. They need to know you can picture them in their new surroundings, just like they need to be able to picture you in yours. So picking them up at home may actually need to include a brief tour on the first occasion. Be careful not to allow this to set a precedent, otherwise you will find you have to come up to their room or visit the cat every time. If the move was necessitated by the divorce itself, insisting you stay for dinner or other "be there" activities is usually a ploy to get you and your ex-spouse back together again. Going along with this scheme in order to humor the kids will not turn out to be a fun game. Let them know you are interested in seeing their home, but don't get trapped in other agendas.

Most of the entanglements happen during the drop-off. Taking them to school or day care or putting them on the school bus is a normal activity for most parents and is quite tolerable, but returning the children to the other parent is always painful, as it highlights how abnormal life after divorce really is. Focusing on the next time you will see each other, while traveling back, can help some kids; for others, it's a tease and they're better off talking about how much fun you've just had together. If you bring them back to the residence where you all used to live, it's tempting for them (and you) to want to extend the time together, with a bedtime story or dessert in the kitchen. Don't do it, because all too often tears result when the fantasy interlude of what was, but cannot now continue, simply makes everyone hurt more, and the good-byes become much more painful.

General Guidelines

A good handover routine reduces the pressures and demands on the parent the kids are leaving, and maximizes the enjoyable time with the parent they are joining.

- Once a child is old enough to be in day care, the best routines avoid a direct parent-to-parent handover.
- Scheduling times for pickup and return requires careful consideration of everyone's commitments. Before you make compromises, get input from the kids. Parents who make unilateral decisions often meet resistance and acting out.
- Pickup times are usually set so the visiting parent has the maximum possible time with the children, but that is not always wise. Giving the children a window of free time between the end of school and pickup offers them quiet time to ease the transition, time to spend with peers that may decrease competitive pressures on time with the parent, and/or lets them complete their homework.
- Partings from each other are less volatile if children are brought back to school or day care in the morning, rather than returned directly to the other parent.
- Neutral locations are the best when meeting the kids or returning them, e.g., school or day care, the library, school bus, community center, etc.
- Neutral locations minimize the problems of "getting the kids ready on time."
- As the children's interests and social groups change, the routine will have to be adapted.
- No matter what the handover routine, there will be some awkwardness and hesitancy around reunions, and mixed emotions in anticipation of saying good-bye.

Transitions

In which Amanda, age eight, describes what
happens when Dad returns them to Mom
after a visit

Child's Point of View:
I Dread the Good-Byes

I got the teacher all upset in class today. It was her own fault. She had each of us talk about what we did over the weekend. I said that I didn't remember much of what happened; but I went on and on about how I hate when Dad picks us up, because we never know what to say to each other for the first couple of hours, and how I start dreading the good-byes, hours before it's time to go home. I described how my little brother usually seems fine until the last moment, and then he stands by the door, looking through the glass, sobbing while Dad walks away. She asked me whether I cry. Well, I wasn't going to admit that in front of the whole class, so I said I usually try to think of the fun things we've done. That's what Mom and Dad advise me to do when I get upset, but it doesn't always work.

I didn't tell her how Dad makes it really tough if it's one of those weekends when *he* starts to cry on the way back to Mom's. He thinks I can't tell, but his voice is different and he looks really sad. Even when he doesn't cry, he's usually a grouch most of Sunday afternoon.

Sometimes I think we should come home earlier and avoid the whole scene, but Mom says there's no avoiding the feelings. Even Mom's getting caught up in this. She used to be all smiles and happy to see us. I thought that was why she insisted we be home promptly at six. But in the last few weeks, she hasn't even come to the door when we arrive home. We were even late once and she didn't seem to care. It's like she can't stand to see Dad cry when he drops us off. She says we'll all get used to it in another year or so. I'd sure like to think so, but it's been almost two years now and it's just not getting a whole lot better.

Parent's Point of View:
The Visits Are Hard; the Partings Devastating

All week I think about seeing my kids. I seem to live for the weekends we can be together. I talk to them on the phone about where we could go and what they would like for dinner, and they always seem to be looking forward to the visit as much as I am. Then what happens? More times than not, when I actually arrive, one of them doesn't want to come. There is a whole lot of clinging to Charlotte and crying. She does her best, but I think she fusses over them for too long. When I finally get both of them buckled in the car and everything should be fine, my problems have just begun. I can't believe how long it takes them to behave normally! I don't know whether to be angry or sympathetic. Amanda usually sulks all through dinner, and Tommy sucks his fingers and tries to annoy his sister by kicking her "accidentally" or taking her stuff. It's all such a waste of our precious time together.

Even when I pick the kids up at school, it's not great. True, the initial moments are much smoother, but the kids still seem distant—their emotions all mixed up about seeing me. I'm surprised that after two years we still take time to fit together. I suppose the "hellos" have gradually gotten easier over time, but the "good-byes" are still as bad as ever. I don't even like to think about those. Maybe, if anything, they're getting worse.

No matter what I do, no matter what the activity or how much fun we're having, acting up always starts sometime Sunday afternoon. I used to think they were afraid Charlotte would be angry if they were back late, since they would start packing up at lunchtime and then, with nothing else to do, pick on each other or me for the rest of the day. I began to wonder whether they might just be feeling bored because it's a small apartment and they don't have many toys here, but recently I have realized that I am also acting differently as the leaving time approaches. I feel myself getting upset thinking about what it will be like at 6:00 P.M. and what I'm going to do to distract myself when I get back home. Nothing compares with the empty feeling that I have when the front door shuts and I walk back to the car alone. It's so unnatural to be shut out of your own kids' lives. The weekend usually ends with me feeling devastated. It doesn't matter how good a time we have had; Monday morning, the sadness of parting is all I remember.

Making Sense of It All

Many parents and their children quickly learn to anticipate the awkwardness of saying hello after being apart for days or weeks, and the angst of saying good-bye before another absence. What surprises them, however, is the duration and the intensity of the emotional reactions leading up to and then following each of these events. Often the difficulties are compounded by the logistics of the handover, but for most families, coming to some resolution of these transition difficulties is more complex than just changing the handover routine.

Anticipation and Accommodation

Parents have difficulty dealing with their children when they act uncharacteristically during the anticipation of parental handovers. All too often, these adjustment periods make both parents feel deprived in different ways. The little girl preening in front of the mirror, isolated in her hopeful fantasies that Dad and his girlfriend will like her pretty dress, may unwittingly elicit strong feelings of resentment in her mother. Mom would prefer having the time together in front of the mirror without feeling that her former husband is intruding. A teenage son, feeling guilty about an expensive weekend raft trip with Dad, may be withdrawn for hours on Sunday afternoon as a way of preparing to go back to see Mom, who he knows is chronically short of money. Dad, expecting to share the last hours of time together recalling tales of their exploits on the river, may become perplexed or antagonistic at his son's display of aloofness.

The period following the transition is frequently as troublesome as the period of anticipation. Parent and child often struggle to get into sync with one another. The process can take hours, even if there are only a couple of hours to spend together. Getting in sync can be complicated by the child's feelings of having betrayed the parent left behind. In the examples given earlier, the little girl may actually ignore her father's compliments and gain little joy from his admiration, as she struggles to recover from her Mom's displeasure. The son may continue in his aloof mood, aware that Mom will only become upset if he shares stories about a great weekend. Following the reunion with the child who has been away on a visit, the receiving parent may be at a loss to know how to interpret the child's behaviors. Do the tears later that night mean Dad didn't like the dress? That she didn't have a good time? That she's worried about getting her homework done? Does the son's refusal to talk about the weekend mean he had a good time and is afraid of provoking jealousy? That he's afraid too much information will elicit another soliloquy about Dad's irresponsibility with money? That he's disappointed because another "good time" can't substitute for a "real" relationship with his often absent father? Transition times are awkward and uncomfortable for all concerned.

Why Children Have Difficulty

The fundamental problem for children is that divorce makes it risky to display or admit to one parent that they are thinking about or missing the other, or that they are anticipating the emotional turmoil of the handover, instead of enjoying the last hours or minutes before the transfer actually happens. Children often feel it is necessary to emotionally detach from one parent in order to attach, no matter how transiently, to the other. This engenders feelings of guilt and stress. Many parents find it difficult to appreciate how hard it is for their children to tolerate repeated separations and reunions when the children come to perceive them as repeated betrayals. It is especially difficult when the children come to realize that actions such as running back for one more kiss before Dad leaves or calling Mom in the middle of Saturday dinner with Dad (see Chapter 11) are usually met with parental displeasure. The children fear that even bringing the absent parent with them in their thoughts will hurt the parent they are with. Sadly, many children find that it is more adaptive to work on putting the absent parent and their life with that parent out of their mind during their time away. In this way they attempt to decrease their own guilt and stress.

Parents: Help or Hindrance?

When transitions don't go well, your first inclination may be to try to analyze your children's behavior and comments or lack thereof. You will accurately perceive your children are behaving differently from usual, but you may fail to see that you are behaving differently also. In many cases you will get a better understanding of the transition difficulties if you look at your own and your ex-partner's behaviors as well as your children's. The adults' behaviors have a critical influence on what is going on. The period of time during which your children appear to be acting abnormally, in anticipation of and following the handover from one parent to the other, will be increased if there is tension or hostility between you and your ex-spouse. Hostile parents ensnare the children in their own angry feelings, and it takes time for the children to discover that it isn't they who are unhappy or worried or angry, but rather the parent they have left behind. For example, if Mom is worried that Dad is not a good parent, or a good person, since she believes he's a cheat and untrustworthy, or she hates him for getting a divorce and leaving her all alone, she can give out all kinds of indirect cues that may produce unease in her child: e.g., "Better eat a snack because Dad isn't a great cook," or "I won't pack your good shoes because Dad's always too busy with his work to take you out," or "Take some real clothes in case Dad decides to do something normal with you, rather than just going from one party to another." The effect of these messages lasts, whether given minutes before Dad comes or when the child leaves for school in the morning. If Mom has tears in her eyes, anger in her voice, or if she clearly doesn't want the child to leave her or see the father at all, then the child will feel added conflict, guilt, and confusion.

When children get these mixed messages, it often takes several hours for them to relate normally to the "new" parent. Of course, none of this is made easier for the children if the receiving parent isn't "acting like himself" either. He may simply be trying too hard with his nice-guy or have-fun persona, but by not being "familiar Dad," he is extending the awkward transition time. Many parents have a hard time with this paradox—they act interested and engaged hoping to get back into the swing of things with their kids, but find the children are still distant despite the parent's own welcoming behavior. Finding the balance between simply saying, "I'm glad to see you," and an act that doesn't ring true to the child, is difficult for everyone.

Minimizing Difficulties

The ideal transition in which both parents are happy and the children totally unambivalent seldom happens. A more realistic expectation for parents and children is that the feelings engendered during the transition will take time to settle and that the handover routine needs to accommodate this time (see Chapter 9). When divorce minimizes your time with one another, there is a premium on togetherness and that in itself generates tension and anxiety. Rather than let anger or false expectations thwart your enjoyment, try to set an example by talking to your kids about your own mixture of emotions caused by the going back and forth, and encourage them to talk as well. If you feel set up by the other parent, there's no point in getting angry at the kids. If you're using phrases like, "I don't care what your mother said . . . ," or "Why doesn't your father speak for himself . . . ," that's a clear warning you're talking to the wrong person and compromising your opportunity for quality time together.

General Guidelines

Bear in mind that:

- The transition period precedes and extends beyond the actual moments of saying hello and good-bye.
- Transition awkwardness can't be avoided entirely, but its duration and impact can be minimized.
- The inevitable transitions that become part of family life after divorce affect the emotions of each parent, both at separation and reunion.
- Changes in your behavior impact how your children feel and behave. They will pick up positive and negative vibrations from your body language and tone of voice.
- You can ease the transition adjustments for your children by setting an example. Openly discuss your own emotional reactions and how they affect your personal behavior.
- An appropriate handover routine can limit the emotional disequilibrium experienced by all members of the family (see Chapter 9).

Telephoning Home

In which ten-year-old Sarah wants to call
Mom from Dad's house

Child's Point of View:
I Just Wanted to Call Home

I didn't think when I asked if I could call home that it would end up as such a disaster! I mean, I just wanted to talk to Mom. All of a sudden I really missed her, even though it was only a day since I last saw her. I don't know why, but I kind of worry about her when I can't be sure where she is or what she's doing—not that I think she'd forget me or anything. . . . But anyway, Dad was getting dinner ready and I really didn't want to help set the table (not that I said *that!*) . . . so I just asked if I could call Mom. Well, first Dad got that irritated look on his face and said it really wasn't a good time. Then he did his why-do-you-have-to-call-Mom-all-the-time speech . . . the one that goes, "We're having a good time, aren't we? You'll be seeing Mom soon, so you really don't have to call *all* the time and interrupt what we're doing." Well I *wasn't* having a good time right then, but if I said *that* I was afraid I'd hurt his feelings, so I just cried. Then Dad got all worried and said he didn't want me to cry and I could phone Mom.

I wish that had been all, but it got worse! I phoned Mom and she could hear from my voice that I'd been crying. She seemed very sympathetic, so I asked if I could come home instead of staying the night with Dad. Big mistake! Mom asked to speak to Dad. Dad wouldn't come to the phone, saying he was "too busy" cooking, and told me I should say good-bye to Mom and come eat. I started to cry again; Mom started telling me that she thought Dad was being inconsiderate; and then Dad snatched the phone, shouted at her, and hung up.

All that because I wanted to call home! Sometimes I really don't think either of them care what *I* want. They're too busy making sure they get what *they* want. I was so mad that I just screamed and shouted and slammed doors. In the end Dad took me home. I bet he was glad really—to be rid of me, I mean.

I hate all this! I hate when Mom and Dad shout at each other over me. And most of all, I hate myself when it's all *my* fault.

Parent's Point of View:
Will Every Visit Fall Apart Like This?

I'm really discouraged. I mean what does it take to get a great day *and* an enjoyable evening with my kids? Take this weekend for example. I tried so hard. We went out for breakfast and I let them have chocolate chip pancakes—their mother would never do that! Then I froze sitting on a bench at the playground, while they swung on the monkey bars and spent an eternity digging in the sandbox—an activity I thought Sarah had given up years ago. The afternoon was spent at the movies with buckets of popcorn and giant sodas—not exactly the movie *I* was dying to see, but Sarah thought it was funny. And I let Noah sit on my lap most of the day, talking and talking—even during the movie! I thought we'd had a great day and then, after all that, the evening was a disaster.

When we got back to my apartment, we played cards until I started to prepare dinner. Sarah looked a little bored, but I couldn't play and make dinner at the same time, so I asked her to set the table. Then it all started. "What are we having to eat?" she asked in that negative tone of voice I hate. "Spaghetti and meatballs, your favorite." I replied, trying to stay cool. "It's not anymore," I heard her mutter under her breath. Not wanting to start an argument, I ignored her, but could see we were heading in the wrong direction.

After another prompt to please set the table, she glared at me and said, "I want to call Mom." Those dreaded words! How my heart sinks when she says that. I know she's only a kid, and of course she loves her mom, but couldn't we have one whole day in which Kathy, or the ghost of Kathy, didn't invade our time together? I suppose a perfect parent would have said, "Yes, of course darling, I know you miss your mommy very much. I'll put all the just-ready-to-eat dinner in the oven and you may talk with Mommy just as long as you like." Instead, I told her the truth. I didn't think it was a good time and it wasn't really necessary. That did *not* have the desired effect. Tears started to flow, and I handed her the phone.

If only that had been all. The next thing I hear is, "I want to go home *now*, and Mom wants to speak to you." Speaking to Kathy these days has to be the most unproductive activity imaginable, so I said I was too busy cooking and invited Sarah to get off the phone so we could talk about it together. She declined. "He won't talk to you and he won't let me come home," she sobbed into the phone. I couldn't see any other way out. . . . I took the phone from her hands, said an angry good-bye, and hung up.

The next hour was pure hell. Sarah crying and slamming doors. Noah pleading that *he* didn't want to go home yet. Me telling them I loved them and just wanted to spend time together. And then, emotionally drained, I looked at my little girl and her tearstained face and took them both home to their mom. Now I just feel empty and hopeless. When will this end?

Making Sense of It All

The dilemma of what to do when the visiting child wants to either call home or go home is one faced by most parents. Calling at dinnertime or bedtime is extremely disruptive, but a request to call at these times is not unusual, because the activity is associated with the absent parent. Unfortunately, the call often only makes the visiting child more homesick. In the example given, we don't know all the reasons why Sarah wants to call her mother: perhaps she misses her; maybe she feels guilty about having such a good day with Dad while Mom is all alone; maybe she thinks Mom may have forgotten her; or she may, like most ten-year-olds, just be avoiding setting the table.

Being separated from either parent is hard for children of divorce. Missing the parent they're not with may significantly interfere with their ability to enjoy themselves, which can lead to acting out in many ways. Even though the left-behind parent may be having as much difficulty with the separation as the children, that adult has the responsibility to decrease the children's guilt and the potential for loyalty conflicts. The left-behind parent needs to reassure the children by saying, "I miss you, but I'm not lonely," and then by sharing with them the stories of what she or he has done while they've been away. A scheduled phone call at the beginning of the day gives an opportunity to share yesterday's activities and today's plans.

Children of divorce may perceive their lives as being dominated by a succession of good-byes—parents leaving each other and parents leaving children. We would caution that encouraging repeated phoning home or being phoned usually does not reassure the children but actually feeds their anxiety about the temporary separation from the other parent. This phenomenon is hardly unique to divorce. A familiar example of separation anxiety being increased by the ambivalent behavior of a parent is commonly seen in day-care centers and nursery schools. The child who clings and fusses while the parent prepares to leave, and then settles down and has a fine time when the parent has gone is a common sight. A brief visit in the middle of the day, like the unscheduled phone call, may actually be counterproductive and start the tearful behavior all over again. Repeated visits, like repeated calls, mean repeated separations and repeated good-byes. This is why most summer camps commonly offer only limited telephone access for campers to call home: frequent phoning home usually increases the homesick child's sadness.

The urge to touch base with the absent parent is understandable in children of any age, but for some kids, especially the younger ones who lack even the experience of a sleep-over, a day or two away from their residential parent may feel endless. To the nonresidential parent, however, a mere two days of contact with their child seems far from endless. Frequently there is a withdrawal around the transitions, so it takes time for the children to warm up, and anticipation of the parting may start several hours before the good-bye (see Chapter 10). Requests such as Sarah's, to phone Mom in the middle of a visit, only serve to highlight the temporary nature of the contact. It can feel as if the visit finishes there and then, even if in reality it is only an interruption.

After a full and fun day together, it is painful for this father to accept that his kids could be thinking of their mother. If he had been abusive, ignored the children, or been absent because of other activities, he might legitimately see a request to call home as a condemnation of his parenting. But even when this is not the case, as in this dad's visit with Noah and Sarah, it is easy to feel guilty and respond inappropriately. The children's need to call the absent parent usually reflects the quality of their relationship with that parent.

Should Sarah's dad have dealt with the situation differently? Maybe, but without a road map it is easy to get drawn onto a side road, which is what in fact happened. Sarah would have done better with a "Yes, you may phone now," or "No, you may not." The attempt to invalidate her feelings by telling her it wasn't *necessary* to phone was a mistake, as was his immediately giving in to her tears. The lessons taught were: 1) we the adults define what you should be feeling, and 2) if you cry for Daddy he'll give in. These are not lessons most parents want to instill in their children.

General Guidelines

There may not be a solution that is equally acceptable to both parents and children for avoiding conflicts over calling home. Most children would like complete freedom to phone whenever they want, most nonresidential parents would like their limited time to be free of interference from the other parent, and most parents would like to hear from their children while they are away on visitation weekends without having to sit home waiting for an unscheduled call. It is important to have ground rules about phoning that are mutually acceptable to the other parent and your child *before* there is an issue. Our advice is:

- Limit the calls to one per day, and discuss together at the outset of the visit the time when calls are permissible. Explain the emotional and logistic reasons for why this will be to everyone's benefit.
- Arrange the call to be after breakfast and before the day's activities start, to guarantee the parties will be available to talk to each other. Midday calls or bedtime chats interrupt the flow of events and tend to shatter any intimacy between parent and child during a short visit.
- Have the kids call, rather than plan to have the other parent check in. That way the kids are ready to talk and the other parent does not disrupt a fun activity or an important conversation.
- When separated from their children, some parents find phone contact difficult to handle. Most adults want to know their children are OK, but they don't want to know that their children are unhappy, lonely, bored, or having the time of their lives. Some parents actually prohibit calls for these reasons. This can make children feel unwanted, so a better way to limit the anxiety is to set up a schedule for calls.
- Don't be tempted to make repeated spontaneous changes in the agreed-upon arrangements. This behavior leads to difficulties, because it invites manipulation by the child and/or the other parent, as well as increases parental hostility, since it forces plans to be changed. Even in an intact marriage there are usually limits to the amount of flexibility each partner allows the other.
- Don't be influenced by tears any more than you would have been before the separation. Giving in to the tears may seem like a kind thing to do, but children rapidly learn to exploit this chink in your armor.
- Don't let guilt be the driving force behind your decisions. Once you start feeling guilty if you don't go along with your kids'

requests to go home or stay home, the result is predictable: you are likely to find yourself with so little contact with your children that you cannot build the relationships within which your children will *want* to visit with you.

- Remain in the parental role. That means sometimes making decisions that your children do not agree with. Once the children start to believe that they can control the flow of events, you have burdened them with a role they are ill-equipped to play.
- Sometimes children may fear that out-of-sight means out-of-mind and that they may be forgotten, despite your verbal assurances to the contrary. Encourage your kids to leave you drawings and other reminders. Set up a system to exchange or send faxes or letters, all of which are more tangible than phone calls. Likewise, a passport photo that kids can carry in a pocket or wallet means a lot—and it is less likely to upset the other parent than a framed picture by the bedside.

Why Not on Thursdays? 12

In which nine-year-old Larry talks about

Dad's one-night stand

Child's Point of View:
So What if They Slept Together?

Life wasn't much fun when my parents were fighting all the time. I thought when they split up things would get better. Maybe both Mom and Dad would be less angry at each other and everyone else—especially me! But I must have been living in a dream world.

Dad had this woman, Vanessa, there this weekend. She was nice to me and she kept Gus laughing about her experience in the second grade—tough to do since he hates school. Sylvia didn't want her to go home on Saturday, because she spent so much time reading Sylvia bedtime stories. But Mom went ballistic when I started talking about the great breakfast Vanessa made on Saturday morning—and then she wanted to know everything else we did with Vanessa, which only made her get madder.

So Vanessa slept there. Yeah, and they probably had sex, but what do I care? Mom's always saying she's lonely, so why should Dad want to be lonely too? Mom acts like Dad is getting married before they are even divorced. I mean he's only known Vanessa for a week. What's the big deal?

Parent's Point of View:
You Can't Humiliate Me Like This!

I thought I was angry three months ago when he said there was another woman and he wanted a divorce, but that was nothing compared to how I feel now. I have to admit I felt some satisfaction when the "Great Romance" didn't last. My friends have told me there have been a couple of less "great" ones in the last few weeks. Sounds like his latest was a pickup in a bar—and he has the gall to have her there when he's with my children! How could he? Doesn't he have any integrity? I feel like he's intentionally trying to humiliate me. It just demonstrates his contempt for us, for marriage, for commitment, and for promises. What does he think this does to the kids' trust in his love for them, or their view of me?

Well, maybe he doesn't think, except with his balls—like many men. After the last meeting with the mediator, I thought he really did care about the kids and wanted to do what was best for them. Foolish me—

believing him one more time. Well, now I'm going to listen to my lawyer. She's right. If I'm cooperative, if I compromise, he'll just take advantage of me. I'll teach him. If he's late to pick up the kids, like he was Friday, then he can forget seeing them. If he touches me again, I'll get a court order to prevent him from coming on the property. I've kept saying that I can't understand why some women seek vengeance, but now I do.

OK Al, want to see who can hurt whom? You're going to get a divorce agreement you'll hate living with every day for the rest of your life. You're not going to walk all over me, and you're not going to do this to my kids!

Why couldn't he just have slept with her on Thursday night when the kids were here with me? I wouldn't have liked it, but I wouldn't feel like I do right now.

Making Sense of It All

Few things in a relationship cause more disagreement than sex and money, so it is not surprising that these are often the focus of post-separation animosity. Although not many adults would claim they expect their ex-spouse to remain celibate for the rest of their lives, parents rarely agree on how and when to introduce a new sexual partner into the lives of their children.

Studies have shown that casual sexual relationships are frequently part of the personal divorce recovery process of both parents. Many men and women, whether the person leaving the marriage or the one being left, feel an overwhelming need to engage in a series of sexual conquests to offset the distressing sense of failure, humiliation, and personal rejection, which is universal when a marriage dissolves. No matter how necessary such relationships may be, however, they should not be part of the children's experience. This father could have spared himself and his family the consequences illustrated in his ex-spouse's diary by concentrating on being a parent while with the kids and confining his social and sexual explorations to the nights and weekends when he's not responsible for the kids' care.

Many parents are so caught up in their own lives that they fail to see the direct or indirect impact of their egocentric behavior on the other parent or even on the children. They see the world only from their own perspective and ignore the enormity of the pain they have caused. There are stages of grieving for any significant loss, and the end of a marriage is one of life's most painful losses. There is usually a period of denial, followed by a phase of anger, which precedes the readiness to move forward. All adults and children go through similar stages, including the adult who "walks out" on the other, but the rate at which they progress from one stage to the next are not the same. Everyone is therefore out of sync. At the time at which one parent wants to introduce other relationships and sex as a "normal" part of life, and a sign of "moving on," the other is seldom ready. The consequence is significant emotional turmoil that all too often stirs latent hostility or precipitates overt anger.

In the period before and after the separation, and often even after the divorce itself, children rarely progress beyond the stage of denial or of hoping that their parents will get back together. If introduced too early to the dating behavior of one parent, not only can the children no longer use denial as a defense mechanism to protect themselves from the pain of realizing their family is disintegrating, they also see that the happiness of one parent is causing distress to the other. Once the other parent realizes the children are being exposed to the presence and influence of casual romances, the children are bound to experience the fallout from an escalation of hostility; whether seen in the body language of their parents, heard in their angry statements, or felt in the acts of retribution that often follow incidents like the one described.

The children are further compromised because the angry parent usually finds it difficult, if not impossible, to help them accept or forgive the irresponsible behavior of the other parent. No matter how much grieving or self-realization has been accomplished, witnessing a series of transient lovers is demeaning and belittles the significance of the marital relationship.

While transient post-separation affairs may be a normal part of the adult recovery process, they are often merely an attempt to paper over insecurities or to get back at a spouse. When consumed by self-centeredness, parents often fail to care what their spouse feels or to notice that their children are being placed in an intolerable series of loyalty binds. If the children feel attached to the "other person," they feel guilty; if they hate the other person, they feel displaced. Once hostility escalates, conspiracies to keep events secret become commonplace (see Chapter 19), and the children are increasingly set up as messengers between their parents, with disastrous results (see Chapter 18). More-over, it becomes easy to make the "other person" the scapegoat for everything that goes wrong, e.g., "Your father could give us more money if he didn't spend it on her," or "Mom wouldn't be late if she wasn't seeing him," etc., making it unlikely the children will ever feel comfortable with the relationship even if it lasts.

Since many of these dalliances are transient, it's ironic that their consequences are often engraved in the divorce settlement document, and that what may seem "normal" in terms of parent recovery has a long-lasting negative effect on the parent-child relationship. A blink-ered focus on "self" heightens the anguish for the children. The par-ent who is consumed by grief, the responsibilities of child care, or the financial demands of the new situation, often feels justified in retaliat-ing. At a minimum, this parent usually starts with overt criticism of the ex-spouse, even if it has been resisted up to this point. The parent involved in the affairs then usually responds by labeling the other par-ent as a mean "sob" or "bitch." It is clear that, at this stage, an alliance with either parent becomes very dangerous for the kids. They are dragged further into the hostility if one or more of the following occurs:

1. Visitation is withheld or contact with other family members is restricted.
2. The parent who is hurt increasingly bad-mouths the other.
3. Communication is cut off in many ways, e.g., changing the phone number and making it unlisted, or changing the lock on the door.
4. Court charges of physical or sexual abuse are pondered or made.
5. Financial arrangements become more contentious.
6. Spurious motions in court increase.

If you are the parent put in the position of the mother in this diary, you are still responsible for helping your children, rather than harming them, however justified your anger. First, carefully watch their reac-tions. If they see nothing wrong in their parent's dating behavior, don't subject them to shows of your personal distress, but address the issue directly with the other parent. If the children aren't upset by the inci-dent, don't then take advantage of their innocence in the hopes they will become your allies. Although you can certainly tell them you find this behavior offensive, don't put them in the position of feeling they have to protect you. Rather, emphasize that even though it may make you uncomfortable, you want them to feel free to continue to talk to you about anything that's on their mind. The last thing you want your children to conclude from such an incident is that they can't trust either of you to place their interests above your own personal problems.

If you are the parent who has acted like the father, don't do it again; it is not worth the risk to your relationship with your children. If you are considering "just getting on with your life" whether or not your children are around, reconsider. Thursday night, or any other night without the kids, is still available. We've provided you with a long list of possible negative consequences, which, if you reflect on it, can hardly be blamed on your ex-spouse. If you think this is the real "love of your life," wait until the kids are ready and your former partner, their parent, has had time to adjust to the idea of divorce. If you are tempted not to wait, remember two things: not only do the courts favor the parent who has not indulged in this behavior when deciding disputes over visitation and finances, but such relationships started in the immediate separation period rarely endure. To risk sacrificing the cooperation of your children's other parent, and thus the terms of the divorce agreement, for a transient relationship simply isn't worth it. No matter what you are trying to prove to yourself or your spouse, you can be sure the kids won't benefit.

General Guidelines

- Don't introduce your kids to relationships that are likely to be transient.
- Don't compromise the chance of getting a divorce agreement that will truly serve your children's best interests, by flaunting your attractiveness to the other gender.
- Don't fail to respect the significance of divorce. Everyone has to recover from this trauma.
- Don't delude yourself that affairs prove you're "over it."

- Don't blame the other parent. If you have involved the kids in transient affairs, no matter how much they liked your lovers, you are "asking for" retribution.
- Don't fail to apologize to the kids and your ex-spouse if you have done what this father did, and don't forget not to do it again.
- Keep your children out of the sexual "experimentation" phase.

The repeated departure of adults you have introduced as people you "love" will cause your children to wonder what "love" means to you, whether they can trust you not to leave them, and which, if any, of your feelings for them can be believed. For children of divorce, repeated separations following even brief attachments are hard to endure, so your children need to be spared involvement in these relationships. In retrospect, most divorced adults say it takes two to three years to be ready to take on the commitment of another long-lasting relationship, although many make the mistake of rushing headlong into another disastrous marriage. Everyone agrees there is a need for a recovery phase after divorce. If, for you, this includes experimenting with new relationships, "Why not on Thursdays?"

The Middle
Phase of
Divorce

Staying in Touch 13

In which Nathaniel, age fourteen, introduces

E-mail to the family

Child's Point of View:
We're Finally Using E-Mail

At last I've convinced Mom that E-mail is the way to communicate. Dad and I have been doing it for months. It's great. I have to check my mail a couple of times a day anyway because all my friends send me messages, so I pick them up at recess and before I leave school. The computer room is real busy these days, and it's not with kids getting their homework done!

Mom brought home a computer from her new job, so I've managed to teach Tommy and Sally to use it. They love all the password stuff, and Tommy's getting the hang of how to type in E-mail addresses. He's a bit slow, but when he sent a message to Dad and got a "You've got mail" message later that day, he went berserk with excitement. I think Sally would still rather use the telephone, but even she had to admit it was fun to send messages any old time and know Dad would pick them up in between meetings or while sitting in the airport. It's neat that we can "talk" even when he's away on business trips. I wonder how I can get a laptop like his?

Today was a breakthrough day. Mom sent me a message for the first time! She knew she would be home late from work and wanted me to put the casserole in the oven at 6:00 P.M. She knew it had worked as soon as she walked in at 7:00 P.M. and could smell that dinner was ready! Maybe, instead of trying to talk to Dad, which always ends up badly, she should E-mail him instead. Better go now as *The X-Files* is on TV, and I can't miss that or I'll have nothing to talk about with Greg on the bus tomorrow.

Parent's Point of View:
Maybe This Will Work

"Plan ahead." "Communicate." "Tell me what's going on." The kids used to think I was a tape recording of these messages, especially after Richard and I split up and life got more complicated. No matter how much we cooperated, there was no way Richard and I could anticipate everything the kids needed to bring back and forth, to schedule, or to communicate to their friends. They had to be responsible, and they really rose to the occasion, but of course I was around to bring things over at the last minute or drive them places if they needed a ride. Now that I've gone back to work, I just don't have that flexibility.

Life seems chaotic now. My day is full of surprises, because I can't be on top of everything here at the office and at home. I told the kids that they had to let me know what was happening ahead of time by calling me at work, rather than leaving me Post-It notes on the door-jamb for when I get home. But sometimes I can't get to the phone, sometimes the message left is too brief, and many times they don't call when something comes up right after school. Last Tuesday, for example, when I arrived at the usual time expecting them to be there, no one was home, and I got real mad. Then Thursday was a repeat, except there was a note from Nathaniel saying he'd taken his brother to Joe's house and would be back by 6:30 P.M. I didn't even see Sally's note about going to the library with Emily, until she phoned, angry that she had been waiting for me to pick her up for the past half hour. She was OK, but clearly the system wasn't. When everyone eventually got home, we went out for pizza to talk about solutions.

Nathaniel convinced me that E-mail was part of the answer and that we were all too dependent on the telephone. I must admit I hate the computer and associate E-mail with work rather than home, but I think it may fill a gap in our communication system—rather like Post-It notes used to! Tommy said that now that he can read (sort of) and write (spelling is a little strange!), he could use it too. I must admit he's been unbelievably quick to master all the games on my computer. To Sally and Nathaniel it's old hat, and since they can get on the Internet at school and most of their friends' houses, that problem is solved. We agreed that when the phone won't do, we'll try using E-mail.

The casserole was in the oven as requested when I got home tonight. Things are looking up!

Making Sense of It All

Communication depends both on having something to say to each other and then making sure it actually gets said, although in modern society, regrettably, fax or E-mail are accepted as substitutes for the spoken word. Divorce in no way diminishes the importance of parents and children being able to communicate, but arguments about the right time to schedule a "conversation" or the preferred mechanism too often become the singular focus at the expense of the substance. When all of the logistic complications are worked out, there may be little left to say if parent and child have drifted too far apart.

We Can Talk Anytime, Can't We?

During the early months of separation and divorce many families go through phases where adults and children are emotionally out of sync. For as long as two to three years after the divorce, adults tend to be literally unavailable or emotionally unavailable. Sometimes they are remote, sometimes overly involved or concerned. These all-or-nothing responses, while entirely normal, make children wary and skittish. Communication appears to be at the whim of and in the control of the adults and revolves around their schedule, leaving the kids with the impression that their needs are clearly secondary to the parents' needs. Months and even years after their parents split up, children cite these early experiences, often involving frustrations with the telephone, as reasons why they are hesitant to share their feelings and uncertain that their points of view will be respected.

This reluctance to talk is often fueled when parents, albeit well-intentioned, increase distrust by being evasive with their children about the reasons for the divorce, living arrangements, visiting schedules, or a host of other items. Because of their own discomfort, parents often inappropriately squelch their children's need to talk about why they feel at fault for causing the divorce (see Chapter 6), or the adult's own emotional needs may lead to inappropriate responses to simple requests, such as wanting to call the other parent (see Chapter 11). Finally, many visitation schedules deny one or perhaps both parents the chance to spend any long-duration blocks of time with their children, thus significantly decreasing the likelihood of having a meaningful conversation or an emotionally fulfilling interaction (see Chapter 7). Children come to doubt that anyone will listen to their issues and constantly wonder what will be the response to their emotional needs. This is unfortunate, because just as the parents may be settling their own affairs and becoming more available to listen to their children, their children are becoming less willing to take the risk of talking with them or any adult. Often, wanting to make up for lost time, parents are frustrated by their children's reticence.

Unfortunately, it becomes all too easy to take offense at or respond angrily to a child's withdrawal that may be just a test of love or a simple protective mechanism against further disappointment or rebuff.

Different Agendas

In many families, the emotional distance is increased because the child thinks he or she is asking for something simple and the adult reacts as though it is horrendously complicated. The child's "simple" problem or question may look like a logistic or emotional nightmare in the adult's view, e.g., "I want to stay home this weekend rather than come to you. So can Mom take me to Andrea's birthday party and then to sleep over at Jan's?" Working out this "simple problem" often requires a major rearrangement of one parent's plans or requires time to coordinate with the other parent. Therefore it's important you receive the request in a way that gives you time to think about the situation and decide what is the appropriate response, especially when such requests may be a child's way of either questioning the schedule per se or your use of time with him or her.

Time together is quite difficult to coordinate in every family but especially after divorce, because children and parents don't think about time and relationships in the same way. Children tend to focus on events and what gets done with them, while time together for its own sake means much more to adults. So for the parent with visitation that weekend, giving up time for the child to go to the birthday party may be OK, but also allowing the sleep-over at Jan's may cross the line into the unacceptable. Simply demanding, "You have to be with me because it's my weekend," will make the child feel more like a chattel than an important person. Saying, "You're very important to me," is a point well worth making, but the response hardly addresses the issue of the party invitation. Perhaps a reasonable response could be, "I know this is really important to you, but our time together is valuable too. How about promising to get your homework finished Friday night. I'd rather have you come here, but if staying there makes that easier, and your mom is willing to take you to Andrea's on Saturday morning, that's OK with me. If I pick you up after the party and we have dinner together, I'll take you to Jan's as long as the homework is finished. That way we'll have time to do something special together on Sunday after the sleep-over. Why don't you think about it and call me between 3:00 P.M. and 4:00 P.M.? When we work it out, then I can let your mother know and confirm everything is OK with her." These rearrangements, which happen in every family, highlight the importance of staying in communication with and cooperating with your ex-spouse, to avoid burdening the child with the job of being a messenger between the two of you (see Chapter 18).

Availability

Such a considered response is difficult to compose on the spur of the moment during a live telephone call. Getting the message some other way makes it possible to consider options. Therefore, in order to establish the emotional rapport most families are seeking, the logistics of communication take on increased importance, though the logistics of finding the "right" time to talk may seem an almost insurmountable barrier. School schedules, extracurricular activities, work obligations, and community and social responsibilities all conspire to make it difficult for any parent to find time to talk with children and vice versa. None of this, however, alters the importance of timing when it comes to communicating and building relationships. If the anxiety, in anticipation of a test, is peaking on Thursday night, then both parents face the need to find a way to be available on Thursday, although the parent the child is away from has to overcome the awkwardness of not having the comfort and proximity of a face-to-face conversation. Clearly there have to be flexible and responsive ways to get in touch with each other. Fortunately there are now many options, some preferable to the telephone in certain situations.

Mechanisms

When parents separate, most adults and children assume the telephone is the most expeditious way to reach one another. The telephone has a certain appeal because it is live and you get to hear a real voice, making it the most personal type of exchange. Telling the kids to "Just call" seems natural and almost guaranteed to be successful—but then there is the meeting or phone call that can't be interrupted. Calling spontaneously on weekday nights may reach the other person, but all too often the timing turns out to be wrong—it's in the middle of the child's favorite TV show or the teenager is expecting his girlfriend to call any moment. The telephone comes to represent both temptation and frustration. Furthermore, all too frequently the residential parent justifiably feels that telephone calls, especially more than one a day, are an intrusion on personal space and a disruption of the harmony of that household. While we recognize that the nonresidential parent wants to keep connected, there are times when the kids just don't want to talk. If you are facing unanswered calls, it may improve your communication to set a schedule for your telephone calls or, for a while, to trust the kids to initiate their own calls.

There are three ways of making telephone communication effective and useful:

1. The telephone answering machine can be part of the solution. The message which is left, however, is critical. "Please call" doesn't indicate how imperative the issue may be, or how long the conversation will take, or when the other person can be reached. A more complete message does provide some time to think of alternatives. When you have planned a special weekend, it's one thing to be able to consider your response to your ten-year-old daughter's request to sleep over at a friend's house, and quite another to contain all of your ambivalent reactions when you get this request out of the blue, during the middle of a hectic schedule, when your daydreams have been about a close, fun time together with her on the weekend.

2. Don't like message machines and don't have one? What about the times the phone rings and you hesitate to pick it up? In some areas the telephone company will install caller ID, or an alternative is to use a code. For instance, when a child really wants to talk with you, the code can be to ring twice and then call back. It identifies the caller and gives the parent a choice of how to respond. One child could have two rings, another three. It's simple, cheap, and takes out some of the element of awkward surprise.

3. The third option, which is surprisingly affordable in many areas, is to piggyback a second line onto your existing phone service. Sort of like the "red phone" in the President's office.

It means a lot to the kids to know they have their own special phone at your home or office, even if you don't always answer. It can also be worked in reverse by installing a "red phone" in their other place of residence.

Ten or fifteen years ago beepers were unusual, now they are every-where. They have enhanced utility because a parent or a child can always be reached (although a child may not respond in the middle of a soccer practice or an orchestra rehearsal). Beepers not only provide access, but also the distance so necessary when you receive a message and may want time to think about the response. Current one-number services will ring first your home, then office, then car phone, and finally the beeper, so you are always "findable." Some beepers will display script so that you not only get a beep but you also get the text message. This makes it easier to decide what would be the appropriate speed of response.

E-mail is appealing to many families like the one in the diaries, especially since everyone can be encouraged to leave a more complete message than can be relayed by a beeper or left on an answering machine. As a result, children get practice expressing themselves and parents get a more complete picture of the overall situation. More than one exchange typically takes place to allow a response without com-mitment to action in an uncertain situation. If there isn't a computer at home, Internet connections are available at work and in many schools, so children usually can find access to this mode of communication, and learning how to use it is seldom a problem for them. Remember, E-mail only works to keep you all in touch if the person who needs to get the message is reliable about checking in.

Finally, don't forget the fax machine. While communication by fax does not offer the access of a beeper or quite the same privacy as E-mail, it has a major advantage: a piece of paper is printed so that instructions and directions are not likely to be "forgotten." Almost all businesses and schools now have a fax machine, and the cost is dropping to the point where having one at each house can be part of the divorce agreement. Especially for parents who travel, although the initial expense of a few hundred dollars may seem exorbitant, over the years it's well worth it. Leaving the hotel fax numbers may be more important than leaving telephone numbers. Many parents fax the list to their kids so they'll have it, and thereby invite them to use it. Getting back from a meeting late in the evening to find a telephone message that requests a call can mean a sleepless night. In the morning you may be hesitant to call, not knowing the nature of the problem or whether it is wise to call before school. You may be trapped in a meeting or catching a flight, making it difficult to call back at the right time. However, a fax can be written in the cab or at a meeting break and sent from just about anywhere. Moreover, people often find it easier to offer options or devise compromise responses when they have to write them down. And while telephone messages are often transcribed incorrectly or left at the wrong extension—even at home the messages are often not relayed—faxes rarely fail to be delivered correctly. Faxes are especially valuable to children who cannot yet write letters, as they can send and receive drawings. These reminders of your mutual love can be carried around by both of you.

General Guidelines

The sound of a voice is very reassuring, so the telephone always has appeal, but as we explored in Chapter 11, it is complicated to coordinate the timing of calls and who should initiate the call. Most families need some other type of communication to function effectively. Each method has certain limitations of security and privacy.

Telephone

- A separate line offers access at that location only.
- An answering machine is effective only if 1) it has the capacity to record a long message, and 2) children can follow instructions to leave sufficient information so the adult can make a decision.
- The timing of live calls presents many problems. Using a code based on the number of rings can identify the caller.

Beepers

- Beepers can provide notice of the need to call as well as a relatively short message.
- With a beeper there is the expectation of a quick response.

E-mail

- Children and parents have access at many different locations and it can be used at any time of the day or night.
- Messages are usually fairly complete and multiple exchanges can occur before any verbal conversation.
- Messages can be printed so instructions or requests can be followed easily.

Fax

- Access is widely available, including the office, school, and home.
- The printed message avoids confusion or misinterpretation that can occur with people's varied memories of conversations.
- When traveling, faxes often function better than telephone messages.
- Younger children can send and receive drawings and "I love you" messages.

Finally, once you have decided what methods of communication to use, make copies of a laminated card which specifically says what to do in a medical emergency and then lists the various way(s) to reach you, including all E-mail or other computer addresses. The reverse side of the card should have instructions reminding children to indicate, at minimum:

1. time of the message;
2. nature of the problem or request; and
3. where they can be reached for the rest of the day and evening— and how!

Each child can carry one of these—in a wallet, a purse, a knapsack, or in a shoe as some preschoolers are prone to do.

Sharing Dad's Bed

14

In which Jillian, age eight, wonders why she
can't sleep in Dad's bed after a bad dream

Child's Point of View:
Why Is It Bad to Sleep in Dad's Bed?

I had a horrible night last night. The day was just fine. Dad and Eric and I played soccer in the park. Then we went to the video store to choose our evening's entertainment. We, or rather I, ended up choosing this movie about two kids who get lost. Anyway, we got home, made popcorn like we always do, and cuddled up on the sofa to watch. Eric was asleep within minutes, so Dad carried him into our bedroom and tucked him into bed. The movie was OK, but I kept my eyes shut during the most scary parts—like the raft tipping over—and Dad told me when I could open them again. In the end, the kids do find their parents and it all works out fine. So when I went to bed, I didn't think I was going to have that awful dream.

But in the middle of the night, I woke up really scared! I dreamed that I had gone swimming in a pool and all of a sudden the pool became very wavy and I couldn't see the edge and I couldn't reach the bottom and then this *huge* monster that I couldn't see but could feel in the water, started chasing me and . . . well, then I woke up. I lay very still for a minute and then went to Dad's room. I told him I'd had a bad dream and that I wanted to sleep in his bed, as I was scared of the dream coming back. I expected he'd pull back the covers and let me in like he used to before the divorce. Instead, he sat up and said I couldn't sleep in his bed and that I'd have to go back to my room. He seemed sort of . . . angry. Even though I was crying, he took me back and sat with me a little while. But I was too scared to go back to sleep. After he left, I waited a few minutes until I heard his snoring. Then I took my blankets and snuck into his room and slept on the floor.

When he found me in the morning, he let me get warm in his bed while he went to shower. When he came back, he said something about it not being a "good idea" for us to sleep in the same bed and that I shouldn't tell Mom I'd slept in his room. I don't get it. I sleep in Mom's bed sometimes, even when I don't have a bad dream—and I know *she* thinks it's OK—so what's Dad's problem? I always cuddled in bed with them when they were together.

At breakfast he said that he was sorry about last night but some people think it's "bad for kids" to sleep with their fathers, and that he might get in trouble with. . . . Well, he sort of hinted it was Mom; or that if somebody found out, then the court, or someone, might make it so I couldn't stay over anymore. So *who is* it? I just don't get it.

Parent's Point of View: It's a No-Win Situation

Sometimes I think people really don't understand the absurd situations fathers find themselves in when they have to look after their kids alone. Last night was a great example of how this process—divorce, that is—actually makes me look bad as a parent no matter what I do. Yesterday Jillian and I made popcorn, cuddled up on the sofa, and watched a movie like we usually do on Saturday night. We had a great time. She had chosen a movie I had some reservations about, because it was the story of two kids who get separated from their parents in a rafting accident, and, even though they are found in the end, there were a few too many images of loss and danger for my liking. But Jillian hid her face in the scary bits, and we talked about it and I thought she'd handled it pretty well.

Then in the middle of the night, she came in crying that she had a bad dream. My first reaction was to let her sleep with me. We always did that before the separation—not that it happened very often—and I knew if she came into bed she would settle down very quickly and go back to sleep. Just as I was about to do it, a little voice at the back of my brain, which sounded suspiciously like my attorney, said, "Don't take her into bed with you . . . the next thing that will happen is that you'll be defending yourself against charges of sexual abuse."

Well, I've obeyed that warning up to now. Jillian and Eric have their own bedroom and I am really careful about her privacy when she gets undressed or bathes, but she was standing there in the dark, frightened and needing me to comfort her. And what did I do? I listened to the voice of the lawyer, dammit, and told her she had to go back to bed.

I took her back still wailing that she was too scared to sleep, sat with her for a while, and left her alone. Is that what the lawyers and the family counselors, or even her mother, really want me to do? The other voice, *my* voice, was telling me that was *bad* parenting and I felt terrible.

I felt even worse when I found Jillian huddled on the floor of my room next morning with just a blanket over her. I was glad when she said sleeping next to my bed felt at least a *little* safer. I hugged her, but I didn't know what to say.

I owed her an apology. I owed her an explanation. But how do you explain to your own daughter that people could think that her father might hurt her or sexually abuse her? How do you explain to her that the mere suspicion might be enough grounds to keep her from visiting with me? I made some halfhearted attempt to explain, but I could see in her face that it made no sense to her. I feel I betrayed her trust in me to look after her when she needs me. But I don't want anything to threaten our time together, and I know from past experience I need to be on guard at all times.

Making Sense of It All

Examples of accusations of sexual abuse being used in divorce cases to influence custody decisions are legion. They are no longer merely the material for novels such as Sue Miller's *The Good Mother* or Richard Patterson's *In the Eyes of the Child*. In acrimonious divorces, even complete hearsay can cast doubt as to the suitability of a parent to have custody or visitation privileges with a child. It is necessary for men to be careful, almost to the point of paranoia, that they do nothing with their children, especially their daughters, that could raise concerns or suspicions of abuse or "inappropriate behavior." Because such accusations are often extremely difficult to disprove and involve so much emotional pain to the child being asked to bear witness and the parent being asked to defend, they are clearly situations to avoid at all costs.

Of course, inappropriate behavior is a subjective thing. The regular sleeping of children and their parents in the "family bed" is controversial, but has been condoned by pediatricians such as William Sears as being natural and beneficial. Few pediatricians and child psychiatrists would argue that bringing a scared child into bed with her parents is to be avoided. However, once parents are separated, any such innocent activity can be subject to a less benign interpretation. Suddenly, "Daddy rubbed my back while I was in bed with him" takes on a sexual tone. "Daddy wanted my whole body to get clean when he gave me a bath," invites questions about what "whole body" means. This, of course, leaves fathers worrying about whether they can give their children of either sex a bath at all—or until what age?

In the diary entries, it is clear that Jillian is baffled by her dad's rejection of her request to come into bed. Most children continue to be allowed into the mother's bed if they were before the divorce and often even if they weren't. Jillian is understandably confused that what is OK with Mom is not OK with Dad, especially as it used to be OK with both of them. She is also now left to wonder why she's been told not to tell Mom (see Chapter 19).

Her father is justifiably angry at being put in this dilemma at all. His awareness of society's bias against single-parent fathering is realistic. And his decision not to do anything that could be misinterpreted is wise. Jillian's solution of sleeping on the floor next to her father's bed is a reasonable compromise in this situation.

If you and the other parent talk frequently, this is the type of parenting situation that should be discussed so you are aware of any concerns your former spouse may have. Unlike disagreements about, for example, giving the kids candy before dinner and therefore compromising what they eat at mealtime, this situation is more inflammatory. Regardless of the status of your communication, you should share with the other parent significant incidents and events that have happened during your time with the children, e.g., illnesses, injuries, introduction of significant others, or "bad dreams" and how you handled them. Although this may engender criticism of your parenting decisions, it is better than using your children as messengers (see Chapter 18).

General Guidelines

In general, it is important for all parents to be aware of the fine line between appropriate and inappropriate intimacy with children.

- Respect the privacy of your children in dressing, bathing, etc., and insist that they respect yours.

- Try to give them a separate sleeping space or at least their own bed, when they are with you.
- The younger the children the more acceptable is intimate physical contact, but once they are able to attend to their own toileting and bathing needs, let independence flourish. Encourage privacy and sleeping alone and make it part of the routine when they are with you.
- Be aware that it is not only *what* you do, it is also what your children *say* you do that is open to misinterpretation. Giving them constant reminders of what to say or not say, and to whom, rarely serves anybody's interest. Children are not good at keeping secrets and should not be made fearful of telling either parent the truth.

Two Birthday Parties

In which Danny, age seven, wonders whether
he really wants to have two birthday parties

Child's Point of View:
Having Two Parties Is Too Embarrassing

I suppose I could have said I didn't want to have a birthday party at her house, but Mom would just have kept asking me why, and it's too hard to explain. Today she kept reminding me it's only two weeks away and I need to give her the guest list, but Dad's already sent out my invitations for the other party and it seems a little weird to invite the same crowd again. At first I thought it was a good idea—two sets of presents, two cakes—but now I'm not so sure. I don't think she'd understand why this is so embarrassing. Most of my friends don't even know about the divorce, and I don't want them asking about it. I don't want to tell people what happened, over and over again. I don't want their parents asking me how I feel, and I don't want them thinking the divorce makes me different—different from them or different from the way I was. It's better that no one knows—except for Jess and Zach. They know because they come over here all the time. Maybe I'll just invite them for a sleep-over, since it isn't my birthday the weekend I'm with Mom anyway, and then I can just have my real party on the real day at Dad's. It makes more sense that way, since I'm there for my birthday and most of my friends think I live there all the time anyway. I was hoping if I kept stalling, something would come up at work so that Mom couldn't do it. But now I've promised her that I'll call everyone tonight. It's so late already. Maybe I'll tell her they were all asleep, or busy, or it conflicts with the big hockey game on TV. I bet if I just ask Zach and Jess she'll get mad. I wonder why this is so important to her. It's my birthday, but it's almost like I'm doing her a favor.

Parent's Point of View:
I Want to Throw a Special Party Too

If Danny doesn't send out invitations soon, there won't be a party, but I can't even get him to make a list. He said he'd call people tonight instead, but it's already after nine. He seemed really enthusiastic when I first suggested that we could have a party here the weekend before his birthday, but now he won't tell me why he's stalling. I suppose he might be embarrassed that Jack's going to be here, but I thought it would make him feel better to have a man around as well as his mom, and he gets on OK with Jack now. Well, I hope he pulls himself together, because I love birthday parties and I would like to make this one really special for him. Last year he didn't get a party because life was so crazy, and I felt so guilty afterward. The year before, though, we had a treasure hunt and made ice-cream sundaes. Danny loved it and was so happy. All the parents said their kids had a great time, and were so impressed at the cake I made him. I'm planning to make his favorite chocolate cake again, though when I asked him if he wanted it in the shape of a soccer ball this year, he just shrugged and said he didn't care. That made me wonder what's going on. He never turns down chocolate cake. Maybe he doesn't want the kids to just hang out here in the yard when his dad is taking the whole class to the video-game arcade. I suppose I could rent some videos, or maybe get a magician or entertainer of some kind, but that's really expensive. I wish I knew what Danny wanted.

Making Sense of It All

Because birthdays do not need to be celebrated "on the day"—like Thanksgiving or Christmas—and because both parents may want to show they have an equal stake in the anniversary of their child's birth, many children struggle with the pressures of deciding how to celebrate their birthday twice in a short period of time. Trying to coordinate two parties on the actual birthday is almost impossible and has the same negative, divisive emotional impact on children as parental attempts to celebrate Christmas or Thanksgiving in two different places on the same day. Often, both parents offer to host a party on different days, but as illustrated in the diaries, this is not always greeted with enthusiasm. The third alternative, joint celebrations, is rarely successful. So for most children there is a party with one parent, while the other parent is usually only able to call their child on the day itself and is left to wonder whether to send a present or keep it for the next visit. What used to be an unambivalently happy day, before the divorce, has become a day full of tension and a sense of loss for all concerned. As the years go on, birthdays, although enjoyable, often remind everyone how disappointing it is to no longer be an intact family.

While most younger kids, say up to six years old, delight in the prospect of two parties and have a great time at both, even at that age there may be reluctance to go along with the idea. Sometimes this is a result of their allegiance to one parent or the other, or the child's fear that the nonresidential parent won't get all the planning and details right. Sometimes older children are unsure whether they want all their friends to come twice or to split them between the two parties, which may end up feeling like having half a party each time. Other children find that their initial joy at the prospect of getting double the presents is displaced by concerns that the presents won't be as special because people have to buy two.

Having two parties can engender some unexpected reactions. There's always some kid who asks if it's possible to bring a present to one party but not the other, or a mother who phones to ask if both parties are real birthday parties, thus implying they don't want to buy two presents. We've also seen times when kids reflect their parents' resentment at the cost of buying two presents for the same kid or the hassle of still more chauffeuring. Regrettably, we've even heard of comments like, "It's a bit much expecting us to buy two presents—sort of like it's our responsibility to make up to their kids for the divorce." Be aware that your child may be subject to some negative reactions.

The desire to make their child happy and the hope that he or she will be appreciative frequently lead to competition between parents to stage the "best" party. After the fact, their efforts are commonly followed by appeals to the child for assurance that "I did better." This clearly puts the child in an uncomfortable position. However, taking advantage of this kind of parental competition, kids can start to consciously or unconsciously exploit their parents' generosity. The expectation that "the parent who loves me the most will give me the best presents, have the biggest parties, etc." can easily get established and extends way beyond birthday parties. This materialism sets the stage for manipulative antics, which can be emotionally devastating (see Chapter 5 and Chapter 27).

The "solution" to the party problem might appear to be to have both parents come to a single "big" birthday party, but this can also create waves. The birthday party is, in many cases, the first time the child has seen the parents together following the divorce. Family members from both sides may be invited and the atmosphere can be tense. Especially if the gathering is held where the child lives, hopes are rekindled that the parents will get back together. Therefore, the end of the party, when one parent leaves alone, often brings on tears. These reactions may be mitigated, somewhat, by having the party at a neutral location, but, even when the parents are together at a birthday party a year or two after the divorce, the child may end up more upset than pleased. Moreover, for families where the parents see each other frequently, but the transitions are often rocky, birthdays have no magic that can prevent the same conflicts, emotional ambiguities, and jealousies from causing clinging, manipulation, or parental confrontations.

As revealed in the diary, the preparations for a birthday often give parents clues that their children have hidden the divorce from some of their friends for weeks, months, or even years. Having to reveal the truth by inviting peers to two parties brings it all out in the open, not only forcing the child to face up to reality, but also to come to grips with the inner doubts and problems with self-image or peer relationships, which gave rise to the decision to hide the divorce in the first place. Adolescents often find it especially difficult to let others know about the divorce, acting out elaborate schemes so friends always come to the original home, picking up phone messages only at the original phone number, even getting left off at that house so they always take the same school bus or walk to school the same way. The creativity is impressive, but poignant.

So if you decide to try having two birthday parties, resistance is often a key signal that friends don't know about the divorce at all, or they don't have the complete story. Perhaps your child feels ashamed or at fault in some way that needs to be talked about more openly. Sometimes the resistance is an indication the child needs more time to talk with a parent or someone else about friendships and the mutuality of support. It may also be time to talk about the parent-child relationships and loyalty conflicts, and to look at the changes which have occurred since the separation or divorce.

Successfully staging two birthday parties often tests the parents' ability to cooperate. It involves coordinating dates, party motifs and activities, gift requests, and even guest lists, to avoid ill will and to prevent competition. It's a tough act. More often than not, it flops. An alternative to "competing" parties is for one parent to host a gathering at their house and the other parent arrange a trip to a special sports event, show, or theme park (alternating roles every year if that is desirable). Sometimes kids will be just as happy to celebrate with a parent and perhaps a best friend, as entertain multiple guests.

General Guidelines

- Having two parties rarely turns out well. It's seldom double the presents or double the fun.
- Celebrating the event twice on the same day rarely works well, as moving between parents gets in the way of everyone's enjoyment, both logistically and emotionally. The same problem occurs when other holidays, like Christmas or Easter, are split between the two families.
- Don't try to orchestrate or purchase the "better" party. That kind of competition produces only losers. Children may end up feeling guilty that the other parent cannot share the fun, or they may come to expect more and more from you every year. Even if you "win" this time, the precedents set aren't worth the cost in the long run.
- If, in the process of arranging a party, you discover that your child has been hiding the divorce, make time to talk about the need for secrecy. It suggests that at some level your child feels at fault or at least unduly embarrassed.
- Having both parents at the party inevitably results in one having to say good-bye. Before it begins, make sure your child understands that this will happen at the end of the celebration.
- Often what works the best is to let your child choose where "the" party will be and then let the other parent celebrate the birthday in a completely different way, with a special outing to a restaurant, movie, or sports event.

Moving from
the Family Home

16

In which Nancy, age seven, worries that she
might end up homeless

Child's Point of View:
Are We Going to a Shelter?

Mom's been crying again. I try to ignore it, because when I ask her what's wrong, she usually says something random like, "I just feel a little sad," or, "Nothing you need to worry about. I'll be fine." She hasn't been fine though. One day she's cuddly and plays games with me and the next she doesn't appear to hear anything I say . . . or at least doesn't remember it. Last week I asked her if I could go to camp again this summer, and she got angry at me just for asking and told me there were more important things to worry about . . . like the electricity bill. Maybe if we're really running out of money, we might not have enough to eat. At school we were talking about all the poor people who live in shelters and how we needed to bring in cans of food for them. I wonder if we'll need to go to a shelter. After all, when I found her crying last night, Mom said we might have to move. If we were going to move somewhere nice, why would she be so upset?

I wish she'd tell me what's going on. I mean, if we move, where will I go to school and how will I see my friends? I couldn't tell them I'm going to live in a shelter; it would be so embarrassing. . . . I haven't even told them my parents are getting divorced yet!

Parent's Point of View:
Should I Sell the House?

There are times when I feel the burden of responsibility is just too much for me to bear. I got married believing that it would be ideal to have a partner in life to discuss things with and to share problems with, partly, I suppose, because I've always hated making decisions alone. Now I do nothing but make decisions alone—and who knows whether they are the right ones! To make things worse, I'm facing a big financial problem that doesn't have a right answer. It's clear that unless I get more child support (which isn't going to happen), I'm going to start going into significant debt. With hindsight I can see that if I'd only kept on working, I would have more financial security now; but when the kids were little, I really needed time with them more than I needed my own money.

That decision has come back to haunt me now. I can't afford to keep living in this house, unless I go back to full-time work (if I can find it), but I don't know if selling the house and making such a dramatic change in the kids' lives would be really harmful to them. They would have to change schools and make new friends all over again. I don't think Nancy or I would like that. She's finally made some good friends this year, with mothers whom I like and who have really been supportive and have helped me out with carpooling and babysitting. On the other hand, in many ways I would love to move to a smaller house and start again with a little more cash in my pocket, free from all the memories that this house holds. I don't know. Is what is good for me good for us? Is what is good for the kids good for me? Who matters more? Well, I know the answer to that one—*they* do . . . but having no money to take them places or buy them things isn't good for me or them. Nancy found me crying over the unpaid bills yesterday, and I told her we might have to move. All she asked was whether she could take her collection of stuffed animals with her. Sometimes I don't understand what she's feeling at all.

Making Sense of It All

"Home is where the heart is." The decision to move from the family home is seldom a straightforward dollars-and-cents proposition. For kids, home is as much an emotional milieu as a physical place, and that milieu has been drastically altered already by the departure of one parent. The question commonly arises as to the benefits of creating a new "home" in the same place versus starting over in a new environment.

Even in the best of circumstances, moving from the home where your children have grown up is an event that raises conflicting feelings. Within a family, the more people involved, the greater the variance of enthusiasm and reluctance to putting an end to a certain phase of life. Divorce intensifies the feelings, because moving is an admission that the marriage is really over; that the divorce is a reality. Even though the divorce decree may have been granted years ago, leaving what was the family home signifies a painful finality.

Logistic Issues

Money isn't the only factor to be considered. Parents, like the mother in the diary, who are forced to make decisions as to the best affordable opportunities for their children, may find it difficult to find a comfortable balance between the dollars available, their self-interest, and the children's interests. Many newly divorced adults fail to recognize that the balance is constantly changing. In an effort to create stability for the kids and themselves, they choose to ignore the rapidly evolving situation and imagine that if they at least keep one aspect constant, i.e., the place they live in, it must be to everyone's benefit. This is frequently not the case.

We think stability is important for children, but would define it as meaning maintaining the integrity of both mother-child and father-child relationships, the continuity of peer relationships, and the opportunity to continue within the same school and extracurricular activities. Therefore, when the economics don't dictate a single option, parents should consider the following in making a choice whether to move or not.

Staying in the School District

To maintain the benefit of staying in the same school district does not necessarily require staying in the same house. If you remain in the neighborhood, your child's peer group stays intact and after-school and weekend activities can be continued. If you move to a place farther away from school, check out the availability of transportation. If a move means a child who hates to get up has to wake up an hour earlier to get to school, or that car pools are a bigger part of your life, don't underestimate the significance.

Coping with Embarrassment

Moving forces children to deal with the public embarrassment of divorce (see Chapter 15 and Chapter 25). If the move results in a lower standard of living, then you have to be prepared to help them cope with that as well. Remember that to live in a smaller place with the same TV, their familiar toys, the canopy bed, etc., is not likely to concern the seven-year-old, like Nancy, as much as it will concern her adolescent sibling, who will be more anxious about what others might think.

Availability of Living Space

Young kids and toddlers require only an easily accessible place to play that doesn't have to be kept constantly tidy. As they get older, private space becomes more of a premium, so while nine- and five-year-old siblings might be able to live peaceably in the same room, that's not going to be true in three years' time.

Closeness to the Other Parent

While it may be tempting to move far away, don't choose a place that heightens the difficulty of having the kids spend time with the other parent. On the other hand, if you are a parent looking to buy close to your kids, make sure they aren't going to move, and be objective about the pluses and minuses of being a short walking distance away (see Chapter 22).

Emotional Issues

Fitting each of the logistic variables into the equation may not produce a simple answer. Some adults further complicate the dilemma by adding another dimension.

Home as a Sanctuary

One of the most common reasons for staying in the same house is the belief that it serves as an emotional sanctuary for the children—a place where a child feels "I belong." That may be true if the children consistently express that sentiment, but more often, the belief in the home as a sanctuary reflects the parent's need to feel grounded. Unfortunately, staying in the same place may not have that much-hoped-for benefit. Children often harbor much of the ambivalence their parents feel. The house holds constant reminders of conflict, of one parent leaving, and, for children, specific memories of doing or saying something that they may feel caused the divorce (see Chapter 6). The home has typically been the site of many arguments or fights, loneliness or emotional suffering.

Home as a Symbol of Constancy

Other times, adults choose to emphasize their hope that their children will feel "safe" if the parents maintain the familiarity of routine. Parents repeatedly use the fact that they are staying in their home to reassure the kids that everything will be fine, and, now that the divorce is settled, there will be no more changes. But the kids will be justifiably suspicious. As money gets tighter, they may find that they are forced to choose between activities they enjoy and want to continue. Certainly as time goes on, children are less concerned with where they live and increasingly concerned with having the latitude to choose activities and interests with the fewest possible cost constraints. Moving may be the answer to freeing up discretionary funds, and staying in the same abode may not provide the constancy the children need.

Economic Considerations

During the separation process of dividing assets and coming to an agreement on child support or alimony, selling the house has to be considered. For many lucky enough to have been able to buy a house, equity in the property is the primary family asset, often exceeding all other liquid and investment assets the couple holds. The decision to keep the house leaves many custodial parents "house poor"—with a familiar place to live, but not enough cash to provide anything beyond the basic necessities, or maybe not even those. Many are advised to take out an equity loan. Since these loans are often variable rate interest, they are quite likely not to be supportable—given the income of a parent who is already "house poor."

When financial demands increase, many respond by suggesting that the parent get a job—that's often the real "cost" of keeping the house. The status of the economy may make that relatively easy or almost impossible, depending on the person's educational level and talents, as well as the almost certain need for time flexibility. Traditionally, this has been a decision forced primarily on mothers, and the message has been that the children need to maintain their standard of living, even if this compromises the time parent and children can spend together. Given their choice, most children under the age of ten would rather have Mom (or Dad) around more, even if it means having a smaller room in a different neighborhood.

Staying at home, however, is hardly a panacea if it means that income to live on is seriously restricted. For some parents, a return to the job market has an added advantage: it can be a way to prove their competence at something or a way to restore self-image. Either avenue may give a mother or a father a certain purpose in life and help them avoid serious loneliness or depression.

Moving House

The prospect of moving house may be a fortuitous opportunity for the residential parent to look at the interaction between "What do I need to do to get my life back on track so I'm happy?" and "What is really best for the kids?" If keeping the house is going to define the residential parent's role in life in a way that is uncomfortable, this can place many burdens on the children. They will certainly feel responsible for keeping that parent happy, in part to make up for the sacrifice that parent has made. Moreover, if keeping the house limits other choices, e.g., there isn't enough money to pay for music lessons and to play a spring sport, then the house becomes a place that symbolizes the limitation of possibilities, rather than a base for exploring new opportunities. That's not good for any child, especially one trying to recover from divorce.

Selling Your House

If you have to move in order to gain access to equity in a property or to reduce your rent, try to make the best compromises. The temptation is often to buy certain things that may make you feel better as you get your personal life back together, or to grant some of the kids' immediate wishes in order to look like the "good parent" or to make it up to them for the move. The biggest advantage to selling is having financial flexibility—spend money carefully.

- Before you sell, make sure you can afford the next "buy." Look at mortgage costs, rental rates, or condo carrying fees. Many people sell and then end up no better off. If you've never purchased or sold property before or your spouse handled all the financial affairs, then ask for the advice of a friend or family member who has experience.
- If selling your home or getting a loan provides some money, get help to invest it to provide income so you can minimize the consumption of capital. Given the current economic world, putting it "in the bank" is not likely to generate sufficient return.
- As children get older, activities become more expensive, especially since many school budgets no longer support extensive

extracurricular activities. Providing for the future will pay immense rewards—so don't spend it all now.

- Children need a broad social network of support and friendships. There may be "more house" for less money elsewhere, but if your kids are older than seven or eight, we'd advise that less will indeed be more if it means keeping friendships intact.

- Divorce leaves kids with a lot to sort out. Having a private space to call "my own" can be invaluable. A new house does not have to be big or luxurious as long as each child gets some personal space.

Timing of the Move

The age of the children and the timing of a move after the separation do influence its impact. Clearly for some, including most toddlers and preschool-age children, a move during the separation process adds to the chaos and the agonizing sense of loss of control and displacement. For others, even children as young as four or five, it helps propel them to a fresh start away from the emotional turmoil and anger that has come to be identified with that building. The transition can be eased for many older children if they are given the chance to articulate what they would want in a new home. The younger child needs to know what is happening and will be made more comfortable by a detailed explanation of the fact that a big moving van (an item of fascination in itself) will come to make sure all of the "valuable stuff" gets to the new house. All the children should be offered a tour of the prospective home, and an adolescent mature enough to understand the trade-offs involved in moving should be given a say in the decision.

General Guidelines

So is there a "right" balance of economic considerations, living amenities, and emotional or physical stability? Yes, but make the decision slowly and carefully. If you don't have to move immediately, don't. There are so many life changes after divorce. Everyone involved needs a period of time to grieve.

If you are contemplating selling a house or moving as part of the divorce process:

- Communicate with the children. Don't present a fait accompli, because it says you don't value their input. If your reasons for moving won't stand up to their arguments now, they will not in the future either.
- Be honest about your own feelings, and give your children the chance to voice theirs. If the house contains too many painful memories for you, be aware that the same may pertain to them. If you feel a sense of shelter and safety from staying in familiar surroundings, you may find they have similar feelings.
- The economic sacrifices you make may be worth it, but check to make sure your children aren't trying to make you happy by agreeing to do what you want.
- Maintain some flexibility so you can adapt to future changes. Evaluate what really matters to your kids and what their future plans are.

Remember that "stability" does not equal "no change." Staying put will not prevent changes in your children's behavior. After the acute process of separation, children's behavior patterns can be very different from the past, even if the children remain in the same home.

17

Grandparents

In which nine-year-old Rob tells why visiting
his grandfather after the divorce is
such a relief

Child's Point of View:
I'd Rather Stay with Grandpa

One more day and I've got to leave. I thought I would be homesick when Mom told me I was going for three weeks this year, but it's just been the best time. No little brothers bugging me, no Mom nagging me, and no Dad correcting everything I do. It's such a relief to be able to get up late and help Gramps make waffles—like, every morning!— and pour on tons of syrup and whipped cream from a can. I'm sure Mom would have something to say about it if she knew, but Gramps said he wouldn't tell if I didn't. Last year we all came up to the lake together and it was really boring. Mom and Dad argued all the time and Gramps was too busy talking with them to have much time for me. I thought he didn't like me, but I was really wrong. We have such fun together. I haven't laughed so much for a long time.

After the divorce in April, I thought the fighting would calm down, but my parents never let up. It's felt pretty lonely since then. Even though Mom and Dad try to spend time with me, they treat me as though I'm a baby. They never tell me what's going on or when I'm going where. Dad bought this dumb comforter for my bed that has stupid cars and trucks on it, and Mom only lets me watch movies that my little brothers think are babyish! Gramps treats me as though I'm grown-up. He bought me my own fishing rod and tackle box, and has taught me how to bait the hook. Now he's trying to teach me to be patient, but he says that's a losing battle 'cause I'm just like Mom!

While we're fishing we talk a lot. I didn't know he'd been divorced before marrying Grandma. No one ever told me that. I wonder why not? He's really helping me understand Mom and Dad better, and why adults fight, and especially, why it doesn't help to take sides when they're squabbling about money or changing the schedule. He said I was entitled to my point of view, but that it is hard for parents to take advice from their nine-year-old, even if he's right! He even told me I should have a say in where I lived. No one else has believed in me that much.

He told me how he was always sure he was right and his first wife wrong when he got divorced, and how he realizes now that it's not that simple. I thought he would stick up for Mom since she's his daughter, but he encouraged me to talk about both of them and didn't mind if I criticized Mom. That's what I hate about going to my aunt's house. She just defends Mom all the time and says Dad is irresponsible, even when he's not. I wish I could stay here another week. I'm getting a stomachache and haven't even packed yet.

Grandparent's Point of View: I'll Be There for My Grandchild

Only one more day to go and then Rob has to go home. I'll miss him. Reminds me so much of his Mom when she was young. Maybe I can help her avoid some of the mistakes I made as a parent. Like this fishing—she needs a special interest they can share to have fun together.

There's been too much anger in that household. All the rows and sulking remind me of how she would treat me when she was a kid and I was traveling for my job all the time. Nothing would seem to be OK, no matter what I said or did, and now she's doing the same thing to Frank, whom she refers to only as "Him" or "My ex." She does have a great job, of which she is justifiably proud. I've told her that I understand that feeling successful helps compensate for all the feelings of failure involved in the divorce, but I also know her schedule makes it tough on Rob and Timmy. I see them looking up at her the way I remember her looking up at me, with the same expression I saw in her eyes when I was off on my travels again. Now I regret missing so much of her childhood.

Sometimes I feel like a traitor when I criticize her, but Rob does have the right to feel angry when neither his mom nor dad is there when he needs them. I think I got him to understand that threatening to run away or asking to go live with the other parent all the time won't work, but I wish they'd listen to what he has to say. He understands so much more than they give him credit for.

Wednesday, the fish wouldn't take anything, and Rob got real mad. I tried to kid him about the fish not wanting to sacrifice themselves, no matter how much we wanted them to, but I couldn't get him to laugh, and then he suddenly started crying. I asked him if he wanted to go home, and the reply was a downcast face and a question: "Which home?" He said he didn't really want to leave, 'cause when he was back in Trentfield, he couldn't get rid of the feeling that whichever house he was in he always wanted to be in the other. When with his mom, he wants to be with Dad, and vice versa. Boy, that's tough for a kid. The smile was weak, but real, when I told him I understood, and he could come for a weekend anytime just to chill out. But now he's sitting on the dock just dangling a line, and I can tell from the droop of his shoulders he's not thinking about fish. He doesn't want to leave any more than I want him to. Maybe his parents will stop this silly fight over always having equal time—it just means the kids are always shuttling back and forth. Maybe they would just let him come up here for the rest of the summer.

Making Sense of It All

When a family breaks apart because of divorce, grandparents can play a pivotal role in helping their grandchildren accommodate to the changes in their lives. For many kids, the caring presence of a loving adult, or just the letters and phone calls from a more distant grandparent, become a lifeline. Grandparents walk a tightrope when trying to stay connected with their own child, the "ex," and their grandchildren. The key to success is not taking sides but offering support as it is needed. While it is tempting to defend one's own child, building such alliances can cost grandparents their most constructive and gratifying role—that of nonpartisan support to their grandchildren. Rob is able to gain much more than a place to run off to, because in his grandfather he finds not only someone who encourages him to talk, but someone who, by being nonjudgmental, can also listen.

For many kids, grandparents are the only people in their lives with a sense of humor about the family situation; they can laugh at or at least put in perspective the antics of both sides. Moreover, they can add valuable wisdom, since many of them have been through divorce themselves. Serving as models to show how to recover from divorce, these grandparents can not only talk about their mistakes, but also set an example of how to learn from mistakes. Since they don't have to be players in custody battles and the other hassles of divorce, grandparents don't have to take sides and are available to provide a much-needed continuity in the children's lives.

Economic support from grandparents is frequently a major contribution to the children's well-being, saving the children from having to sacrifice too much of their quality of life. Benefits may take the form of free child care while a parent is at work or at school, or "chauffeur" service to get to a piano lesson or a soccer game. Perhaps the grandparents grant a loan; give a gift; make possible some special wish, like going to camp or getting new clothes; or pay for extracurricular activities the parent(s) can't afford. Other times they may pay for a vacation when everyone needs a break, but the dollars or an affordable place to stay just aren't available.

In an era when some children continue to live at home until their late twenties, many grandparents provide a place to live. Sometimes the divorce cripples a family financially so that there is no option of independent living. In other situations, the grandparents may live in a better school district or staying with them may allow an older child to finish at the same high school, maintaining the crucial social network adolescents depend on. Living with grandparents can also be a refuge from continuing parental hostility or serve to lessen the oppositional behavior of many adolescents toward their parents, which is exacerbated by the loyalty conflicts generated by the divorce.

Sometimes, grandparents can unintentionally start to compete with their own children for "perfect parent" status. The tendency to be over-solicitous, combined with the multiple opportunities to "spoil" the grandchild, invites intergenerational tension. It is important for the adult children to set limits with their own parents and make clear the role they wish them to fulfill.

General Guidelines

- Grandparents shouldn't take sides if they want to be helpful to their grandchildren. They can provide respite, escape, explanations, financial help, and caring. Those are very big and very important roles that can make them critical players in their grandchildren's lives for years to come.
- By providing financial assistance, vacation homes, money, babysitting, chauffeur service, or a place to live, grandparents help families bridge the awful emotional and financial gaps that result from divorce.
- In the unfortunate situation where a divorce leaves one or both parents uninvolved with the children, overly committed to work, or departed in pursuit of other romantic relationships, grandparents can provide the caring all children need and deserve.

- Grandparents can open new lines of communication or serve as critical intermediaries. This is easier to accomplish if a strong attachment to the son-in-law or daughter-in-law balances the instinctive reaction to side with their own progeny.
- Grandparents who exclusively defend one parent or engage in character assassination of either or both create loyalty conflicts for their grandchildren.
- Occasionally, grandparents unintentionally displace their own child as a parent. This generates feelings of antagonism and incompetence in that child and confusion in the grandchildren.
- Grandparents are for many children the ideal individuals to help them gain perspective and maintain a sense of humor so that the divorce, while momentous, doesn't become as scarring and limiting as it would otherwise have been.

Playing Messenger 18

In which Angie, age fourteen, asks to go to a
party with her mother and is disappointed
by the angry response from her father

Child's Point of View:
Why Am I the One Who Has to Ask?

I knew this wasn't going to work . . . but when Mom said she thought I should call Dad about the weekend, I didn't know how to refuse. I mean, I knew she was right that he would automatically say "No" if she asked him to change weekends again, especially for a family party . . . and I knew he would be angry with her if she called, but I still think Mom should have offered to make the call. She could have explained that it was a surprise party, and nobody knew 'til today, and that I have very important personal reasons for wanting to go with her. I mean if Alan is going to be there and I don't go. . . .

So I agreed. I called, and just as predicted, got shouted at again. I said exactly what Mom had told me to say. She even stood next to me and prompted me when Dad started to object. But all I got in the end was, "The answer is *no*. I'm tired of your mother thinking that I should just change all my plans for her convenience. I have a life too. Tell your mother she can go to her brother's party alone, and that I expect to see you as arranged at 6:00 P.M. on Friday . . ." and then he just hung up. I hate it when he calls Mom "Your Mother."

He didn't give me a chance to explain that it wasn't only Mom's request—I wanted to go because Mom said my cousin's best friend Alan would be there. It's been a month since I got to see him and I think about him all the time. He's so cool! And I'd much rather see him than Dad. But I couldn't start to explain that to Dad! So I suppose I'll just go as usual for the weekend, and we'll have a lousy time together: he'll be mad with me for asking to miss the visit and I'll be mad because I won't want to be there.

Parent's Point of View:
A Lose-Lose Situation

Boy, do I hate it when Angie phones up with that edge in her voice, sounding just like Ellen, and proceeds to tell me that once again her mother has found a way of undermining our weekend together. Well, that's not exactly what she said, but telling me she had to go with Ellen to her Uncle Bob's birthday party felt like the same thing to me. If Bob had minded his own business, there is a chance Ellen and I would still be together; good old Bob could never resist an opportunity to humiliate me. Ellen knows perfectly well that I loathe him, so using his birthday party as the excuse is really inflammatory. To make it worse, I could hear her whispering to Angie, telling her what to say on the phone. It feels like Ellen would do anything to keep Angie from seeing me. I bet Ellen told her that kid Alan, who Angie thinks is so great, will be at the party. I wouldn't put it past her. It's not that I don't want Angie to meet new friends, and she's dying to have a boyfriend like everyone else, but why does it have to be all mixed up with Ellen's family?

Now I'm in a lose-lose situation. If I insist Angie comes here, she'll sulk all weekend and refuse to talk to me. If I let her go, I won't see her for another two weeks, and Ellen will gloat and start thinking of the next obstruction she can put up. Maybe one day Ellen will grow up enough to actually be able to discuss plans with me directly, instead of use our child as a messenger. Poor kid! I wonder if Angie can possibly understand the feelings of anger that get stirred up when she talks to me like her mother used to. Sometimes it's like they're one person.

Making Sense of It All

When parents live apart, kids inevitably become participants in the day-to-day wrangling or negotiations caused by a fixed visitation schedule. Most of the time, this process is benign and entails their communication with a parent about minor adjustments for their convenience. Children are forever wanting to change the schedule to accommodate their needs—they want to be picked up from a friend's house, not the gym; or at 7:00 P.M., not 6:30 P.M.; or need you to bring them the jeans they left at your house over the weekend. Sometimes, however, they are hijacked into communicating not on their own behalf, but on their parent's. As a result, they find themselves in the cross fire of disagreements. The diary illustrates how, in asking for a schedule change, Angie has been placed in the middle of a long-standing argument between her parents about family priorities and changes in visitation. Parents need to be careful not to place their children in the "line of fire" like this, as the kids are likely to get hurt.

Why Do Parents Use Children as Messengers?

Kids are generally put in this awkward position of playing messenger when their parents won't face up to the need to resolve lingering hostility and differences of opinion between themselves. By avoiding the emotional burden of addressing the situation directly, or the payments necessary for the services of a mediator, the parents force children to be players in a complex situation they often don't understand and that inevitably causes pain and distrust.

Despite feeling justified, the parent who instigates the messenger service does so at great risk to the parent-child relationship when the child realizes how she or he has been manipulated. The parent who uses the child as a messenger to ask for more money or to change visitation arrangements, constantly subjects the child to feeling like a failure when the requests are refused. That's a function of children's "logic": If Dad loves me as much as he should, then he'll do this for me; if he doesn't, then either I'm not good enough or he doesn't really love me.

How to Respond

Parents frequently use their children to convey information that will upset the other parent. If you suddenly find yourself set up with an unexpected demand from your child for a major schedule change; a request to provide more money to the other parent; or unsettling news about whom the other parent is dating or about to marry or did marry, try not to fall into the trap of venting your emotions on the child for delivering the message. To spare the child, the parent who receives the message must not overpersonalize it or dwell on the unfairness of the gamesmanship. In this instance, the father shouldn't think about Bob as his "ex-brother-in-law, the marriage breaker," even though the characterization may be fair. Nor will he ultimately gain by trying to convince Angie that her mother's family is vindictive and always wanted the marriage to fail, even if it's true. Retaliating in that kind of tit-for-tat manner demands the children make a painful loyalty choice in which they are always the losers.

This dad's angry response is unproductive. His weekend with Angie is likely to be difficult, and in the future she will be more hesitant to share any information about her life that might elicit the sort of knee-jerk response she received this time. If this was a first-time incident, this father would have been better off making no editorial comments about his ex-wife and her family party, and deciding whether to allow the change without a lot of debate. Although these diaries suggest that this request is another instance in a pattern of the mom using her daughter to manipulate logistics and emotions, the dad still needs to address Angie's request directly. At a later time, he should encourage Angie to voice her objections to playing the role of messenger and help her communicate her feelings to her mother. Unless the children object for themselves, complaints on their behalf seldom work.

Many parents go even further by engaging in an especially dangerous game, either consciously or unconsciously, in which the child ends up being used as a mouthpiece to communicate anger and hostility toward the other parent. Constant bad-mouthing of the absent parent can alienate the child from that parent, as the child identifies with the anger of the parent sending the messages and begins to feel it as his or her own. For example, if Mom continues to repeat that Dad is selfish, then over time, the child who identifies with her will likely move from saying, "Mom says you're selfish," to both saying and feeling, "You're selfish, Dad," when he refuses to accommodate a request. If, every time something needs to be addressed, Mom keeps reiterating that "Dad can't be trusted because he committed adultery," or "I wish we could ask Dad, but he's too irresponsible," the child will adopt the tone of voice and then the words, not just in reacting to a response, but also in making the request. Suddenly, as the child begins to identify more and more with the mother, the child starts sounding and acting just like the mother (see Chapter 29). Hence, Dad is likely to start treating the child more and more like the ex-spouse. The unfortunate child has been manipulated into becoming the inappropriate target of Dad's reactive anger to the mother's ongoing hostility and manipulation.

This high-risk situation for the child most likely develops when the parents "don't speak to each other," as it leaves the child no choice but to be the one who asks for changes in the arrangements. The child feels she or he is the one who has to solicit more money for support or extracurricular activities, since the residential parent has told the child it's the only way to meet her or his needs. The child's "power" is often transiently confirmed when legitimate requests are initially met with acceptance. However, things change if it becomes clear that this ploy is a calculated effort by one parent to circumvent the provisions of the divorce agreement, or that the child is being used as a provocateur in ongoing emotional hostilities between the parents.

Putting an End to Inappropriate Messages

The language your child employs—the actual choice of words—most commonly is the tip-off that the child is being "used." Kids don't think about parental "responsibilities" or talk about "adultery."—they hear these terms from adults. If you're the target of such statements, don't play into the game. Keep telling the kids you wish they were not being put in the middle of issues that are not theirs. Be specific about how you've tried to arrange changes in the schedule or the ways in which you provide for their needs, so they know you are concerned about how they feel. If you did have an affair or behaved badly, it doesn't hurt to say you're sorry it happened, but you've learned your lesson about the importance of being honest and truthful with the people you care about—and make sure you are as good as your word!

But telling the children you understand the bind they have been put in isn't enough. Notwithstanding the actions of the other parent, it is your responsibility to make sure the burden of communication is lifted from your children's shoulders. While it's true that many divorced spouses literally never want to speak to each other again, and they may want to believe it can be done, it's difficult if each wants to continue to be an involved parent. While it is true you don't have to be friends, and you may have no contact about anything else, as parents you will at least occasionally have to talk with each other about the kids. It may be very tempting to punish the other parent with silence. You may be able to enlist the kids by manipulating their world to show them how horrible their departed parent really is, but the children are the ones who always get punished in such tactical maneuverings. They are the ones who get shouted at, and they are the ones who suffer when a parent finally retaliates by cutting support or failing to visit, even though the retaliating parent feels more than justified after sufficient provocation.

When parents are hostile toward each other, communication is a burden, since arguments often cut short any constructive exchange. If you really can't manage more than a few words, e.g., "Hello, this is Fred and I want to talk about the kids. . . .," before there is an explosion, then see if a mediator can help you. Unable, or unwilling, to pay for that service? Perhaps a friend, a member of the clergy, or someone who is close to the children, can be a conduit for messages and replies. If none of these options are available, use fax, E-mail, or even snail mail—none requires talking to each other. But don't send the kids with a note.

No solution will work if hostility, bitterness, and anger linger and continue to influence your decisions and actions or your willingness to deal directly with the other parent. If you don't address these emotions and pay the cost in terms of dollars as well as time and emotional effort, the kids will inevitably be thrust into the messenger role. Communication is a parental responsibility. Taking advantage of a child's naïveté and trust is clearly a situation bordering on abuse.

General Guidelines

The following suggestions should allow you to avoid repeatedly burdening your children with the emotional baggage that is always a part of being the messenger between parents.

- Work out a mechanism to communicate about the inevitable need to make changes in the schedule or meet unanticipated financial demands as children develop new interests. Any experienced lawyer should help you incorporate this into the divorce decree. If that didn't happen, set some guidelines in writing now.
- Incorporating a periodic review of the financial arrangements into the divorce settlement, say on a biyearly basis, often minimizes the temptation to use the children as messengers.
- Schedule changes often occur with sufficient advance warning that they can be negotiated in writing, so try to look ahead and anticipate problems.
- If talking to each other leads to anger and acting out, use an intermediary or fax, E-mail, or snail mail.
- When you find your kids are being used as messengers unnecessarily, help them to understand that this is not their responsibility and reassure them that they can refuse.
- Take constructive action to halt the process. Tell your children what you are going to do to take them out of the messenger role. Above all, don't get mad at them, and don't make them listen to character assassinations of the other parent. It won't improve your limited time together or their opinion of you.

Keeping Secrets from Parents

19

In which eight-year-old Kevin is forced to tell
the secret he was keeping from Mom

Child's Point of View: It Wasn't My Idea or My Fault

Why is it that anytime I get really happy, something spoils it? The weekend was awesome, and now everyone is mad at me because I told Mom it was the best weekend of my life. After all, I did have a great time at the rock concert.

When Mom knew the Ragers were performing this year at the stadium, she got us tickets so we could go. Then there was some problem with the weekend schedule to see Dad, and it ended up that we had to spend that weekend with him. Kerry was hysterical that we would miss the concert, as it's Mom who does their local public relations, but Mom gave the tickets to Dad, so I thought everything would be fine. I mean, I knew Mom might be disappointed to miss the show, but she can see them anytime she wants.

In the intermission, Dad bumped into this guy Mom works with and he took us backstage. We got to talk with Mark, Pete, and Dave in their dressing rooms, and when Mark heard I had started to learn guitar, he let me play my chords on his famous guitar! Then he signed a huge poster of him playing the blue guitar and gave it to me. *Wow!* I couldn't stop talking about it all the way home, I was so thrilled; but Dad and Kerry said although it was all right to be excited with them, it would be better *not* to tell Mom about the backstage bit. It should be our secret.

It wasn't my fault I told her! I was practicing my guitar, and Mom came in to say how good I sounded. I wasn't planning to tell her why I'd gotten so enthusiastic about practicing, or what Mark had said about maybe playing with him next time . . . until the door blew shut, and when Mom turned around to open it, she saw the poster with Mark's "Dear Kevin" message on the bottom. I had to tell her then. I mean, what was I meant to do? Lie? How? I thought she would be happy I'd had such a good time, but all she did was shout at me for not telling her earlier.

Ten minutes later, Kerry came storming into my room, swearing at me for being such a fink and upsetting Mom. She said she'd never tell me anything because I couldn't keep a secret and I was "immature." Then Dad called me tonight—I think Mom called him—and he was upset with me too. He said he was "disappointed." It's not fair. I wish I'd never gone to the stupid rock concert. I think I'll tear up the poster; it makes me cry whenever I look at it.

Parent's Point of View: Do My Kids Ever Tell Me the Whole Truth?

I'm so mad at myself for feeling angry. I don't know if I'm angry because John and the kids colluded to deceive me, or that John used my professional position to enable him to play the good guy and get the kids invited backstage. I suppose the first worries me and the second really ticks me off! I *think* this weekend is the first time they have come home from a visit with John and told me an edited version of the truth . . . but maybe they *never* tell me the whole truth. Now I feel I don't know what is going on in my kids' lives when they are not with me, and it's probably my own fault. I suppose I've made them scared of telling me they've had a great time with their dad. I'm worried that my tendency to get tearful, especially in the early days of the separation, has made Kerry think it's better to lie than risk hurting me with the truth—and her father seems to have condoned her lying. But that's not surprising; lying always came naturally to him.

Worst of all, I feel guilty that I took my anger out on Kevin who doesn't even understand why he was meant to keep the secret! If I was a good mother, I'd be thrilled he had such a fabulous time, even though I wasn't there, but . . . I'm not that good. I don't know what to say to Kevin to make him feel better, or to Kerry to ensure lying to me doesn't become a habit.

Making Sense of It All

Keeping secrets sometimes sounds like a harmless game to kids, but it isn't. It inevitably causes pain to the party excluded and a feeling in the children of having been manipulated, especially if they have hidden something from one parent at the instigation of the other. The fallout from telling the truth may be difficult to deal with at times, but it's vastly easier than living with the recriminations and doubts that deception brings.

Children Lying

Unfortunately, the culprit who gives away the secret and takes the greatest heat is often the least-deserving target. In this event, Kevin, like many "younger" children, was the one who got "caught"—ironically because he did all the right things: he practiced his guitar and eventually told the truth. He's bewildered because he can't see what he's done that's so wrong, and feels set up by his father and big sister. To make things worse, he also feels guilty: guilty that he enjoyed himself in the first place, guilty that he betrayed a secret, and guilty that he upset his mom.

Kerry isn't in quite the same position. As an adolescent, she cannot deceive herself that she is completely innocent of the reasons for covering up or the consequences of hiding the truth. Most teenagers have some sense of the complications that can ensue when secrets are unmasked. In the family and in the peer group, Kerry is undoubtedly familiar with the tensions, the allegiance conflicts, and the pain of exclusion that always occur with conspiracies. Moreover, while Kevin might be able to console himself that he was protecting Mom from feeling jealous when he agreed to keep the secret, Kerry is old enough to know there's more to Mom's potential reactions than simply being envious that they had a good time. Dad certainly should know that using his ex-wife's professional contacts to his own advantage could cause trouble, and letting the kids take the heat is clearly unfair. Poor Kevin, the innocent, who believes he is the betrayer, has also been betrayed.

Lying has different meanings to an adolescent and an elementary-school-age child. Younger children are more likely to think lying is OK if it's to avoid hurting someone's feelings, or if it keeps themselves from getting into trouble. Adolescents like the "avoiding trouble" excuse, but may also enjoy the charge they get out of putting things over on an adult. Many feel like "good" lying is just part of learning to play adult games—after all, Dad is on the far side of forty, and he never tells the truth about *that*. But being asked to lie to a parent never really feels right and parents should not encourage it, nor set children up to keep a secret they do not understand or want to keep.

Adults Lying

Adults do keep secrets and do lie, and in many cases the ease with which they have done so has precipitated the divorce. Parents will often justify their lying or deception, especially when they think it is "for the sake of their children." Lying is a dangerous behavior in all spheres of human relationships, but especially in the divorce situation, as it jeopardizes the children's ability to trust their parents' word. Children model their moral behavior on that of their parents and depend on their parents to be trustworthy. As we emphasize repeatedly in this book, since divorce itself represents the breach of a promise, trust within the family becomes very precarious after divorce. In day-to-day events, trust is based on the expectation that the truth is the only valid currency of communication. Secrets are "anti-truth," and though they are often presented to kids as the ultimate in faith keeping, as in "It's our secret," when exposed, the deceptions spoil whatever joy or pleasure might have been shared together and create a lingering doubt about the future.

Throughout twenty years of helping families, we have stressed the importance of honest, reliable communication between parents and children, even when its expression can create anxious moments and tense feelings. Secrets undermine communication. They almost always place the children in vulnerable positions, caught out in the multiple layers of a game they can't understand or play as equals. Enlisting children in plots to keep secrets almost always takes advantage of their naïveté or puts them in loyalty crises, much like using them as messengers takes advantage of their innocence and jeopardizes their relationships with both parents (see Chapter 18).

Is Lying Ever Acceptable?

Despite all these warnings, there may still be times when you're tempted to enlist the kids in keeping secrets from their other parent. Usually it concerns a new romantic relationship or a change in finances. Revealing anything this personal appears to run the risk of upsetting the other adult or creating waves you don't want to handle.

But if you want the kids to meet your new friend and are tempted to say, "Please don't tell Dad about Jim, because it will just upset him if he gets the wrong ideas," or you want to spend your bonus, and plead, "Let's keep it a secret that I got you new skis, because Mom will think that I should have given more of my bonus to her," we would advise you to think again. Are you asking them to lie if they are asked a direct question? Whom are they betraying if they tell? Whom, if they don't tell? Whose feelings are you trying to spare: Yours? Your ex-spouse's? Your kids'?

Even when these pleas are based on bad past experiences of truth-telling and seem reasonable, they make the children coconspirators, while labeling the other parent as jealous, selfish, or insecure. These directions, even when honestly given to protect the ex-spouse or to shield the kids from reactions they shouldn't have to weather, place limits on whom the children can talk to. If your children can't talk to their other parent, whom can they talk to when the introduction of your new significant other makes them worry that they'll be replaced, or when they feel guilty that they have all sorts of hidden gifts from you?

Illness sometimes needs to be an exception to the rule. Many times the children discover there is a serious problem, despite your efforts to hide it from them. They may be concerned, they may feel they have to do more to protect you or care for you, so they'll be tempted to tell the other parent. Yet for reasons of custody, visitation schedule, or personal finances you may not want the information divulged. This may be one time when it's reasonable to ask them to say nothing until further notice. Tell them honestly that you'd like to have them wait so you can tell the other parent yourself when the situation is clearer. And then do it!

General Guidelines

- The best advice about secrets is to avoid them once you move beyond surprise outings and surprise parties.
- Keeping secrets models that you are willing to breach someone's trust, and in the context of divorce that is very risky.
- Particular social situations and financial events may put you in the position of not wanting to inform your ex-spouse. Prevent the children from feeling trapped in a loyalty choice, by letting them know when and how you are going to tell the other parent.
- Personal illness can create a unique set of circumstances which compromise your future, your health insurance coverage, your job, etc., if your ex-spouse finds out. Try to keep the children in the position of coconspirators for as short a time as possible.

20 **Therapists**

In which Barbara, age thirteen, tells why she
doesn't think her brother's visits to a
psychologist are worth it

Child's Point of View:
I Don't Want to Go to a Therapist Forever

I got in a big argument today with Dad because he's wasting his time—and my time. Every Thursday afternoon we spend almost two hours going to the psychologist so my brother can play games with Dr. Smith. That's what he says he does, and I know it's true. I saw her a couple of times when my parents separated, and we just played with a dollhouse every week. She was nice enough, and I liked her, but being there meant missing a whole afternoon playing with my friends. Thankfully, we only went a few times and then stopped because she said David and I were doing fine.

But then, about a year ago, David had to go back to see her when he got sent to the principal's office twice in one week. The principal told Dad that he thought David might be disturbed about the divorce. Dad talked to Mom on the phone, and they decided David needed to see Dr. Smith again, even though I don't think Dad was too happy about it, as he has to take time off from work. Dad says that he and I can both use the time there to do our work, but it's hard to do that with all the people in the waiting room. It's kind of aggravating, because while we're having to wait, David keeps answering the same questions about how he feels and whether he still misses Mom. He told me that mainly how he feels is that he wants to get out of there and go home to ride his bike. He tells me he knows what Dr. Smith wants to hear, so he says it—just like I did!

I don't know why, but finally today, David decided he'd had enough—and that's when the arguments started. He didn't just complain about going, he refused to get in the car! Dad told him he had no choice. Since I didn't want to go either, I thought I could help out by telling Dad he should just drop it. I told him it would do us more good to play with our friends. He got really mad, saying that when he wanted my opinion he'd ask for it and he didn't need me making life more difficult. So with everyone steaming, we went as usual, but this time David refused to say or do anything. Dr. Smith ended up calling Dad into her office for "a talk." Dad was pretty mad on the way home. He told David that refusing to participate was not the way to prove everything was OK. Then turning to me, he said that continuing to side with David might get me some appointments with the psychologist too!

The atmosphere settled down at dinner—sort of. Dad explained that it was really important to continue, and that Dr. Smith thought she could help David sort out some things. David wasn't about to give up. He protested he felt fine and that other kids got sent to the principal's office, but they didn't end up seeing a shrink for a year, so why should he have to? According to him, some of those kids are in trouble all the time and all that happens to them is their parents get called in for a conference, or they get sent to some lunch group to talk about things with the school counselor. Dad kept saying that going to see Dr. Smith wasn't meant as a punishment. I don't think he gets it, because it sure feels like one to David, and I don't exactly love it when I have to tell friends I can't come over on Thursdays because my brother is "in therapy"!

Parent's Point of View: Does My Child Really Need Therapy?

I can't decide whether today was a day to try the soul or some kind of strange wake-up call. It's been three years since the separation, almost a year since the divorce, and considering what we've been through, I'm basically pleased with how everyone has adapted. The kids seem happy and are doing well in school, and we seldom fight or have major disagreements. Arguments like today's make me wonder whether I'm completely off-base. Maybe the kids are right; maybe the psychologist isn't necessary anymore, but I know Diana is still worried about David.

It's hard to believe these weekly visits started over a year ago. At that time Diana was very concerned the finality of the divorce was the reason David kept getting sent to the principal's office. She wanted him to see the therapist we had seen as a family when we first decided to separate, although I was ambivalent. I have never really trusted this psychologist's biases, since she started off our first meeting by saying she thought mothers should always be supported in the divorce situation and assumed the kids were going to live with Diana. I remember she was speechless when she heard we had already agreed that I was going to have physical custody, and then she kept encouraging Diana to voice her doubts about it, as though somehow Diana must have been pressured by me to give up living with the kids.

Somewhat against my will, I found myself back in the office a year ago explaining there were some worrying incidents at school. I told her I personally didn't think this had anything to do with the divorce, because the kids were behaving fine in general, but that Diana was concerned and I wanted to make sure. The therapist indicated that divorce could cause these sorts of behavior problems in kids and she thought that moving quickly was a wise idea, especially since this was an unusual situation where the mother had been the one to move out. I wasn't sure what to make of that! There's no question our divorce has had more impact on David than Laura—he's the one that's sadder when Diana has to change the schedule; he's the one with the nightmares. So I started to bring him every week. I must admit Diana and I both felt better that we were doing something, and there haven't been any more problems at school.

At first David treated these sessions like playtime, which I guess is what they were. But in the last few months he's gotten increasingly resistant to going, and the questions in my mind about the benefits of all this have increased. Today David refused to talk to her, so she sent him out and called me in. I told her about his increasing resistance, but she interpreted David's behavior as indicative of his still being afraid of something and repressing his feelings. I didn't come away feeling she had helped me understand David any better or that she can say what's really going on in his life—it's all the same stuff about the "difficulty in getting kids to talk," and she "doesn't want to rush to conclusions." *But,* she said darkly, there are certainly "indications" that he still needs to continue to see her.

I couldn't help but be struck, however, that David was fine as soon as we got out of there, and Barbara kept reminding me how well he is doing in school. Now I'm beginning to wonder whether Dr. Smith is convinced David has to have problems because his mother doesn't have custody! Or is that just my paranoia?

Making Sense of It All

Many parents become frustrated, confused, and skeptical trying to determine if their kids need therapy, and, if so, with whom and for how long. The work of the therapist has no obvious end point, so goals need to be agreed upon at the outset. Many times, families are left in the situation illustrated in the diaries, in which it is unclear whether children's resistance to continuing therapy is a symptom of its necessity or a sign that it should be stopped. Frequently, one parent is more invested in continuing than the other, but the parent who bears the financial burden may not be the parent who feels therapy is necessary. This disparity often leads to major disagreements as to what is in the best interest of the child and which parent "cares" the most.

There is no question divorce can lead to behavior problems and difficult emotional adjustments for children, although it is not always clear whether the problems commonly seen are related to the family dynamics that lead up to a separation, or to the separation itself. Other events such as a remarriage or an attempt to blend two families may precipitate the need for additional psychological support. Sometimes, the first indication of adjustment problems occurs at school, rather than at home. A psychologist or other professional therapist can be of immense value in helping children express feelings and in assisting parents to devise strategies to deal with problematic behavior at home or at school.

On the other hand, divorcing parents often jump to the conclusion that all their children's behavior problems are precipitated by the stress of the divorce. It is important to remember that mood swings, sibling rivalry, or difficulties in peer relationships occur in all kids. Be careful not to read more significance into the behaviors than is warranted, just because you are feeling depressed, angry, guilty, or lonely. Starting a child on long-term therapy is a move that parents need to consider very carefully. Children may think that having to see a therapist means they must be crazy or disturbed. It usually gives the children the message that something is wrong with them and makes them feel more "different" than they already feel. For parents, it may provide an uncomfortable and expensive reminder that their decisions have had negative impact on their children.

Therapy sometimes needs to be short-term, sometimes long-term. Resistance may occur at any time, but as illustrated in the diaries, does not necessarily mean that therapy should stop. It is not unusual for a child to balk at seeing the therapist, before a strong therapeutic alliance is established; and, as in adult therapy, appointments are frequently avoided when the child faces a dilemma or acceptance of a personality characteristic or behavior trait that has previously been denied. An occasional visit without your child is important so you can update the therapist with your observations and get some clarification of where the therapy is headed. If you are not happy with these feedback sessions and your child is requesting a break, you need to listen carefully to your child's argument. If the behavior that resulted in the referral is no longer present and no new problems have occurred, then perhaps the child is right and it is time to stop. While parents don't usually want to terminate an activity that has potential benefits, it is important to determine whether any benefit is actually being provided. We frequently refer children to therapists, and have seen remarkable progress. However, we've been involved in cases where the child has been seeing someone for years, yet neither parent nor child has any better understanding of the issues, nor has there been appreciable change in the troublesome behaviors. While the child may need further therapy, a different person or a different approach is clearly called for in such a situation.

General Guidelines

There are few general guidelines, as each family's situation is unique, but the following are worth remembering:

- No one is the perfect therapist for everyone. Chemistry is everything.
- Short-term therapy can be of immense benefit to a child in adapting to particular situations, such as the news of the separation or the demands of living with new step-siblings.
- If your child is in long-term therapy, a minimum of three sessions a year should be used to give you and your child a sense of progress. Effective therapy should result over time in a decrease in unwanted behaviors, as well as additional insights into the child's character and social style.
- During the separation and often after the divorce, behaviors, which in other circumstances would be attributed to sibling rivalry, peer struggles, or school adjustments, may get considered in an overly pathological light.
- An increase in the frequency of risk-taking or self-destructive behaviors, an increase in the intensity of hostile, angry, or withdrawn reactions, or an uncharacteristic slump in academic performance should not be ignored in any child.
- If they are overly depressed or angry, children often need reassurance that seeking help is not a weakness, but a necessary step to getting back on track.

- Being in therapy can be a stigma for the child that says "something is wrong with me," and a stigma for the parent that says "I caused this." The negative effects of these stigmas need to be balanced by the positive benefits of the therapy.
- Resistance to therapy needs to be taken seriously, not just overcome. Early on, in the first weeks, it may mean that a therapeutic relationship is slow to be established. Later in the process, it may be a sign of the child's reluctance to face important issues. However, if all is going well in school, social, and family life, resistance may be a valid sign that the therapy can be terminated.

Last-Minute Cancellations

21

In which six-year-old Alice tells of her
despair when Dad cancels

Child's Point of View:
I Was All Ready to Go

I put on my party dress today. Daddy likes it the best. Mommy brushed my hair. I was so proud I was ready on time. I waited by the window. I like to see his car come. It is so shiny. I waited and waited. Then the phone rang. I was scared. Mommy got it. Her face went all frowny. It was Daddy. I hoped he was just late. I said, "Daddy when are you coming?" But there was no answer. He was gone. I cried and cried and cried.

Parent's Point of View:
My Child Is Devastated

I knew it was Daniel the second the phone rang—and I knew he was going to cancel another weekend with Alice, and I knew he would have some very plausible excuse, but I still felt sick. She looked so cute sitting there—she'd gotten all dressed up for Daddy and even packed up her little knapsack. She was watching me, wondering why I didn't answer the phone. Finally she said, "Mom, I can't reach it," so I picked it up. At least this time he was in Italy, not Kansas City or some place where he really could have managed to get back in time. Hearing that he was trying to get back, but now it would be midweek, didn't make it any better.

He wanted to know if it would be OK if he came to see her as soon as he returned. What could I say? It's been almost a month since he's seen her; therefore, part of me, but only part, wanted to say yes. I told him I had plans, she had school, and I had already paid for after-school care for this month, so I asked, when did he intend to spend time with her? Of course, he didn't know exactly. I felt sorry for Alice, but I just couldn't help feeling like he was jerking *me* around again. I would be the one to have to tell her that he wasn't coming today; I would have to make the alternative plans. Most dreadful of all, I would have to deal with the fallout, especially the sleep problems this weekend and then again, after he comes to see her for what always seems to be a few hours instead of the oft-promised couple of days. He loves to put on the good-time-Charlie act, complete with presents and staying out past her bedtime—she loves it, but she's an emotional wreck and physically exhausted afterward. I should have said, "No midweek visit." I should have told him to learn to stick to his commitments. But I looked down at her expectant face and I gave in, still believing it's important for her to see him as much as possible.

He asked me to apologize to Alice, and I think he was surprised when I said, "No way. You tell her." But when I handed the phone over, she listened a second, looked puzzled, and held the phone up to me. Nothing but a dial tone. I was steamed. I wasn't sure whether he had hung up, or whether we had been disconnected. As I turned back from putting the phone on the wall hook, Alice, tears running down her face, realized, "Daddy's not coming, is he?"

The rest of the night she was just terrible, wanting affection and attention, while pushing at every limit possible. Like the last few times when this has happened, getting her to bed was a real battle. In the end, she slept in my bed. I hoped she would be better this morning, but she just picked up where she left off. I knew she was upset, so I kept trying to be compromising or forgiving, but I finally blew up, and then felt worse than ever for her.

When she calmed down, I told her I felt she was trying to make me mad and I wished she would tell me what was wrong. She hemmed and hawed, and then it started. It was all I could do to listen. She had been looking forward so much to his coming back. She hoped it would be like when we were all together. Now she was angry and sad. "I wish Daddy was here. I don't want to keep wanting him all the time and then crying when he doesn't come. Why can't you make him come home?"

Why not indeed? If I'd had my way, he never would have left.

Making Sense of It All

Divorce itself highlights the differences between a husband and wife, but last-minute cancellations of visitation always result in drastically divergent views of the facts, motives, and consequences. In this instance, Alice's father would probably claim that he really wanted to get back on time, but it was impossible. Since it is his job that supports everyone, he would assume he deserves more understanding and flexibility on the part of his ex-wife to accommodate to the demands of his long hours and unpredictable travel. On the other hand, feeling taken for granted, his ex-wife would likely assert that she is unfairly burdened and her own plans devalued.

People who travel a lot or have demanding careers are often just as frustrated as everyone else in the family when work interferes with visitation responsibilities. If the visiting parent's delay results in the residential parent retributively canceling the visit, resentment and hostility will build. Meanwhile, the children take repeated tardiness or cancellations as the visiting parent's sign of not caring, and the custodial parent almost always develops the feeling of "my ex is out to get me." Attempts to make up for the cancellation by having an extra good time at the next meeting often compound the mixed emotions and the difficulties, especially when the visit is over.

In the end, it is the children who suffer the most. They will, at a minimum, be disappointed and feel rejected, their sadness often turning to anger, which may be directed at the parent they're with or a sibling. Life for the children becomes very lonely if they are left with the feeling that they don't matter very much. This is especially true when parents use cancellations as one of many ways to get back at each other; the children feel like pawns in the game. No child deserves to be the victim of this kind of hostility.

Even if every effort has been made to avoid unscheduled changes, they may still happen. The critical issue is how to tell the children that the timing of the visit has been changed. Parents need some type of agreed protocol. The first step, and the only acceptable option, is for the parent who is changing the schedule to be the one who tells the kids. What actually gets said to the children can be crucial as well. Start with the truth, but adding comments like "I couldn't help it" usually results in the child feeling anxious and vulnerable. Your contingency plan should try to make the crisis into a delay rather than a forfeited visit. If that is not possible, part of the protocol for an unavoidable cancellation should be some agreed-on automatic make-up time. This is more likely to be acceptable, however, if sudden changes are infrequent. A future date enables the parent making the change to give the kids something to look forward to.

Remember, if you are the parent who has transgressed, you are in the position of being the supplicant, so apologizing not only to the kids, but also to your ex, is prudent. Being polite and considerate fosters a better outcome than being demanding, or acting entitled, or suggesting you are the victim, e.g., "I pay the support," or "It's my right to see the kids." Finally, don't fall into the common trap of believing the kids can be bribed by gifts (see Chapter 5) as a way to make up for the time. Having a big FedEx box show up, instead of an apology, simply won't cut it as a substitute. The first time, a gift may transiently ease the pain and disappointment, but repeated gift giving will be seen as representing your lack of caring.

Sadly, a pattern of repeated delays and cancellations often develops as a result of a very preventable phenomenon that occurs when the schedule of visitation is first set up. Competition for "best parent" status, combined with guilt, drives many overcommitted parents to make unrealistic promises. When faced with the reality of being separated from the kids for long periods of time, many parents desperately fight for the maximum time they can get. The desire to appear the better of the two parents leads to unrealistic promises of availability. Unfortunately, the adult who was rarely available or reliable during the marriage, despite vowing to change and become a better parent, frequently fails, and continues to create the same tensions as were generated within the marriage.

Understanding the evolution of the problem does not diminish the difficulty faced if you are the parent who remains with the child who is stood up. While you may want to be caring or comforting, your own emotions of anger, sadness, and resentment may be almost unmanageable. You're likely to feel sympathetic for the child, yet also resentful and perhaps taken advantage of, for many reasons:

- You have no control over the situation; that demeans you and undermines your role as parent.
- Your own plans need to be abruptly changed and your social commitments put on hold while you look after your children's emotional needs.
- If you follow through on your own plans to go out, it's with the knowledge and guilt that your children are likely to be even madder with you than with the parent who cancels, because you will be seen as the one who left them in the lurch.
- As this pattern of negligent behavior was probably established long before the separation and almost certainly contributed to the divorce, you are likely to face a flood of painful memories. These make it difficult to focus on the present without being overly critical of the other parent.

All these factors combine to make character assassination tempting. Many parents give in to the frustration with their ex-spouse, acting out

in ways that neither set a good example nor help the children overcome their own disappointment. Indeed, many fathers or mothers,
faced with telling their children the bad news and weathering the
aftermath, find themselves acutely wishing they weren't parents on
this particular day; a message that's hard to hide from the children.

Not all last-minute changes are preventable. Not all are part of a
conscious or unconscious hostility directed at the ex-spouse. Last-
minute delays do occur—planes are late, work demands vary. Certainly, if a delay is unavoidable, e.g., you are supposed to pick up the
kids at six but can't make it until the next morning, try to at least see
them for the shortened weekend rather than canceling and trying to
reschedule. Even if the weekend isn't quite as conflict-free as you had
planned, at the least you will be the one who takes the flak from your
kids while they are still angry, and you will be the one who will be able
to apologize to them and your ex-spouse. The last thing you want to
encourage is negative reactions, like, "Well, as your dad doesn't care
enough to be on time, he can't see you this weekend." Distrust and
hostility only increase the likelihood that you will get to see your children less and less.

If you've been guilty of a last-minute cancellation, or a whole series
has resulted from your actions and perhaps those of your ex-spouse,
the toll on your relationship with your children most likely isn't worth
the gain. It is too high a price to pay for getting a little more work done,
satisfying the urge to get back at your ex-spouse by ruining his or her
weekend plans, or protecting yourself because the thought of a weekend alone with the kids leaves you feeling inadequate. Make it clear to
your boss which weekends you won't compromise because that's your
time with the kids. If something does come up that you can't avoid,
don't play the long shot that somehow you might get "free" by the
time you're supposed to pick them up. See if a friend or a relative can
take care of them on Friday night until you are available, or arrange
activities with friends on Saturday or Sunday where they have responsibility for your kids if you need to catch up on some work.

Especially if you are aware of the possibility earlier in the day, don't
wait until 4:55 P.M. and then call, expecting the other parent to tell your
children you won't be there at 5:00 P.M. As in Alice's case, it dramatically increases the intensity of the negative feelings. Even if you do
call ahead, but especially if you don't call at all, don't complicate mat-

ters further by sending a gift as an apology or using the time when you do arrive to participate in some expensive extravaganza with the kids. While they may temporarily forget their disappointment, that's not the "solution" to the problem you have to solve.

If you find that you just can't meet the commitments of the current visitation schedule, better to temporarily revise it than to perpetuate a series of disappointments that may define your image for months or years to come. A revision that gives you less time may have a certain element of risk if your ex-spouse or your ex-spouse's lawyers seem intent on making you appear to be the inadequate parent, but your repeated failure to meet commitments has a greater risk. Try proposing a schedule with a decreased time commitment for a set period of time followed by an automatic return to a schedule that provides you with more time with the children. Such a written agreement puts you in a more advantageous position if there is a legal battle over the visitation schedule.

Unfortunately, most divorce agreements do not provide for such revisions without ludicrous legal expenses as well as significant time and turmoil. Therefore, for a variety of reasons, last-minute cancellations may be occurring in your children's lives. If you're the parent they are with, rather than feeling like a victim, do some anticipatory planning. If you really, honestly, truly need to plan your social engagements for Friday nights, have a contingency plan. You'll probably be surprised how many friends and relatives will help out if they're asked ahead of time and if you develop a "rotation" so you're not always reliant on one person. If that's not possible, explain to the kids that you know how important the weekend time is to them, but that similarly it's also important to you. If your kids are mature enough (and legally old enough) to stay by themselves for limited periods, get a special video for them while you are out on Friday, or make arrangements for them to go somewhere after church on Sunday so you have at least part of the day free. The scheme may vary from weekend to weekend, and it helps to have it in place by the preceding Wednesday to avoid last-minute panics.

Finally, don't forget that your children can be your allies in trying to precipitate positive change. They usually want to see the visiting parent, and they'd rather have the weekend begin Friday, not Saturday afternoon. Kids often create solutions of their own, showing surprising willingness to do homework while they wait for the visiting parent at the library on Friday night, so they can stay out later on Sunday evening; or designing cards to send saying the visiting parent has to pay for pizza and a movie to entertain them every Friday that he or she turns up late. We don't often advocate kids playing such a role, but in these circumstances they are generally the ones who get both parents to listen.

General Guidelines

Last-minute cancellations have a much bigger downside than the loss of time with your kids. The negatives have significantly greater impact if the news comes on the day the visit is supposed to commence, or worse still, if it comes an hour or a few minutes before you are supposed to arrive. If a pattern develops, parental hostility increases and the children begin to feel unwanted and uncared for.

- If you have to cancel a visit, don't wait until the last moment. Procrastinating is not a sign of how much you want to be there; it's just inconsiderate.
- If your job requires unpredictable demands on your time, try to make the reality bearable by setting up an agreed protocol with the other parent.
- If changes are likely because of travel, etc., then take the responsibility to set up alternative people to care for the kids until you can be there. A delay is better than a cancellation, and these efforts will produce big dividends, since they remove unfair burdens from the other parent.
- If you have to cancel, tell the children yourself. Offer them an explanation that is truthful, but also one that doesn't cause them undue concern or make them feel unwanted.
- Don't demean their affection for you by sending a surprise gift, no matter how lavish, especially if cancellations and delays have become a pattern. Being there is the only real sign you care.

The Late
Phase of
Divorce

Reading the Agreement

In which Andrew, age fourteen, tells why
reading the agreement would
clarify the future

Child's Point of View:
I Need to Know My Choices

It was exciting when Dad moved into a house two blocks away last week. It felt really alien seeing him in a hotel room and then an apartment. We were all tripping over each other, and everyone wanted the weekends to end so we could get back to our own rooms. We're supposed to go over there this weekend, according to the "schedule," that great pronouncement from on high, but I decided to walk home from school today and go by Dad's house. I never expected him to be home, but his car was in the driveway. So I figured I'd say hello. I rang the bell. There was no answer. I tried again. No answer, but I couldn't hear the bell. Thinking maybe it didn't work, I knocked and tried the door. It was unlocked and I went in.

I called "Dad" just as he walked into the hall. He seemed to be getting dressed. I said "Hi," but he didn't even smile. He finally asked what I was doing there. His tone of voice was, well, not just that he didn't expect me, but that somehow this was really the wrong time to visit. I told him I was just walking by and saw his car. I could hear someone in the bathroom upstairs, so I took a hint and left.

When I got home, I was pretty upset and didn't want to tell Mom what had happened. She came up at dinnertime and, after I told her the story, tried to explain why I can't expect to drop in on Dad whenever I like now that he lives almost next door. Mom tried to make me feel better by saying that Tuesday afternoons weren't on the schedule and she was sure he was busy with preparations for his next recital. Well, she was right about him being busy! I guess I felt rejected by both my parents and kind of put off, so I told Mom again that I wanted to see where on the piece of paper it says I can't see Dad whenever I like and where it states how much money he's supposed to give her, as she always says we're in debt. Mom keeps telling me it's all settled, even though she doesn't seem to be too happy about the balance, and Dad says it's too complex to understand. If that's true, then I won't understand any of it anyway, so what's the harm? Every way I turn, the agreement seems to get in my way. Makes me wonder what else is in it that's going to affect my life next week, next month, or next year. What choices do I have, or have they all been made for me?

Parent's Point of View:
Should the Kids Read the Agreement?

Andrew blew into the house yesterday, stomped off to his room, and slammed the door. I left him alone, but when he didn't come down to eat, I went up. When I asked if he was having dinner, he replied, quite tartly, "Is it approved on the schedule, Mom? I don't want to do anything not on the schedule. Besides, if I don't eat, then we'll save money."

Eventually I got the story out about what had happened at his father's. I think we both know Sam was with some other woman, so it made the rejection hurt even more, especially since Andrew just felt unwelcome, with no explanation offered. But it's made him get even more focused on reading the settlement. There doesn't seem to be anything I can say. He's decided that the agreement is the key to understanding all the limitations on his life and that it's all documented on the paper. But the thing is so complicated and written in language that makes it impossible to understand. I'm reluctant to share it with him, as I can't help feeling it's a private agreement between me and Sam, and I'm not sure I want to reveal everything to Andy.

I suppose that as it determines what happens in Andy's life, he's entitled to read it. But if he reads it, the other kids will want to as well, and, as it's gibberish to me, it will definitely be pure gibberish to them. I can't decide if Andrew needs to know the financial terms as well as the schedule. What if he thinks the agreement is not fair? He is not in a position to change it, so it will probably make him even angrier than he is now. Does he really need to know the terms if I remarry? He already hates me dating.

I'm so tired of all his anger though, and maybe reading the document will let him come to grips with events like yesterday. He can't just assume we can drop everything for him. Both Sam and I agreed we should plan our "off" days as days off. Life must go on, and both of us want to meet new people and start up our lives again after having put everything on hold for so long. Maybe letting Andrew read the settlement will set the stage for us to begin to address that issue with him.

Making Sense of It All

In their attempt to come to terms with their parents' divorce, many kids ask what the divorce agreement actually says. Too often, parents deny them the opportunity to read it themselves or gain any detailed understanding of it, on the grounds that it is "private," or "too complicated," or "not necessary." From the child's perspective, the settlement comes to define life at the moment and life in the future, so it's unsettling when they are kept in the dark about its terms. They know that this piece of paper restricts their freedom, limits their financial resources, stifles flexibility, and causes friction between their parents. They know it took time and money to devise. They know it specifies when they will be where and how much money each parent has to spend—the latter being perhaps most important of all. Many also sense, or they may have been told, the settlement is unfair. Yet parents will rarely discuss the details, although they intimate the details are cast in stone. Following all the turmoil during the separation, this hardly makes children optimistic or more trusting of their parents. More than one child has remarked that though this piece of paper may be a settlement, it rarely ever sounds like an agreement.

Even for the youngest children, after many months of being in limbo, the announcement that there is now a "settlement agreement" signals the end of a long period of anxious anticipation. To be told that they can't see this document, read it, or be privy to its contents—when it's quite plain even to a five-year-old that this will be the "bible of life"—generates a broad range of reactions. Rarely are any positive. Withdrawal, anger, confusion, and hostility are typical and expectable.

Drained by the whole process, often fearful of exactly how they'll manage the future, parents are taken aback by the reaction of their children. The adults, believing things are settled, are now facing another volcano. It's therefore tempting to try to end the fuss quickly. Many parents tell their children the legal details of the document are too complicated, or say "you wouldn't understand," and deny their children access to the document itself. This tends to stifle an open dialogue between parents and children. Other parents try to get themselves off the hook by hiding behind the authority of the court. These parents are prone to say there is no point in reading the agreement as they can't change it once the judge has made the decision. Having had their lives turned on tilt, children have difficulty coping with the concept of an unaccountable and unknown authority like "the judge" or "the courts." It makes life feel threatening and leaves them distrustful of their parents' ability to control the future. It is even more confusing when they discover the truth, which is that their parents, not the court, actually decided or at least agreed to the provisions. We've heard many children say, "I don't get it. If they made the rules, why can't they change them?"

The best way to answer your children's questions about the future is to read the document with them. As you do this, you can explain it is an agreement between adults about how to conduct family life after divorce. It is not divine intervention, nor is it the ultimate evil. If there are particular financial provisions you don't want the children to see, e.g., trusts or reserve funds, then clip the provisions out or mark over them, and explain to the kids that you wish to keep personal financial matters private. However, since the financial terms of the agreement affect their lives as much as the visitation or custody provisions, you're on somewhat shaky ground if you do not share at least some financial information. The visitation provisions and, especially for older children, the money allocation are always issues. Hiding the truth usually leads to trouble in the end; occasionally a serious breach in the relationship. Knowing the realities of family finances can make it easier for the kids to accept limitations that seem unfair. At least it's better than believing a parent is simply saying, "No," out of spite. Given all the dissembling that goes on in the early stages of divorce, trust is always at a premium.

At a practical level many divorce documents are long and complicated, written in the language of lawyers—"pursuant to paragraph 1, pro rata shares, and schedules D-1, D-2, D-3, etc." This tradition can be broken, just like the tradition of not telling children what is in the settlement agreement or excluding them from any of the discussions of the visitation schedule. The divorce agreement should be written in plain English, so it is comprehensible without an interpreter. If you have ended up with a document full of legal jargon, a summary that you prepare is a good substitute to share with your children. Time with each parent can be written out on a yearly calendar. If there are arrangements for changing the schedule (e.g., a request to change weekends has to be made by the preceding Wednesday), that should be included. An explanation of the family finances can be a simple statement of each parent's monthly income, as well as special arrangements to pay for summer camp, extracurricular activities, after-school classes, or college education. As your children's interests change, they should know which parent to go to for extra funding or to initiate a change in the schedule. High school students need to know who will be responsible for future education expenses.

Be prepared for awkward questions when you try to explain the words on the paper to your child:

> Why doesn't Mom get more money?
> Who decided we could do only one after-school activity each term?
> Why can Dad remarry, but Mom can't without losing money?
> If Dad gets a promotion, do we get more money so I can buy new skis?
> Why can't Mom take us out of state without Dad's permission?
> Why can't Dad see us more if he wants to?

Although such questions are ones many parents want to avoid, they are indicative of what's important to your child, so at some point you need to address them. No matter how imperfect the answers you give, especially in the first few months of the separation or divorce, offering some definition of what is happening and what will happen is generally comforting. Generalities like, "It's all agreed and we can't change it," or "We did what is best for you," are seldom reassuring. Most children are concrete thinkers and they want concrete answers. Uncertainty makes it difficult to adapt. For most children who have endured months or years of unpredictability and pain as their parents split apart, the anxiety surrounding even the immediate future becomes unbearable. Once a settlement is reached, the children want the uncertainty to end. They want to know what it means for them; they want to know what the world within which they will have to build their emotional lives looks like. Keeping them in the dark engenders fear, which leads to anger and acting out.

General Guidelines

Why should you consider sharing the divorce agreement with your children?

- Reading the settlement helps children look to the future with a sense of certainty and decreases the fear that parents are hiding something even more dire than the divorce.
- Letting your children read the settlement agreement lets them know there are rules that govern your post-divorce actions, and which you have agreed you are legally bound to obey.
- Even for the young children who want the document read to them—and that usually lasts for about two paragraphs, since most kids think it's very boring—just hearing it and seeing it are reassuring.

When you have decided to go ahead:

- Make sure you have a document that is written in plain English, not "lawyerese"; it will be easier to explain and leave less room for misinterpretation in the future.
- Don't hide behind the agreement. If there are sections neither you nor your child like, explain your point of view and how it differs from your ex-spouse's. Rather than criticize the other parent, have the child talk to him or her directly, but forewarn the other parent!
- Be prepared to answer your child's questions and criticisms, especially if there was no prior consultation about scheduling, transitions, or finances. Children often have good ideas that deserve consideration.
- Try to minimize loyalty conflicts. Many children will think a certain provision unfair, either because they don't like it or the provision makes them feel as if they're being forced to choose between parents.
- Tell the truth.

23 Individual Time

In which Tony, age fifteen, wonders how he
can get some private time with his father

Child's Point of View:
I Need Private Time with You

I wish I could find more time to talk to Dad these days. He's always too busy looking after the twins. It's so frustrating because there are endless interruptions. I realize they are younger and need more attention, but it doesn't mean I don't need time too. Dad says I can talk to him about anything; but with the twins around, I can hardly launch into a conversation about the party I went to, and whether I should break up with Mariko, or the really weird advice my friends have given me. I mean, sex is not exactly a topic for a family dinner table conversation. What I would really like is either extra time with Dad alone or a time when the twins could go back to Mom early and I could stay.

Unfortunately, I know what will happen if I ask for that. I'll get a lecture about "the schedule," or the twins will say it's not fair if I get "special time." Maybe we should all get "special time"—like, each give up one afternoon with Dad every month so we can go individually. Problem with that is most of the time I don't have anything I particularly want time with Dad for! It's just *now* that I need it. Everything is so regimented in our family. Sometimes I feel like opting out altogether.

Parent's Point of View:
How Can We Make It Fair?

Today, when Tony wanted to talk about staying Sunday nights at his Dad's place without the twins, I was willing to listen. But then when he said he thought the little ones should come home in the afternoon on Sundays, as his Dad was usually out doing errands, my first reaction was to be furious with Richard for dumping Tony with the job of babysitting. Then I felt angry at Tony for not realizing that maybe I might need some time for myself on weekends. After all, I do have all three of the kids to manage most of the month, and sometimes I really need a break!

I can see the writing on the wall. This is a no-win situation. There's no way of making it fair, and that's what the girls whine about all the time. If we let Tony stay with Richard on his own, then the other two will want that privilege too, and I know Richard will refuse. He finds it hard enough to entertain Dana and Rose for the limited time he has with them already—hence the errands without them on Sunday afternoons. And the last thing I want to hear is more complaints about not seeing Daddy enough. It always makes me feel as if they are totally unappreciative of all the time I spend with them—as though that's just "my job." But if Daddy spends time, *that's* special.

It's clear that, as far as Tony is concerned, the visitation schedule we thought would stabilize everything doesn't work, because it lumps him together with his siblings all the time. He's probably right; he's really much older and has completely different interests. Richard and I did try to avoid this problem and came up with some quite creative ideas, but we gave up because we got sick of the lawyers telling us "it's not done that way" or "that's hard to get on paper" (ergo: more money for fees). The schedule worked fine for the kids at first, or at least nobody complained, except me. I felt really lonely when they were all away. But now I've gotten to like it this way. At least I know when I can go see my friends, or just sleep!

I've been thinking more about what Tony said, but, selfishly, I want to say he can't change the arrangement to suit himself. I guess I'm jealous. I hate to think there are things he wants to talk about to his dad that I'm not good enough to handle, or maybe that he just likes him better than me. Maybe this is a time in his life when his dad is more important than I am, but I don't really want to admit that. What makes it worse is that I bet Richard will gloat. He is longing to do "guy things" with Tony, which he knows I can't do. I just wish Richard would pay more attention to the girls. He doesn't seem to relate to them nearly as well as he did before we separated. He never knows what to buy them or where they would like to go. It's pathetic sometimes how they draw him pictures and make him little gifts and he doesn't seem to notice. Maybe Tony could stay there some Sunday nights alone, and Richard could manage one night a month with the girls without Tony's help. He'd have to listen to them then, and it would give Tony some extra time to see his friends or, with luck, to spend with me.

Making Sense of It All

From infancy through adulthood, everybody needs periods of time alone with each parent. Such times are basic building blocks for any relationship. Attachment in the young infant builds security in the toddler; five-year-olds are full of fears and self-doubts that only their parents can be told; every adolescent deserves the opportunity for guidance through tough moral, sexual, and education choices from both their mother and father; and what adult hasn't been thankful to have a parent to turn to on occasion? In any family, divorced or not, such quiet uninterrupted times together don't occur often. If you are not living with your children, a chance to be alone with one of them may only be possible every couple of weeks. It is important, however, that the resource be made available when it's needed.

Individual time is rarely built into the initial schedule recommended by the courts, mediators, therapists, or Guardian-ad-Litems (GALs), because it is complicated to structure and encode on paper. Regrettably, this type of flexibility frequently does not even get incorporated into the schedule as the years go by. Yet parents and children have told us over and over again that far from being a "no-win situation" as the mother's diary suggests, the opportunity for each child to spend time alone with a parent, as Tony suggests, is a win-win situation for everyone. The children have their individual needs met, both parents find the times alone enhance their relationships with their children, and everyone feels special and better able to share each other's companionship.

Maintaining stability and predictability for the children does not preclude introducing appropriate flexibility into the visitation schedule. Because conventional wisdom says that consistency is everything, parents, believing they are doing what is "right," often discount their kids' pleas for flexibility and individual consideration, and dismiss their imaginative suggestions. The age of the child who doesn't like the schedule may vary from family to family, and how that dissatisfaction is expressed varies with their age—from the teenager withdrawing, to the grade-schooler manifesting aggression, to the toddler becoming clingy. We urge you, however, not to miss these behavioral signals of frustration—or you'll end up depriving your children and yourself.

In some families individual time does occur, but it evolves in ways that make the children uncomfortable. The most common story we hear from children is that time alone with a parent is used as a reward for being "good"—assuming some new responsibility, abandoning hostile or regressive behaviors, or improving school performance. Such a reward system causes the children to believe that they are lovable only when they behave compliantly, and increases their fears that they could lose the love of that parent (just like the departed parent has). To their children, parents often appear to be granting individual time at their own whim, e.g., when a parent (either the one the children are leaving or the one they are visiting) waits until the last minute to unilaterally decide how many and which of the children will be seen that weekend. Such an action usually increases the children's anxiety in anticipation of "the choice" and makes them feel like "things" to be parceled out according to the adults' convenience.

If you offer individual time, maintaining equity is not as simple as making sure each child has equal time with any one parent over a given period, e.g., six months. Being responsive may require spending more time with your adolescent applying to college or extra time with the eighth grader whose first "love" hit the rocks. To manage this so that the others are not ignored requires more than superficial involvement in and knowledge about your children's lives. They need to trust that you know enough about them to recognize when they need extra time, love, or attention. If you don't have the mechanisms to stay in touch and know what's going on with each individually (see Chapter 13), if you lack time with them as a group when you can hear their arguments and complaints as well as share their fun times, then you will be inviting manipulation and engendering potentially harmful competition for your attention.

If parents are reasonably communicative and respectful of each other's needs, it is possible to offer each child individual time without obliterating all free time for the residential parent. If your nine-year-old is moody and belligerent all week or your adolescent rebellious, a brief message of warning to the parent they're about to be with may be extremely beneficial. Of course, managing to incorporate responsive individual time into everyone's busy lives also requires personal objectivity. If your child needs more time with the other parent, it is not necessarily a personal rejection of you. Similarly, if the "shoe is on the other foot," it's not a reason to gloat. Hopefully, you can communicate sufficiently to ensure that both of you are aware of the children's problems. Adjusting your own schedule to meet your children's needs is part of the responsibility of any good parent—despite the inconveniences.

General Guidelines

- Time alone with each parent is not an honor; it shouldn't be used as a reward or be subject to parental whim.
- Most parents adopt a fixed rotation if they have more than one child, since it minimizes manipulation. There will be times, however, when it may be prudent not to follow that strict schedule in order to meet an individual child's requirements.
- Ongoing contact with all the kids and workable mechanisms of staying in touch when you're apart are critical to making individual time valuable.
- Requests to spend individual time with one parent often provoke feelings of rejection or exclusion in the other parent. If this is happening to you, try to use every opportunity you are offered to spend more time with your other children, if you have more than one—or use the unexpected free time for yourself.
- The quality of the companionship and the reduced competition are important benefits of spending time alone with one child.

24

Assuming New Responsibilities

In which sixteen-year-old Judy wonders how she'll resolve the conflict between her social life and her home life

Child's Point of View:
I Do Too Much Around Here

I think I do much too much around the house. It started out as just helping prepare the occasional meal or cleanup, but now somehow it's become my job to do everything. The problem is that if I don't do it, nobody will. Mom is always busy or too tired, as she's been working two jobs since Dad left, and the boys create more mess if they try to help. I'd really like to go to the party Sally invited me to, but Mom already booked me to baby-sit on Friday while she goes out with Dave. Come to think of it, I'm tired of hearing how "cool" Dave is. He looks like a fat, middle-aged man to me! I really don't want to know their problems, but Mom seems to think I can help her sort things out. I'm having enough trouble trying to sort out my own almost nonexistent social life—not that she seems to care.

Anyway, tonight I'd had enough. What with my social studies teacher yelling at me that my report is overdue and my soccer coach saying I would be cut from the team if I didn't show up to practice more often, I've decided I'm not playing Cinderella any longer. It was frozen dinners all around tonight, even though they are expensive and nutritionally bad news. When Mom came in late, I was talking to Sally about the party. When we finished, I went down to tell her I was going out Friday, but there she was glaring at her dried-out dinner in the oven, so I didn't dare! She seemed torn between wanting to complain about the food and needing to talk about her day, but I didn't care. I want my own life! Can't she understand that?

Parent's Point of View:
I Can't Manage Without the Help

I got home late again tonight and I was looking forward to some of Judy's cooking. She's gotten really good and does a great job of staying within the budget. She's even been talking about going to a professional cooking school, and I've been trying to give her lots of praise. So I was disappointed to find a frozen dinner in the oven and some rice in the pan. Last week she made chicken pies from scratch and even the boys had seconds. She was so proud that it cost her about half what ready-made ones cost.

Tonight I was puzzled that she didn't come down when I came in. When she finally got off the phone, she apologized about the dinner, but said she was really tired. She didn't say anything else except she had to go study some more. So I had a cold dinner with no company. Since George and I split up, she's become so mature that I really enjoy talking to her, but I know she has school stuff to do. I like to listen to her perspective on life; it's so refreshing, and she can be so empathetic when I'm depressed. I hope she's learning some valuable things about how to deal with the workaday world and relationships by listening to my stories; I'm certainly learning a lot from her.

Maybe she's just having a bad couple of days. She works really hard. Without her, I know I couldn't manage both jobs and the household, and I certainly wouldn't have any personal life—it makes me feel almost her age again to be going out on dates. I can't wait till Friday—dinner with Dave at Chez Martine. Maybe I'll try to save enough money to get her something extra special for her birthday next month to say thank you.

Making Sense of It All

After a divorce, many parents are left with no choice but to ask their children to take on extra chores around the house. Often the younger children will revel in being given new roles to play that result in some extra thanks from Mom or Dad, as well as a sense of privilege at being permitted to do more "grown-up things." Older children may enjoy being given increased responsibility, but it is important to stop short of exploiting your children's willingness to help out and eagerness to generate praise. Perhaps if requests for help stayed as simple as clearing the dishes or folding the laundry, then things would be OK. But often extra chores become part of the daily grind, so what is at first a voluntary effort becomes a "responsibility," and then gets taken for granted.

If it was only household chores that were expected, almost all children would cope quite successfully and even benefit from the hands-on domestic skills education, but the demand seldom stops there. In many families there is a slow, almost imperceptible, change from the children helping the parents, to the children directly or indirectly attending to the parents. The children start out looking after the physical well-being of the family and end up taking on the role of support-ing the family emotionally. It is easy to see how this happens. If the children remain in the family home with their mother, and their father has left, the remaining sons become the "men" in the family. Not only do they take on household duties—taking out garbage, moving heavy boxes, cutting the grass—but they commonly feel they should "pro-tect" their mother and support her emotionally and financially. The remaining daughters similarly start by performing domestic tasks, but as their mother's dependency on them increases, they may find them-selves in the roles of confidant and companion.

An additional attraction for the children, in what they come to see as an "alliance of equals," is finding that they can make many of the important decisions just as competently as the adult. In fact, the thrill of the challenge may induce them to focus on the problems at hand and try their best to be helpful; hence, they actually find they can do many things even better than their parent. Parents in the acute divorce situation are never at their best. They are emotionally distracted and/or physically exhausted from the time conflicts of holding down a job, working out a settlement agreement, or perhaps trying to find emotional comfort and security in a new relationship. Certainly if their child seems ready and willing to do more, the parents often become quite self-centered: e.g., "I deserve to have a life too, so is it too much for Judy to watch the kids an extra night while I'm out?" or "I can see why Judy feels put upon having to watch the kids, but this new job will give us all a better life and she needs to contribute."

The alliances forged between parents and children can be positive and mutually supportive, but when adults are traumatized and emotion-ally needy, as they are after a separation, they may lean too heavily on their children. This growing dependency of the adult on the children not only deprives them of the parental support they deserve but also eventually generates resentment. When a child, such as Judy, is obliged to provide emotional support to everyone, especially her parent, then the chores become a burden much larger than the domestic work involved. Forced into or having assumed a very adult role, it's often hard, if not impossible, to go back to being a child—let alone enjoy childhood.

What's confusing for both parent and child is how easily a partner-ship that seemed beneficial can quickly turn ugly, with both people feeling angry, resentful, and betrayed. As each parent may be using the child for support, all too often the child ends up managing two households. It is this lack of a break that often pushes the son or daughter beyond the point of emotional tolerance, especially when the realization dawns that, "I'm taking care of my father and mother, more than they're caring for me. I don't have a life of my own." The willing participant, feeling taken advantage of, may suddenly break the alliance with an unprecedented show of noncooperation, which immediately brings the issue to a head, but rarely fosters a positive resolution.

Some change in roles is inevitably caused by the divorce. It takes most adults a minimum of two to three years to recover sufficiently to function effectively as parents. Meanwhile, someone has to do the work and the caring, and it is often the kids who assume that role. While they can gain immensely from taking on certain responsibilities, they should not be doing most, or all, of the domestic work or acting as the emotional mainstay in the family.

General Guidelines

As a parent, you need to establish some safeguards:

- Maintaining or building a strong social network for your children and encouraging extracurricular activities will give them appropriate peer involvement and support. It does, however, mean they may be out a few afternoons or evenings a week. Don't intrude on that space, even if it requires eating frozen dinners or making other compromises.
- If you simply can't manage without help from one or more of the children, give them all something to do. Don't make one child the exclusive provider. This is true even if you've been offering all kinds of positive reinforcements, such as extra allowance and verbal encouragement like, "You're so mature, you're so grown-up," or, "You're the man of the house." These statements may initially be music to their ears, but the tune won't stay melodious very long.
- Learning to cook, clean, do the wash, etc., are all necessary skills every child can master, but don't make them do everything alone. Sharing the work with them will give you an opportunity to offer appreciation of their efforts and to spend time together. Doing

something like making a special meal together may inspire the "cook" to experiment alone another time, or using a rainy Sunday afternoon to prepare some meals to freeze may free up time later in the week.

- While you and your children may have logistic needs in common, such as food on the table, clean clothes, or scrubbed bathrooms, there will always be differences in your emotional needs. Kids bring a lot of fun and joy into the lives of adults. They shouldn't be asked to support adults, make adults happy, or take over the role of emotional nurturer that rightly belongs to you.

- Don't put children in the position of repeatedly disciplining younger siblings without your knowledge or involvement. It's a clear indication you've assigned them a parental role they shouldn't hold.

- Despite your need for companionship in times of loneliness, don't forget that your children need you to be their parent more than you need them to be your friends. If you are using your children as your source of support, you are in danger of putting in jeopardy the very relationships you wish to foster.

Finally, there are some clear signals that indicate a major change needs to occur:

- The older children spend more time on nights and weekends with the family than you do.
- You realize you're saying, albeit proudly, that "I couldn't manage without their help."
- The kids are your only interest in life and the only relationships that "make you happy."
- You find that your child is your best friend and the only person you can talk to about important decisions.

All of these are situations in which the parent's needs take precedence over the children's. It is important not to exploit your children's willingness to help, and jeopardize their freedom to revel in the joys of childhood.

Sleep-Over at Dad's

In which Lizzie, age fourteen, faces the social
stigma of divorce

Child's Point of View:
What Are My Friends' Parents So Worried About?

I can't believe it! What is wrong with these people! I only invited them for a sleep-over party! One night!—and now they're making all kinds of excuses as to why they can't come! They have to get up early to go to church on Sunday, or they have an aunt coming to stay, or they might get allergic to Dad's cat—give me a break! At least Susie is coming, but Kate and my other so-called friends are all "busy."

I was so upset tonight, that I couldn't eat, and Mom was worried enough to miss her meeting to stay home and talk. I think she guessed what was happening. Before I sent out the invitations she tried to persuade me to have my birthday sleep-over at home, but my birthday is on a weekend I'm with Dad, and I really wanted the party on *the day*. To my surprise, Dad said it would be great to have the party at his apartment. He said he'll clear the living room so there will be space on the floor for all our sleeping bags, and get a bunch of videos from the store and lots of food, and he promised to let us stay up as long as we like. Actually, it sounds better than having the party here, because Mom would keep checking in on us and "suggesting" we go to sleep soon. Dad will just hang out with us for a while, then go to bed. He's been so great to me through all the turmoil of the divorce. He's always there for me, always has time to listen and help me, puts up with my moods, and is the only one who can cheer me up when life seems really dismal.

So tonight I couldn't believe what Mom was trying to explain to me. That it's not that my friends don't *like* me anymore or that they don't *want* to come, but that their *parents* are worried about them sleeping over at Dad's if there's no "mother" there! They have to be kidding. Why does that matter? Maybe I should tell them that Dad's girlfriend will be sleeping with him—that will really freak them out! I mean what exactly do they think? That divorce is an infectious disease that their children will start spreading? Or maybe that now Dad is divorced he's turned into a child molester and their darling daughters are going to be abused? This is so stupid and so insulting. Mom listened to all my ranting and kept saying that she had talked to Kate's and Susie's mothers, who had phoned her to ask what she thought, but the other moms hadn't called. I can't understand why they would call Mom anyway; I mean, it's Dad who's hosting the party. Why don't they call *him*?

I think what really hurts is that no one understands what a big step it was to invite friends to Dad's, or how long it has taken me just to be able to tell people that my parents are divorced. Like, it's three years now and I still feel uncomfortable talking about it. When Dad first moved out, I pretended nothing had happened, and when he came to pick me up from school on Fridays, I used to hide my overnight bag in the nurse's office so my friends wouldn't suspect anything. When Mom and I had to move too, because Mom found the mortgage payments too high, I stopped inviting friends over, because I was ashamed of our new, poky, little apartment. I took the school bus to my old house, and *then* the regular bus all the way back just so I could pretend nothing had changed. It took me half an hour extra just to get home! Now at last, I don't need to pretend anymore. In fact, I know I need my friends to understand what my life is really like—two parents, two homes, and countless complications. That's why I'm so ticked off. I mean, if I'm adult enough to handle it, why aren't my friends and their parents?

Parent's Point of View: How Can I Prove I'm a Responsible Father?

After three years of this divorce roller coaster, I suppose I shouldn't be surprised, but even *I* hadn't anticipated that Lizzie's friends would be afraid to stay the night here. What sort of adult do they think I am? What more do I have to do to be seen as a responsible father? I've cut back on work and travel enough to really enjoy parenting. I cook, I shop, I vacuum, and have time to do fun things with my daughter. Somehow, when I was married and Lizzie potentially had two parents available, she really had neither parent's attention. I was always too busy to play, and Roberta, who had plenty of time, was always complaining that chores took up her entire day and she was too tired to do anything extra with Liz.

I look back on those years before the divorce and regret how many opportunities I missed to share time with Lizzie. Instead, I began to feel pretty unimportant to her. After all, her mom was the one who shopped with her, and took her to ballet lessons, and got her hair cut, and bought her first bra. What was left for a mere dad to do? Mowing the lawn and changing the lightbulbs became my contributions to family harmony . . . and nobody even said thank you.

Well, I don't feel redundant as a parent anymore. Admittedly, it was tough at first. Lizzie was always angry with me for leaving and saw me as the "bad guy" and her mother as the "wronged woman," but gradually we have gotten beyond that. She is able to understand more about the complexity of relationships as she gets older and has really started to enjoy our time together. I never knew how to get close to her when Roberta was always there, but now I wouldn't change this for anything—only I'd like more time together before she's all grown-up and goes away to college!

When Roberta phoned to say there was a problem with the sleep-over party, I was devastated. I try to forget that most people see me as a monster for leaving Roberta for another woman. Lizzie has become so comfortable here with me over the years, and gradually she has introduced me to more and more of her friends. I was looking forward to hosting them and listening to them laugh and have fun. Now I'm afraid her friends' discomfort will trigger her ambivalence again, and I'm not sure her mother is helping by suggesting we move the venue to *her* apartment. I could kick myself for not phoning around to reassure all those suspicious parents that I can handle this. I am so mad with them, but I suppose they are just thinking of their own daughters, while all I can think of is what a blow this is to Lizzie. She has struggled so hard to overcome all her feelings of being different and being an outsider. Poor kid.

Making Sense of It All

Fathers are painfully aware of society's unspoken assumption that fathers somehow lack nurturing ability and compassion and therefore, at best, should be the auxiliary parent. Prejudice runs deep when it comes to fathers bringing up daughters. Although mothers are vulnerable to parallel criticisms about their ability to bring up boys, in this era when boys are being encouraged to show more of their nurturing selves and to participate more in general household tasks and responsibilities, mothers are often seen as the best parent to modify the unemotional, macho stereotype that has been the cultural norm.

This gender bias discriminates greatly against fathers, especially when so many men who separate from their wives find great pleasure in discovering that, even if they were not previously aware of it, they do indeed have the capacity to parent and nurture effectively. The father depicted in the diary has built a great relationship with his daughter. She tells him her problems, she shares with him her feelings, she is proud of him, and she trusts him to support her. He, in turn, has worked hard to earn her respect and trust. He is justifiably hurt by the reaction to the party invitation, both because he correctly sees it as an unfair criticism of himself, and as a rejection of his daughter.

There is no instant solution to the prejudice of society against men as responsible, nurturing parents. Courts are increasingly granting residential custody to men, but progress is slow and judges reluctant. The "best interest of the child" is still assumed to be met by living with the mother and visiting with the father, despite the fact that it is far from clear that gender is the defining characteristic of a good parent. Looking purely at the effect of gender, there is some data to suggest that girls do better living with their mothers, but equally compelling is the data that says boys have a better long-term outcome living with their fathers. Each situation should be looked at individually and all the options evaluated. The age, sex, and preferences of the children are all important factors in the decision. We would support the contention that, irrespective of the sex of the children, residential custody should be given to the parent who will best facilitate free access and visitation with the other. All experts agree that, in all but the most abusive situations, children of either sex do best if they have frequent and reliable access to both parents with a minimum of friction and conflict around visitation.

Parallel with the gender issue raised by this daughter's diary is the potency of the shame children feel when forced to expose their family's disintegration to the outside world—especially to their peers. Unfortunately, although divorce is affecting an increasingly large number of families, the "shame" of divorce does not appear to be decreasing proportionately. Most adults going through divorce feel acutely and painfully aware that, in their own eyes and the eyes of others, they have failed. They will go to extreme lengths at times to blame the other spouse and vilify him or her in an attempt to separate themselves from the stigma of blameworthiness, but these public displays seldom eradicate the guilt and doubt that most divorcing adults feel. Rationalizations such as, "I would never have had an affair if the marriage had been good," or "If my ex-spouse had paid more attention to my needs, I would have been more loving and responsive," may be true, but do not excuse the less than 100 percent effort to rectify the problems that so often characterize a failed marriage.

Inevitably, this adult sense of failure is communicated to the children. Perhaps this is why they try to hide the news from their friends. Children have to face the fact that their parents are at best fallible and confused, while at worst irresponsible and untrustworthy. No wonder the children are angry and embarrassed. They feel they have lost a crucial anchor in their lives. They, like the adults, try to find an explanation in order to decrease their sense of loss. They start to apportion blame to everybody, including themselves (see Chapter 6). Guilt about their own contribution to the family breakup makes them reluctant to reach out to peers or teachers for emotional support. As they become more isolated, their friends may in turn withdraw from them.

Many people naively think that only the players involved go through this process of assigning guilt and blame, but it is clear to us that to some extent everyone the couple knows gets pulled into the vortex. Eventually, friends, family, school personnel, and even acquaintances develop opinions based on a combination of fact and hearsay; then they take sides. Individuals find it is seldom possible to remain supportive of both parties and be credible. Friends begin to polarize. Families close up. As more personal information is offered, what starts off presented as a failed relationship begins to be painted as a failure of one or the other party to maintain the relationship. There emerges in people's minds a "guilty party," and guilty parties are not to be trusted. Hence, people may be hesitant to put their children in that person's care, even if only for a brief social event. If you have engendered support because you are truly the "wronged parent," it may be reassuring to you, but the polarization of support is uncomfortable for your children, who will have more difficulty maintaining a positive image of their other parent when surrounded by detractors.

It is worth reflecting on the possibility that the consequence of convincing your friends that you are "in the right" is that it forces them to see your partner as "in the wrong." That may feel supportive to you, but as your children's peers become aware of their own parents' negative feelings about your ex-spouse, they may be unable to offer much needed nonpartisan support to your children. Ideally, both parents will generally try not to vilify the other, either to the children or to their own friends—although it is the rare adult who can stay nonjudgmental of their ex's behavior at all times. In the diaries, Roberta tries to dispel any lingering concerns about Lizzie's father's ability to manage a slumber party appropriately and encourages her friends who bother to phone to send their daughters to the party. There is little she can do to change the attitudes of those who only know about the divorce through the grapevine or who don't call. In a hostile divorce, inquiring phone calls may ignite an angry parent to reiterate all the complaints about the ex-spouse's irresponsibility, without taking into account the consequences on the children. Even without encouragement, mothers are prone to believe that only they have sufficient nurturing "instinct" to manage a houseful of teenagers, and that a father might act inappropriately with a houseful of giggling adolescent girls.

General Guidelines

Both parents have a role in helping their child minimize any social embarrassment caused by the divorce:

- If you are aware of a reluctance in your children to invite friends over, accept social invitations, or engage in extracurricular activities following the separation, it is important to discuss the issue with them. Shame and embarrassment may silence your children and deprive them of the opportunity to derive support from teachers, coaches, peers, and other family members.
- If your child's social withdrawal is accompanied by failing grades and sleeping, eating, or mood disturbances, it may be a sign of a significant depression. Professional counseling should be considered.
- It is usually helpful to empathize with your children by sharing how you deal with your own feelings of embarrassment.
- Before invitations for a party are sent, a call to the parents of the invitees opens the lines of communication.
- If the father is the host, he is the one responsible for making the calls, as he is the one who is more likely to be "suspect." In that case, the mother should be made aware that invitations are going out, and her support for the event solicited.
- Before the refusals start arriving, discuss with your child the possibility that some of the friends' parents may not be comfortable with their children sleeping over.
- Inviting one of the parents of the invitees to cohost a party, especially a sleep-over, may make everyone relax more.

- We strongly urge fathers to offer their daughters all the opportunities that their ex does, be it ballet lessons, heart-to-heart talks, karate classes, soccer coaching . . . or sleep-overs.
- It is important to remember that it is not the gender of the parent that is the defining factor in whether a parent can nurture children appropriately; rather it is that parent's capacity for love, respect, and communication.

Gender Stereotypes

26

In which Laura, age thirteen, is hurt by her
father's lack of interest in her ballet class

Child's Point of View:
Does He Want Me to Quit Ballet?

I've been so disappointed recently, because I think Dad wants me to give up ballet. That's not what he says, but I don't believe him, since he sure acts that way. Yesterday, I ended up crying on the way home from ballet lessons. That's happened almost every week lately. It seems the better I get, the less interested Dad gets. He tells me it's not true, but he's always grumpy in the car going over to class, and we're often late because he won't get off the phone. I'm sure he doesn't really want me to join the advanced class at the City Ballet School. I think he only lets me keep going at Danceworld because he feels guilty when I cry.

He must think ballet is sort of a waste of time. But I've been dancing for six years and I practice every night at home, so he knows I'm serious about it. It's been my dream to dance professionally ever since Mom took me to *The Nutcracker* the first time. When I was younger, Mom used to come and watch every class . . . but now she's too busy to ever come. All the other moms come and stay. I don't see why Dad can't. Why doesn't he treat it like soccer practice? He comes to that, and he never misses a game, even if he has to leave work early to drive me to away games. I like him standing on the sidelines yelling louder than everyone else at the field! I suppose he can't exactly yell during ballet practice, but just being there would help.

When he does come to ballet he doesn't talk much with the other parents, and sometimes he goes outside and walks around, rather than watching. That's pretty disappointing, because I'm better at ballet than soccer and I certainly feel more beautiful when I dance! I admit he does look kind of funny sitting there when he is the only man—but that hasn't stopped him from doing anything else with me. I wish I could get him to watch the whole hour, just once. Then I could get him to comment on what he thinks I'm doing right and what I'm doing wrong, like he does after watching the game. Maybe I could show him some of the exercises at home. I need to find some way to make him more interested. Crying and fighting with him is clearly not the right answer.

Parent's Point of View:
I Can't Fit in the Ballet Scene

I hope Laura knows I think it's wonderful she loves ballet. But now, although I'm really proud she's been invited to join the City Ballet School, I'm also really worried . . . classes three times a week. I don't think I can take that! I find it very uncomfortable trying to look inconspicuous among the leotards, the hair spray, and the gossip about whose daughter entered what competition, and who *ought* to have won. Laura says that when she sees me fidgeting or walking out of the waiting area, she gets concerned I really don't want her to do ballet anymore. Today she ended up crying on the way home. It was the same litany as usual. She accused me of wanting her to play more soccer and do less ballet because I liked soccer better. I tried to tell her that I do like soccer, but I want her to keep doing both. I hate for her to feel that her love of ballet is forcing us apart.

I can see why she's angry, but I don't know how to get her to understand my predicament. It's not really the ballet that's the issue. It's just that I'm bored hanging around at the ballet school watching something I don't understand, and I'm tense and anxious, in part because everyone reacts as if I'm an intruder. You can tell from the expressions when I walk in the room, and the way the conversation changes, that the mothers there feel uncomfortable. I suppose if I could join in the conversation a little more it might help, but I'm not into clothes and I don't buy jewelry or have the time for manicures. It's no more comfortable when the focus is on me. I've already answered endless questions about what it's like being a father with custody. I've explained that there is nothing wrong with my ex-wife—that she didn't disappear, or run off with another man, or become an alcoholic as they all fantasize. I'm tired of the puzzled facial expressions when I say that in fact we get along quite well and we both agreed to have Laura live with me to let Tricia pursue her career. Moreover, I'm sick of hearing all that gushing about how they wish their husbands would show the same concern for their daughters that I do. I know they mean well, but without their husbands working their butts off, these mothers wouldn't have time or money for all the clothes and manicures they seem to love so much. And then there's the redhead who keeps asking me to come to dinner . . . she's not my type and Laura doesn't even like her daughter.

Today we were late for the class and I didn't feel like going in. Rather than join, I decided to review some computer code I'd written. When Laura came out, and I was still sitting in the car, the criticisms and tears started. I felt unjustly accused, so I decided to tell the truth. I tried to explain that it wasn't her ballet that I didn't like; it was the ballet environment that I found unnerving. I think she understood for the first time that the mothers' chitchat and all the personal questions were driving me nuts. I told her my leaving during practice time had nothing to do with her. The explanation made sense to her, but she wasn't entirely sympathetic. Clearly she still wanted me to stay when she practiced.

In the end, we came to a compromise I can probably live with. We agreed she would always dance in one of the two spots where she would be visible through the doorway, so I wouldn't be forced to catch fleeting glimpses of her foot or a hand for a whole hour. We adopted a signal—if I waved, it meant I couldn't take it any longer and I was going out and would come back later.

We both felt better after we talked. She suggested that I borrow one of my mother's dresses and come in drag so I would be less conspicuous. We both howled with laughter. She told me I was a kook, but a kook with guts, since I was still the only dad there. It was great to see that smile after all the tears. I never want to let her down. She makes me so proud.

Making Sense of It All

There is nothing that highlights the male and female stereotypes like ballet class: an archetypal "girl thing" where "ballet mothers," like "stage mothers," can be quite intense. It's no surprise to anyone, except perhaps this daughter who doesn't see the world in terms of traditional gender roles, that in such a predominantly female environment, a man would feel out of place. Even this father, who has overcome the legal, personal, and professional barriers necessary not only to have residential custody of his daughter, but also to spend significant time with her, finds he can't fit in.

Many fathers surprise themselves by overcoming the daunting challenges presented by cooking meals, doing laundry, and meeting complicated schedules, while still finding the time and energy to nurture their children. But feeling comfortable at a ballet class, or at a birthday party with a room full of six-year-olds . . . and their mothers, is often an even greater challenge. It is hard to overcome society's biases that fathers aren't good enough or don't belong in the position of being the primary parent, and many men resent that obstacles created by these prejudices continue to be put in their way. Single fathers are painfully aware that if they decide to bring their child to school late (because she overslept), or in "unsuitable" clothes (because she refused to wear anything else except her party dress), or with her hair unbrushed (because she threw a temper tantrum), it is likely the reasons for his decisions will be overlooked and the results overly criticized. If he spends time with his kids in the park, he can expect to get comments about whether he has a job, or even more threatening, be taken for a stranger with dubious motives for watching children. Men are seldom welcomed to share the park bench where the mothers trade stories of parental frustration. Somehow, mothers are far more forgiving of each other's failures than they are of fathers' shortcomings. In parenting, fathers have a definite glass ceiling to break through in order to be acknowledged as fully competent to parent.

This feeling of being constantly judged can be hard to explain to daughters without seeming overly defensive, but explaining does help them understand why fathers don't stay at certain activities as frequently or for as long as mothers, or why they look so uncomfortable and distant when they do stick around.

General Guidelines

- We are encouraged that gender bias appears to be lessening in many communities. A generation ago, only mothers pushed babies in strollers and only mothers brought their children to the doctor for checkups. That is changing as fathers are increasingly asserting their right to participate in all their children's activities.
- Certain activities will always create awkward situations for the parent of the opposite gender. Tell your children how you feel, so they don't misinterpret your behavior. If you're bored or uncomfortable, and there is no way to take part in the activity, explain it to your children beforehand so you're able to leave without hurting their feelings.

- Always tell the truth. Demonstrating that you can work through problems by talking is an invaluable lesson about relationships.
- Sometimes compromise works. You can get involved in an activity in indirect ways, such as learning the technical aspects of ballet, or helping to build theater sets or designing the lighting.
- It is worth noting that Laura sees ballet as a way of pleasing both parents at once. The pursuit of a sport or hobby can be a way of engaging a parent or staying linked to one who is absent. For all children in divorce situations, this dimension may take on added significance. Occasionally, children find they gain more parental attention by insisting on an activity that the parents have no interest in or that appeals only to one parent and not the other. Being supportive of even the most unlikely pursuits opens a path to discussing what your child is hoping to achieve.

If you are the only male in a room full of "female wisdom," remember that even though it may not be comfortable at first, such awkward afternoons frequently provide invaluable information and support, if you step forward and ask for help.

- Most women are delighted to share their solutions to household problems or coping with taxing childhood behaviors, if asked.
- Mothers are often very willing to offer advice to men as to how best to talk to daughters about everything from female-to-female peer relationships, to dating, or menstruation.
- Many women will have excellent ideas on how to manage, or parry, the more annoying habits of your ex-spouse!
- These gatherings of mothers are often the source of ideas for inventive and relatively inexpensive gifts for the epidemic of birthday parties to which your kids get invited.
- Mothers' groups are also the source of practical help. Like many mothers, fathers often require backup, or car pools, or play groups to free up time for work, household chores, etc. Although some people will initially be uncomfortable with a reciprocal agreement in which a father will take care of their children, many women will be sympathetic to your need for free time and may be happy to take a younger child for the occasional afternoon, or watch your child after school for an hour or two on a more frequent basis.

Fiscal Responsibilities

In which Chris, age fifteen, resents his
father's spending money on himself

Child's Point of View:
No Pizza, but Two Suits?

My parents are always going on about how they can't understand why kids insist on spending so much on famous-label clothes. Yesterday, Dad noticed my new sneakers and criticized me for buying them, even though I explained the old ones had disintegrated and these were really cheap. He went on and on until he actually succeeded in making me feel guilty about not saving my money for "more important things." What a hypocrite! Today he goes out and spends a fortune on clothes for himself, claiming that it was "different" because he "needed" them for work. I don't get it. He refused to take us out for a $10 pizza last night, saying he would "rather eat at home," and then went on a massive shopping spree today!

It was so annoying! We were on our way to the movies when Dad said he had to make one stop. I thought he was just going to get a shirt or something. But, no. We spent the next hour sitting around getting bored, while he got not just one, but two designer-label suits! It took so long we had to wait for the next movie time, which made everyone antsy. So while we were waiting around, I said something about the suits and how I was peeved I had to baby-sit the other two while he was trying on clothes. I think I overstepped the mark when I asked him who he was trying to impress! Maybe it was rude, but it just didn't seem fair: no pizza, but two suits? He claimed he needed them to greet the customers at the restaurant. I find that hard to believe, as he spends most of the time in back managing the kitchen or pitching in at the bar. It seemed to me that $1,500 was worth commenting on, but Dad looked like I swore at him.

Then he accused me of saying what I did because "Your mother told you to!" That's ridiculous! She doesn't even know what he spends. Besides, Mom's opinion has nothing to do with it. I'm the one who has to spend my weekends packing bags in the supermarket in order to have enough money to buy stuff that I need; that, hopefully, will enable Mom to save enough from her meager earnings to send me to college. I told him he should think about spending all his extra money on me or Mom, instead of himself. He was furious! Said if I was so concerned about money, we could just forget about going to the movies. That produced tears from Alex and Susie, so I shut up. But no pizza and then two suits? Something just isn't right.

Parent's Point of View:
The Kid Sounds Like My Ex-Spouse

It's hard enough when you only see your kids every other weekend, but it's not something to look forward to when they start questioning every decision you make. I've explained to them about the money, so I didn't think I deserved a lot of guff from my fifteen-year-old when I took the kids with me to buy some new clothes for work. I was just trying to include them in some normal family things! Alex actually got a big kick out of helping me pick out new suits. But Chris was scowling the whole time; looked just like his mother when she doesn't approve of something. Same kind of sarcastic comments too: "Real dapper, Dad," "Might look better if you lost the twenty pounds you've been telling us is going to happen for the last year," "Makes you look like a gangster—that will impress somebody."

Then, when we were waiting for the movie, he started in about why we couldn't have pizza the night before. I told him I liked having some meals at home—sort of like a real family. That just made him more determined to make me admit I was wrong to buy the suits. Talk about a scene with everybody looking on. The way Chris was yelling at me you'd think I beat him or something! I just wanted to go home and watch the TV, but then the younger ones started to cry. It all seemed to blow over after the movie, but I wish Chris would stop trying to be the referee all the time, making things "fair" for his mother.

Making Sense of It All

Since almost every divorce results in financial limits and restrictions, kids quickly become more aware than their peers about the importance of money and the financial compromises parents have to make. They watch their parents juggle the reallocation of the family finances as (typically) Dad is now "supporting" Mom with a check that comes once a week or month, and Mom is trying to keep life relatively stable. By observing and listening to both father and mother, the kids come to have a very accurate concept of how the pieces of the family economic pie are apportioned. Inevitably one or the other parent is better off, and this inequity is both emotionally and logistically troublesome to most children. When one parent suddenly goes beyond the normal spending boundaries, the children are likely to question whether that single expenditure, and even the overall division of wealth, is fair.

Of course, this raises the obvious question of what is "fair." Having overcome the financial setbacks that follow a separation or divorce, most parents feel justified in rewarding themselves for their own perseverance and hard work, if it has earned them some added financial security. Usually they do not spontaneously think of sharing their good fortune with anyone else. But as the size of the pie increases, making sure everyone benefits will certainly minimize the friction that inevitably develops when only one person is the primary beneficiary.

While the advertising industry and the current cultural ethos may encourage consumers to make a show of their new acquisitions, when you can move from clothes you have worn for ten years to designer-label couture or from used cars to a new one, it is usually destructive to your relationship with the kids to make it too obvious. Who are you trying to impress? Your work wardrobe hardly needs to be a focus with your children, and you can enjoy the car without a big song-and-dance routine. If you involve the children in the discussions of exactly how much you are spending on yourself, you should expect them to raise objections, especially if their lives are being compromised by a shortage of money for their own activities. They see the total amount of money you and your "ex" earn constituting the "pie," which, in their eyes, should be shared equally. The fact that the courts do not support them in this view does not decrease their moral conviction that fairness is paramount.

Is it possible for everyone to believe they are getting their reasonable share? Chances are increased if:

- parents do not use expenditures on themselves as a way to show off to the kids,
- parents don't involve kids in the actual purchase of big-ticket items,
- parents don't deliberately flaunt their money in order to hurt the other parent, and
- parents ensure that a rise in income does benefit everyone.

While these statements sound egalitarian to some, they may sound offensive to those of you who honestly feel you're paying sufficient support or that the other parent squanders those funds on himself or herself rather than use the money responsibly for the children. There may seem to be no reason to give more money to the other parent if it won't benefit the kids. But when the raise, promotion, or stock option allows you to buy the new car, balance that indulgence by putting some additional money into the kids' college funds or by offering to pay for an additional extracurricular activity or holiday. Specify to the other parent and the kids what you have done and whether this is likely to happen again (if you have received a substantial pay raise) or is only a one-time enterprise (if you have received a generous bonus). Giving away your earnings may not be quite as enjoyable as using them to have a good time with the kids or to buy things for yourself, but it shows them you're thinking of their interests and undercuts any attempt by the other parent to compromise their feelings toward you. If you have a hard time voluntarily handing over money to your ex-spouse, you can always find ways of allocating money that benefit your children directly.

So when a child creates a scene over money, how does the parent determine what is going on? Is the child being used by the other parent in a game of emotional blackmail? If so, then the proper response is to talk with the other parent. But if the child speaks out as an individual on his or her own behalf, it is a mistake to be overly dismissive. One of the best indications of what drives the child to challenge you is the timing of the child's questions or criticisms. The child who starts chiding you about support payments at the outset of your weekend together is more likely voicing the words and demands of the other parent than the kid who raises a question, albeit angrily and not too tactfully, during a quiet moment on Saturday afternoon. The six-year-old who wants to know, "Why don't you spend it on me instead of new clothes for yourself?" deserves your attention to address the issue. When kids talk for themselves and defend their own interests they will speak in the first person singular "I," not "We"; they will label the adult as "mean" or accuse the adult of "never letting me do what I want." When young children use words like "irresponsible," "untrustworthy," or "out of proportion," the vocabulary indicates they are voicing the absent parent's issues. In contrast to the younger child who uses the same words as the adult to speak on behalf of the parent, the angry adolescent who, as a result of your change in spending decisions, is unable to participate in activities with his peers represents his own position when he berates you for "not caring about us," "living better than we do," or "taking vacations that we can't have."

Children are often inappropriately used as messengers to ask for more money or other forms of economic support when a parent believes the child can exercise emotional leverage unavailable to the adult (see Chapter 18). Likewise, children can be used to flaunt the advantages of the "good life" to the parent who is less well-off. Neither of these roles benefits the child in any way. While kids can learn some important lessons in economics as a result of the divorce, they shouldn't be used as negotiators nor be encouraged to render judgments about how either parent spends money. In order to ensure that their children do not feel neglected, parents need to tune in to the children's changing needs and interests and to try to meet any new economic demands within the framework of the divorce agreement. The kids themselves should be encouraged to have some say in certain decisions, e.g., teenagers be given a yearly allowance to manage their own clothes expenditures, or allowed a voice in choosing their extracurricular activities.

A significant rise in financial resources has an impact on any family—sadly, in families of divorce it is often a negative impact. Rather than improving everyone's lot in life, the "good news" often increases resentment and provokes manipulation of the children by the parents. Parents need to rise above their own selfishness and resentments and use their good fortune to benefit their children.

General Guidelines

- Children of divorce often become quite sophisticated about money and the financial trade-offs in adult life, including how to balance work versus personal life.
- Children often cope better with any necessary limitations when they are given some control and responsibility, e.g., if only one after-school activity is affordable, then let them make the choice about which one they'll pursue; older children can manage budget items like clothes expenditures.

- Try to use a sudden rise in financial resources, especially one-time bonuses, to help meet long-term needs such as college funds. It is possible to help the child without feeling it will automatically benefit the other parent.
- When a major raise or a promotion means total resources are increased, don't put the kids in the position of being messengers or negotiators. While you have every right to benefit from your hard work, share the wealth spontaneously so it increases the well-being of the kids and the other parent. At the very least, such a move prevents the other parent from painting you as selfish and unloving.
- Hard work and determination do merit some type of reward, but "showing off" insults all the other family members whose lives haven't been improved by your gain.
- Don't use money distribution as a weapon against your ex-spouse. The children will suffer.

Introducing
the Significant Other

In which Robert, age sixteen, talks about
meeting his dad's new girlfriend

Child's Point of View: Does This Mean We'll Have Less of You?

I guess part of me was hoping that this wouldn't happen. Dad never talks much about his social life or what he does on the weekends when we are with Mom, but I sort of wondered.

This weekend we found out there was more going on than we thought. And Dad sure was different. Friday night Dad picked us up for the picnic he had planned for just the four of us. Then Dad suddenly turns off the radio and tells us that he wants us to meet Toni—a woman he has known for years who works at his company. It was clear from his tone of voice that Toni was more than an acquaintance. I thought he would give us more notice, but Toni turned out to be pretty nice. Dad was like a new person once we got beyond the first few minutes when no one quite knew what to say. He laughed! He seemed to be having fun and enjoying life! He hasn't been like that in a long time—three or four years.

Actually this was about more than meeting Toni. I guess they are going to live together. That's sort of OK. Toni is very active, likes to do lots of things, so I doubt there will be many of those "what are we going to do with each other" weekends anymore. She really made Saturday fun—she's got so much energy. And she's a great baseball player. She even knows the standings in the majors!

By Sunday, though, I wasn't quite so sure about things. Sometimes Dad and Toni are in a world of their own, even though they may be talking with us or sitting at the same table. Kind of like we're there, . . . but we're not there. He's about as obsessed with her as he says I am when I have a new girlfriend. He tells me that when I'm "in love," nothing else seems to matter. Now he's behaving the same way. That makes me happy for him, but when I think about Toni always being there on weekends, I still feel sad and confused. I've gotten to enjoy the weekends when we have Dad all to ourselves. And after Sally and Tommy go to bed, I get to talk with him, or watch TV, or play games. Just the two of us.

I never got to do that when he was with Mom, so in some ways it made the divorce better. Now it seems like there will be three of us again. But it feels different than when he was with Mom. He pays more attention to Toni. And Toni pays more attention to him than Mom ever did. She was always doing things with us, or going to PTA meetings, or working in the garden.

So I can see why he's happy with Toni. And I'm pleased about that. He deserves it. But I wish that just being with us could make him that happy as well. Dad was so excited telling us about his plans for the next few weekends—all the things we would do together. It sounds like fun, but I keep thinking to myself, "If I ask him, will he agree to take the three of us somewhere without Toni coming along?"

Parent's Point of View: How Will They Accept My New Relationship?

A lot has happened in the last few days. Maybe the biggest weekend of my life.

Last Thursday we decided to tell the kids—not just that Toni and I were dating, but that we've known each other for years and are going to start living together. Toni's been here most of the time since I moved out of the house, but she hasn't spent weekends here, so I didn't think it was necessary to tell the kids about her. The idea sounded great over a bottle of wine at dinner. But as the evening wore on, I started to have some misgivings. Would it bother the kids that the divorce wasn't final? Or was the actual piece of paper much less important to them than to me? What would happen to Sally when she was faced with the stark reality that Ellen and I might never get back together?

I contemplated simplifying the story and telling them that Toni was only my date. I realized I was afraid of what would happen if the kids didn't like her. What if they put me in a position where I'd have to choose? Around midnight I heard Toni pacing around. Somehow I had overlooked that she might be just as anxious as I was. She kept trying to devise the perfect answer to the inevitable questions about what our relationship meant, how long we had known each other, whether we were going to get married (Sally was bound to ask that), and whether we were sleeping together (a Robert special). She kept fretting over the stories we'd heard about kids getting angry because they felt like the "other woman" was trying to replace their mother. She suggested getting them gifts, but we decided the kids would think she was trying to bribe them into liking her.

By Friday, when I picked them up, I was so ambivalent that I didn't know how to begin. Then I just blurted out that, "We're going to have a picnic at the park and . . . someone-else-is-going-to-join-us!" It all came out in one word. Tommy hoped it would be the Smiths and their kids. Sally thought it might be Mom. I mumbled that it was someone from work, but no one responded. Maybe they couldn't hear over the radio, which Robert had turned up to the earsplitting level he enjoys. We drove to the park and I pointed toward Toni, who was sitting on one of the swings. "That's who we're having our picnic with. Her name's Toni and she's a friend from work. I really like her—(maybe I said "love her")—and I want you to meet her and get to know her this weekend." There was a pause, and I watched a frown go across Sally's face. No frown for Robert. "Nice, Dad!" he grinned, and we all climbed out of the car.

Most of the weekend went pretty well. Toni is on the company softball team, so she had fun playing catch with the kids that evening. Saturday morning they enjoyed the breakfast she made, and, as she had to go to work, we had the day to ourselves. Saturday evening, however, did not go very well. I forgot how peculiar our family gin rummy rules are, and Toni kept messing up the game. Sally got annoyed and went to bed early. Then Tommy had a temper tantrum when I said he should go too. Robert made polite conversation with Toni, but I think he missed just being able to tell me all the gossip about his friends at school without having to explain who everyone was. He seemed a little withdrawn the next morning, until Toni offered to help him with his math homework—although I think they spent as much time talking about the pennant race!

Sunday afternoon we went to the beach, walked hand-in-hand, built sandcastles, clambered over the dunes, and watched the sunset. All too soon we were back home and everyone was getting ready for bed. I read to Tommy, while Toni played cards with Sally and Robert so they could teach her *our* rules. It made me smile to hear them laughing together.

Now that the weekend's over, I don't know what I feel. I'm all jumbled up inside. . . . It's almost as if I resent Toni's intrusion into my relationship with my kids. . . . But on the other hand, I'm really happy, because for a whole weekend I could believe that one day I'd put the pain of this divorce behind me. Feels like I've taken a big step, but there's still a long way to go. Can't wait to talk to Toni tonight.

Making Sense of It All

The first time children meet with the other adult in a divorced parent's life, the event is likely to cause a wide variation of emotions in all concerned, in anticipation of, during, and after the introduction. The parent is anxious to ensure that things go smoothly and the relationship gets off to a good start, but it is sometimes hard to know how to achieve this when feelings of ambivalence about close relationships and their durability may still be unresolved. The "new adult" wants to be liked and accepted without putting on an act or bribing the children. Meanwhile, children experience a feeling of loss of control over what will happen now that the parent has someone else. They fear both losing their parent's love and having to compete for their parent's attention. In most divorces, especially those with a high degree of parental conflict, there can be intense loyalty issues, e.g., guilt if they do like Dad's new girlfriend because they are "betraying" their mother, or anxiety if they do not like her because they are letting Dad down.

Competing for the attention of a parent who is "in love" is a new and frustrating experience for any child. Old strategies for getting attention from "warring" Mom and Dad are no longer effective. However, if the kids feel included and if sufficient time has gone by since the separation, most will admit they are actually relieved to see their parent enter a stable relationship. When children begin to see the parent has rebounded emotionally from the divorce, it helps them to be more optimistic about the future. It removes some of the uncertainties, and it certainly feels less isolating than watching casual dating activities from a distance. Bear in mind that being introduced to a series of casual dates in rapid succession is not reassuring at all, so keep your children's exposure to your transient love-interests to an absolute minimum.

The parent in love faces the difficult task of meeting the kids' needs, those of the significant other, and his/her own needs. At times, these are incompatible. Keeping time and attention for the children as your primary priority during the early stages of the child–significant other relationship is a wise investment for the future. If in doubt as to the long-term significance of a given relationship, there is no need to involve your children (see Chapter 12).

General Guidelines

A positive start needs sensitive planning and flexibility. While one child in a family may be fine, another may react very differently. With a little anticipation and preparation, the first time together can be both fun and reassuring.

- Don't spring introductions on your kids as a surprise. Such a strategy indicates you are afraid of dealing with their reactions and you run the significant risk of being perceived as being defensive about the relationship.
- Find an open space on neutral territory to do the introductions. The idea of a picnic is a good one because it lets the kids come and go, with plenty of space to "escape" and return when they feel ready. Sitting in a booth at a restaurant can be very confining.
- Introductions in either parent's home are emotionally threatening. This "home territory" may only have been recently established as something special that Mom or Dad and the children share, or may be the place that represents security and stability (see Chapter 16); the invasion can make the child fear displacement.
- Don't be disappointed if the kids don't immediately love your significant other. Try not to pressure the kids to show more affection than they feel. Allow the relationship to build slowly.
- Expect mixed emotions—from everyone. Make sure you are around to answer the inevitable questions. Make sure you inform the other parent before the introduction. Keep the lines of communication open. Being available and being truthful are very important.

An ideal scenario for a first introduction might run as follows:

Friday: Tell the children beforehand, perhaps Friday night, so they have the time to ask you questions. (Telling them too far in advance encourages them to discuss the news with your ex-spouse first.) Questions may run the gamut, from asking what you like about the person, to "Why she or he is better than Mom or Dad?" "Do I have to love him or her?" or "When are you getting married?" Children may voice concerns whether you will still love them. Tell the truth. Then make it clear that there will be lots of opportunities to talk about how they feel, not because they have approval rights, but in order to help you help them build good relationships with this person. Finally, let them know you have already told their other biological parent about the proposed introduction, so they don't get caught in the middle.

Saturday: On the day itself, not only is space important, especially for younger kids, but timing is helpful. Meeting first thing in the morning puts an unwanted emphasis on the activity and prevents the children from asking whatever questions occurred to them in the middle of the night. Better to meet in the middle of the day for lunch, which is more relaxing. Try to keep the first meeting relatively short, say three hours. If things don't go well, the time isn't so long that it gets unbearable; if it does go well, you may decide to extend the visit, but better yet, consider taking a break. This conveys to the kids *they* are still your primary focus, not this new person you love. During this interlude, stay actively invested in an activity with them, even if you are tempted to take a nap! Maybe have the other person join you at home for dinner later, but try not to let your adult relationship dominate the atmosphere; you'd obviously rather have the children further *their* relationship with the new adult. Having your significant other stay the night is not a good idea. It is usually too big a leap for the kids on the first day, and is likely to increase their feelings of conflict when they tell their other parent.

Sunday: In many families, this is a very important day together. Each family generates its own Sunday morning rituals, whether it is a lazy breakfast, a trip to church, or watching cartoons on TV. The morning also gives you the opportunity to talk about the past (including new questions about the divorce), the present ("Will the visiting schedule stay the same? What should I tell Mom or Dad when I go home?"), and your hopes for the future. If everyone had fun Saturday, you could consider doing something Sunday afternoon that includes your significant other.

The next few weeks: Make sure the kids know your schedule and how to get in contact with you. Don't miss opportunities to be with them and don't forget to return their calls. They need to know more than ever that you are thinking about them when they are not there.

"Just Like Your Father"

In which Ted, age eleven, wonders whether
Mom is right that he is as worthless
as his father

Child's Point of View: I'll Never Be Good Enough

Boy, what a day. It doesn't seem anyone likes me. My homeroom teacher is all over my case; the math teacher says I could do better. The soccer coach told me at practice to get more focused, so today I played like I had something to prove, and I scored a goal! It was nice to be able to give myself a little cheer. Of course, the coach said that he expected me to score every game from now on!

But Mom sure isn't cheering for me; it's one criticism after another. I told her I wished she had gotten to the game so she could have seen me play so well. Rather than saying she wanted to or she was sorry she got held up, she just went into her usual: "You expect me to be able to do everything and be everywhere. You're just like your father." She's told me a hundred times he didn't appreciate how hard she had to work to keep her job and manage the house, so I wasn't surprised when she went on to accuse me of being unappreciative of how hard she works in order that I can have things like new jeans and soccer cleats. She said she wished she had enough time off to play soccer too—sort of like I was just goofing off rather than going to practice every day and training in the gym on weekends! I wish she had the time to come watch and see how much better I am than last year, but I wish even more that she wouldn't yell at me. I was hurt that she couldn't even congratulate me on my goal, but I've learned to shut up when I need to. I just said I had really wanted her at the game and offered to set the table for dinner.

Of course, if she had been at the game and seen me "living up to my potential" as everyone lectures me, then she probably wouldn't have gotten so mad at me at dinner when I told her I got a B– on the science report. I admitted I left it to the last two days; "A procrastinator, just like your father," was her only response, but I did the same thing with the last one and still got an A. She keeps telling me that in the real world you're only as good as your last performance, and that's what makes you successful. I don't want to hear again how if I want to go to a good college I better start getting A's. For once she didn't tell me I was going to end up with an inadequate job like Dad, but I've heard it so many times before that she doesn't need to say it anymore.

Anyway, she exaggerates about Dad. He's not perfect, but he still seems OK to me. He may not earn as much money as some people, but when he comes to the games, he tries to encourage everyone, rather than yell at them like some of the other fathers. He always points out the good things I've done. I know I complain when he's late so often to games or to pick me up; and Mom's sort of right when she says he's unreliable. But I think he tries, and at least he never tells me I'm "just like my mother," meaning I'm not good enough.

Recently Mom's been on me every day. Like yesterday, when I knocked over a glass of soda. Mom had to tell me I was, "Clumsy. Just like your father." I didn't do it on purpose, and I said I was sorry. So when she told me I was making excuses just like him, I yelled at her, "I'm not perfect. I'm me. I can't try any harder, and you make it sound like I'll never succeed." She said that wasn't the point, but that she didn't want me to get into a pattern of "running away from my responsibilities."

I guess Dad could get a better job and give us more money, but then he might start being like all the other dads around here—working all the time, pressured, drinking a lot. I don't want that. I can see that Mom really wants the best for me, but I'm trying to figure out my own system—not be like Dad, but not necessarily do it her way either. Seems my being around irritates her. Probably makes her feel like Dad has moved in again, because I seem to remind her of him and she hates that. If I tell her that I'm working like crazy to not be like Dad, at least when I'm around her, will that make her happy? Dad wasn't good enough and she kicked him out. I know parents can't divorce their kids, but will that happen to me?

Parent's Point of View:
What's Bothering My Boy?

I wonder what's happening to Ted. Maybe it's just preadolescence. He seemed to be in some kind of weird mood all weekend. At first I thought it was because I missed his soccer game, but he seemed OK when I apologized and told him I couldn't help getting stuck at work. Weekends with the kids aren't the same anymore. Most of the time, Ted's off in a world of his own. The younger kids are fun to play with, but he's the only one I can really talk to; so when he's withdrawn, the weekend drags.

Usually Ted's moodiness wears off, but Saturday afternoon I thought he was a reincarnation of his mother, going around cleaning everything up, trying to straighten life out. He did do a good job of vacuuming and it freed me to clean the bathroom, but when I thanked him, he just sort of grunted, more like I'd insulted him. I told him he'd done enough and that the weekends were for fun. That didn't get anywhere; so I asked him if anything was bothering him. Not much yardage there either. Reminded me of his mother, who would never talk until she would explode—yelling at me that I wasn't good enough for her because I couldn't buy all the things she wanted.

He continued to be sulky through Saturday night. Nothing was acceptable. A video wasn't good enough; he wanted to go out to dinner, not eat in, and then go to the movies. When I was his age, we didn't even have videos, so why isn't it good enough for him? The other kids and I had a good time. Made some great nachos.

Everyone laughed when I suggested we have nachos for breakfast on Sunday morning. It was a bright sunny day, and we all played soccer together at the park. I thought Ted was back with it, but even at the park I could see him start to drift off. When we got back, he worked on his homework. I told him I was proud of him for getting the work done. He said he was concerned about his grades—got a B last week. He didn't think it was funny when I told him that B's looked pretty good to me when I was his age. I was trying to pick him up, make him think he was doing well. Just seemed to get him in a grumpier mood. I asked again what was really going on, but he didn't say much, and I didn't push. Maybe that wasn't good judgment. He and I used to connect, now I feel like I'm doing something wrong all the time.

By six, I was sort of glad I had to take them back. Greg and Lydia cried as usual. I felt like they were really sad. I was too. I'm glad they still care. Ted got out of the car without saying much.

Now today I feel lonely. Ted being like that takes away a big part of the weekend.

Making Sense of It All

After a divorce, few children want to be compared to either parent. They know all the warts, every fault. Being compared to a parent often injures the child's self-esteem and typically weakens the relationships with both parents. Rather than motivate the kids to behave positively, negative comparisons will likely foster anxiety, anger, and tests of affection and caring as the kids struggle to work out the questions of whether they are doomed to the same kind of rejection that their parent suffered and whether they are worthy of any kind of love or admiration.

All parents have disappointments—sometimes kids don't do as well in school as hoped—and all parents cringe when they see their kids display the other parent's less desirable character traits or habits. However, criticizing your ex-spouse and then reminding your children of how they resemble him or her hardly reassures them. Depending on the strength of their allegiance to the criticized parent, your children may either heed your words of warning and allow their self-esteem to drop even further or alternatively, reject outright your criticism of their behavior, even if it is justified.

A divorced parent who labels the child as being like the other parent creates a real dilemma for the child; e.g., Ted wonders with some trepidation, "If I'm just like Dad, then will Mom also throw me out?" Too often these concerns result in sibling rivalry increasing to an intolerable level, because the concerns raise the fear that the other kids, who aren't labeled, are more loved. Even children much younger than Ted, subjected to constant comparisons with the criticized parent, will start to wonder what their good characteristics are, and the anxiety can cause their overall academic and athletic performance to fall. Self-esteem plummets and social relationships suffer. Relationships with peers may change for the worse and risk-taking behavior increase, as these children have a tendency to want to please the members in the peer group at all costs, rather than work out their own identity.

Parents who have divorced, often harbor aspirations for their children that are above the children's capability. It is as if they want their children's achievements to compensate for their own imperfections. Since many adults doubt their own self-worth following a divorce and tend to feel uncomfortably out of control of their own lives, they react to the avoidance of a chore or a single academic lapse as if the child's whole future, and their credibility as a parent depends on righting the situation immediately. Often the parents' anxiety results in excessive punishments or restrictions, and angry warnings that this is the same slippery path down which the other parent trod.

Our experience, supported by many research studies, indicates that this pattern of comparison can take a dangerous toll over time. Just as Ted feels pushed away and criticized by his mother, he may find himself also moving away from his father, as Ted becomes increasingly focused on his dad's less worthwhile characteristics. In order to reject those characteristics that his mother finds objectionable in him, he must also reject them in his father, thus forcing an emotional distancing. Not only does this cycle deprive children of both parental relationships, it can make the children hypercritical of themselves and others, leaving them unwilling to commit to any relationship.

General Guidelines

- Telling children, "You are just like your mom or dad," is rarely taken as a compliment and even more rarely produces improved behavior.
- Singling out the other parent as someone who is not worthwhile emulating stirs up tremendous loyalty conflicts and emotional turmoil. Children generally strive to maintain relationships with both parents. Making the task more difficult for them benefits no one.
- Within the context of their relationship, children always eventually discover their parent's faults without having them pointed out by the other parent. Rather than indulging in endless finger-pointing and criticism, modeling more agreeable or successful behavior is always a better way to influence your child's development.
- If you hear your children saying things that clearly were planted by an adult, e.g., the six-year-old who says, "Dad, you're not an adequate parent," or feel your children drifting away because of comments by your ex-spouse, it's tempting to take radical action such as going back to court or changing the custody arrangement. Those options are costly, time-consuming, and generally not successful.
- In relationships in which one parent consistently bad-mouths the other, requesting a change in that parent's behavior is likely to be humiliating, but acknowledging your own vulnerability to critical comments may be enough "reward" for your ex-spouse to diminish the frequency of such remarks to your children.
- Talking with the children about your shortcomings can be a buffer as long as you admit your deficiencies, rather than get defensive, and as long as you do not try to prove the other parent is just as bad a human being as you have been made out to be.

- If your relationships with your children are suffering because of the criticism from your ex-spouse, develop a plan with goals you can achieve. In this family, the father would do well to speak frankly about the money issues—maybe a video is the limit, even though he would like to do more. Even more important, the father should assure Ted that he will be on time for meetings and will get to Ted's next few soccer games, perhaps even on nonvisitation days if possible. The father's efforts will be appreciated and will show that he can play the supportive role Ted values. This demonstration of caring and respect will give father and son the platform from which to try to reopen real communication.

- Take advantage of any opportunity to point out ways in which your children exhibit the positive traits of their other parent, e.g., "You draw so well, you must get that from your father."

- If your children are exhibiting the negative traits of the other parent, address the behaviors, but refrain from making judgmental comparisons.

- Too often, as in this story, neither parents or children say much, out of fear of an argument or opening a Pandora's box of criticisms. This is not a good strategy. Better to face the issues when they are fresh, than let them fester.

Refusing to Spend Time with a Parent

30

with a Parent

In which fifteen-year-old Holly pleads for

some understanding

Child's Point of View:
I Have Other Things I Want to Do

It's been five years since they split up and both my parents continue to think that their divorce and the divorce agreement have to determine what happens in my life. It's really simple: I want to make my own decisions and the one I'm making now is that I don't want to go see Dad every other weekend. It's not that I don't like him; we just don't like the same things. He's an engineer and likes sports; all I really care about is my music. I just want to be with my friends on the weekends and sing with the band as often as I can. We're good, and one day someone's going to notice us and offer us a recording contract, but it won't happen if we don't perform whenever we can. Every weekend for the next two months we have some gig or we need to practice. If I'm with Dad, someone has to drive the extra twenty miles to come get me, and that's not fair. If I'm at Mom's, they just pick me up on the way.

Maybe if Dad and I had more in common it would be different. But he can't even stand to come to the shows—says it's not really music. But there's always been an excuse why he wouldn't spend time with me—he had to work or he wanted to do something else, like go see my brother's soccer game. The message has always been clear: I didn't count for much in his world before the divorce and I don't count now. When he and Mom split up, sometimes he didn't even bother to talk to me when he phoned—only to Mike; other times he worked all weekend when I was at his house. Yeah, yeah, I know he wasn't making as much money then and it was for a good reason—but what about my feelings? Did he ever really show he cared? Most of the time, he said he was the one who was hurt and lonely. I was supposed to feel bad for him! How did he think I felt?

Maybe when I was nine, visiting him every other week could have led to us having a good relationship. But it didn't. I had to go then, even though I didn't want to. When I got older, I realized they could make me go, but they couldn't make me be cooperative. I certainly wasn't about to be pleasant to that awful girlfriend he had and her prissy daughter. Thank goodness she's gone. Now I'm old enough to decide and I don't think I should have to visit at all if I don't want to. None of my friends spend much time with their fathers, and they live together all the time—so why can't my parents start treating me like a tenth grader, instead of a little girl?

Parent's Point of View:
How Can I Convince My Child to Go?

This is the third time in a row that Holly has announced she won't go see her father. A month ago the excuse was that she had a weekend show and needed to rehearse. I thought it was legitimate, and she was considerate enough to give everyone a couple of days' notice. Then two weeks ago she announced she wasn't going to go to her dad's, an hour before she was due to leave, and I sort of thought it was an adolescent mood, because she had been sulking all week. So both times I called Russ and told him maybe he should just see her brother; he agreed, albeit reluctantly.

This week when she objected, I told her she had to go for the weekend. I reminded her that her father really cared about her and if she had something to work out with him, then staying at home wasn't the way to do it. I thought she had gotten the message. I was wrong. This afternoon she came home and shut herself in her room and said she wouldn't go with her brother when he was ready to leave at five. At first I tried to be reasonable and talk it out. That didn't work, but I couldn't tell her tactfully that I didn't want her around this weekend. What I did tell her was that I didn't want to have a scene with her father, but that's exactly what happened. Russ wanted to make her come, but I couldn't see physically dragging her out of the house, so we had another of our shouting matches in the driveway, and he left without her.

Of course, he thinks that I put her up to these refusals, since they used to occur when we first separated, but at that time Holly and I were both so angry that it didn't take much for me to let her stay home—maybe I even encouraged her. I'm over that now. Anger just wastes emotional energy. Maybe Holly isn't as forgiving as I am. He was never a very attentive father to her when she was little, and she's never really given him a second chance. He blew it years ago, as far as she's concerned.

Tonight wasn't a good night for me—I was too distracted at dinner to be anybody's definition of a good date, and I couldn't blame Steve for feeling like he was playing second fiddle when I sent him home. That's hardly what either of us had in mind for the weekend. Holly is still in her room, talking on the phone. Do I get in the middle of this? Do I try to talk to her? Do I tell her to see the school counselor? Should Russ try to come visit her here at the house—or will she just barricade herself up there again? Maybe she's upset that Steve and I spend so much time together and she knows we sleep together. I don't know how to decide, and I don't believe I'm going to get much help from Holly.

Making Sense of It All

When a child refuses to go with the other parent, everyone is put in a bind and there are no easy solutions. When it happens early in the separation or divorce, one parent usually feels rejected and is suspicious that the relationship is being poisoned by the other parent through negative comments. Yet, even if this is not the case and there is no hidden agenda, the parent whom the child is leaving is rarely comfortable forcing the child to go against the child's will.

Refusals happen for a variety of reasons other than a dislike or fear of the visiting parent. At times, refusals occur because the child feels that refusals will make the rebuffed parent come back "home" to live, pay more support, or do something else for the family. Older kids may want to establish some independence, especially if they had no say in making the schedule and it has been rigidly enforced. Adolescents, while not only wanting to have more freedom, also find ways to spend less and less time at home, regardless of whether their parents are married or divorced. Hence, as they get older, even a schedule that worked before simply doesn't fit into the logistics of their lives or their peer relationships anymore.

Given all the possible reasons, there is no one "right response" to a refusal to spend time with a parent. Over the course of the first year, refusals generally occur because one parent has been labeled as the "bad" guy—usually the parent who has moved out. Sometimes, however, the residential parent, who has the majority of the child-rearing responsibilities, can be put in disfavor because his or her "strict" rules contrast starkly against the free-for-all during the children's brief times with the other parent, leading to the children's refusals to go "home." In such instances, giving in to the children's objections, especially ones made at the last minute, just opens the door to further manipulation on many fronts. If it is clear that resistance to visitation is increasing, arranging the handovers in a neutral location (see Chapter 9), without a parent-to-parent handoff, minimizes the temptation for the children to act out and the parent to give in. It's easier to pick up children from school on Friday afternoon than to pull them screaming from their bedrooms and physically drag them into the car, which we do not recommend. If the children act out at the neutral location, the parent with whom they need to talk is forced to address the issue, without leaving the other parent as mediator.

Parents can bring on ambivalence in their kids by repeatedly telling them lies about what happened to the marriage or by inculcating distrust of the absent parent. Such actions breed a sense of insecurity that makes children constantly uncomfortable, no matter how many disavowals they hear from the other parent. Children will come to distrust whichever parent they perceive is lying to them, so even if the lying has been done "for their own good," the relationship will be marred. Trying to insist on the schedule, telling them that you won't discuss the divorce because it's "none of their business," or developing further elaborate deceptions, does not substitute for setting up the next visit and clearing the air. Of course, you can't clear the air by asking the kids what's bothering them, because the answer will usually be "nothing." So try sharing with them your concern that your relationship is too distant and inviting them to tell you what's bothering them, even if it is painful to hear. Many parents are surprised to find that what they thought was their biggest sin was actually forgiven, but some other transgression has yet to be settled.

Of course, younger kids can be unhappy about visiting because you don't devote the personal time and attention to them they've come to expect from the residential parent. For the adult who has never been the "primary parent," this is demanding and requires humility to learn to fulfill that role. Sometimes a confined new living space means that the kids don't have much "fun," even after you buy more toys or computer games. If the other parent won't help you out, talk with teachers or the parents of the kids' peers for suggestions. By the time the kids are in the third grade, however, they will want not just you, but also time during weekends to spend with their peers. Building this into the schedule may compromise your time together. Saying, "I only see you three days out of every fourteen, so why can't you play with your friends on Mom's time?" may sound reasonable to you, but your kids probably won't concur.

Finally, there may be occasions when a certain child wants to spend more time with the residential parent (see Chapter 23). The feeling that you, as the other parent, can't play some vital role may hurt a lot, but no parent is the perfect match for all their kids' demands in every developmental stage. If you are patient and continue to state you want to get together, it is likely that the exclusive phase will pass and your turn to be the "favorite" parent will come.

Suppose the other parent is cooperative, suppose you didn't abandon everyone for two years, suppose you don't verbally or physically abuse the children, yet the refusals continue to occur. If you and the other parent are firm, you can make the seven-year-old come, and at that age usually the protests quickly turn into a good time. Things will get even better if you can find out what the reluctance is about, e.g., "Do we always have to go visiting your friends when I come over?" and make appropriate changes.

But it's hard to make adolescents visit with you, and if they only come in response to threats about withholding support or school tuition, the gain is minimal unless you can get a dialogue started. Use a "special meeting" with the children or a series of meetings to try to break the ice. Enlist help from wherever you can, especially the peer group. One remark during one telephone call to one of the child's friends can be an invaluable clue to what is bugging your teenager. Tempting as it may be to exert your authority, it is counterproductive to your long-term relationship to make your teenager comply and to have the time be nothing but an ugly standoff where he or she stays in the bedroom all day and refuses to participate, ultimately ruining everyone's time together.

General Guidelines

If a single incident does become a pattern, don't forget you potentially have a "surprise" ally in the other parent, who may be desperate for the time off a weekend provides and who may have more luck or ability at getting the child to talk. If that resource doesn't work, think about getting professional help. When you don't have time together, relationships tend to slip away in a hurry, and that's a devastating loss for everyone.

Clearly the best solution to this problem is to prevent it.

- Make sure the kids are involved in the process of setting up a schedule. Listen carefully to their needs and realize that their outside interests are a competing force that needs to be accommodated.
- Design a mechanism to change the schedule if necessary; one that requires sufficient notice to avoid manipulation but creates necessary flexibility.
- Using neutral locations, rather than parent-to-parent handoffs, avoids much of the acting up that leads to the refusal to see a parent.
- Almost all children go through one or more periods of wanting to spend exclusive time with one parent. As long as the favored parent does not try to turn the child's refusal to see the other parent into a sign of allegiance, and the other parent does not take the refusal as a sign of rejection, all the relationships can end up stronger for the willingness to allow this to happen.
- Changes in parental marital status or the failure to share financial gains equitably according to the children's points of view (see Chapter 27) may also cause children to refuse to visit. Talking them through their ambivalence about your new relationship or explaining your financial decisions will usually end the boycott.
- If you feel the relationship is being poisoned by the other parent, try to avoid anger while explaining the situation. Believe it or not, sometimes it's unintentional or the parent is willing to change when the effects are made clear.
- If refusal to see a parent continues beyond a few dates, then both parents should encourage the child to participate in discussions to work this out. That doesn't have to result in forcing the child to go, but requires a strong message from both parents that spending time with each one needs to be a normal part of life, even if that requires substantial changes in the schedule.

Adolescent Dating Anxiety

In which Harry, age fifteen, struggles over
dumping his date for the dance

Child's Point of View:
I Wish We Could Talk About Dating

Why can't I treat this like a regular date? We have these dances every other Friday at school during the spring. A year ago, before the divorce, I would have just asked Karen to go, like we always do. I still really like her, but since the divorce I've had all these doubts. Are we really in love? If I keep going out with her, does that mean I want to marry her? I don't think I want to marry anybody. So I thought about taking Abby, just this once. Of course, the person I really want to go with is Marisa, Abby's best friend, but I don't know whether she'd go with me instead of Chuck. Karen keeps talking like it's automatic we're going, and I kind of resent that. Not that I want to hurt her, but maybe I should just tell her I want a break. I told Dad that I would need a ride, and he asked if Karen and I were going someplace afterward, since we walked to the dance the last time. I told him I didn't know, but I was thinking of taking someone different. He looked at me kind of funny and said he thought Karen was a great girl. Made some crack about making him jealous. Then later he told me that it's always hard to break up a relationship. I told him I didn't want to do that; this was just a one-time thing. He shook his head and told me he thought that once himself too, and I knew he was talking about the affair with Susan that caused the divorce. I suppose he was trying to help me, but it just made it worse. I can't get this out of my head. I mean, I'm not married, so surely I'm allowed to go out with someone else. Then tonight Mom says that Karen's mom has invited her over for dinner on Friday and wants to know whether I want to eat with them. I chickened out and told her we were going to grab a pizza before the dance, but since it's Tuesday, I guess I'll have to make up my mind pretty soon.

I wish I could talk more with either of them about girls, but it's almost like they're worried they'll reveal too much of how they feel. Sometimes I want them to give me their opinion. They usually just give me the standard line about responsible behavior and commitment and looking after the other person's feelings. The guys say I'm crazy. They say that Marisa would drop Chuck for me without a moment's hesitation. Why am I waiting? None of the other kids I know talk with their parents about dating and sex. It's my life. Why do I keep looking to them to tell me what to do?

Parent's Point of View: Do I Dare Give Advice About Relationships?

I thought it was nice when Karen's mother called to invite me to dinner on Friday, but I wonder if she did that to find out what's going on between Karen and Harry. The kids have been an item for more than a year, but I don't see her parents socially—the old third wheel problem. When I mentioned it to Harry tonight and he was evasive, I began to question what was going on. I got the feeling he wasn't intending to ask Karen to go to the dance this week. I can't believe he'd just do that at the last minute, but ever since I discovered the affair his father had, I have to admit I'm suspicious of men. Another pretty girl makes eyes at them and away they go! I know he's not the same as his father, and I think he really cares about Karen, but I'd hate to see her get hurt. I don't really think they're old enough to make a long-term commitment, yet I know what it feels like to be in love for the first time. If it's not going to last forever, I guess I should be asking myself whether I want him to be the one who breaks it off, or her. I'm fond of her, but I'd hate to see him get hurt the way I was.

Some people would say he's only a teenager and it's "puppy-love," but David and I met in high school, and we believed we were made for each other. Maybe we should have explored other relationships before we married. Maybe David would have been able to resist getting involved with other women if we had waited. I suppose I should be encouraging Harry to play the field now before it's too late. But how do I do that and help him understand that a girl like Karen would be devastated by a breakup?

David and I have both tried to talk with the kids about relationships and sex, but it's hard not to get all tied up in your own emotions. I know I'm not very good at it, and I'm never quite sure what message David is getting across—after all, he did leave me during an affair with Susan, and Harry knows it! Every time I think I have some pearl of wisdom, I always wonder if it is more about me than about relationships in general. I'd better try to talk to Harry again before I see Karen's parents, otherwise this could be very embarrassing and painful for everyone.

Making Sense of It All

What a predicament for both Harry and his parents, especially following a divorce! Trying to help an adolescent understand the intimacy and the emotions that are the highlights of being "in love" is almost impossible if you haven't set the precedent of discussing all types of relationships and feelings. When facing a particular dilemma your child brings to you, without this background experience, any advice you offer may seem too close, too personal, too sudden, and intrusive. Feeling comfortable exploring such areas as dating and sexual behavior is all the more important if you suspect that your son or daughter is acting out in response to the divorce.

Conversations between parents and children about these topics are seldom easy in any family. The differences in experience and values between parents and children or the similarities and/or differences adults incorrectly assume exist make it hard for parents and children to get on the same wavelength. The questions are complex. Rush ahead or wait? Stay committed or play the field? When is sex OK—especially when it's the first time? Should boys get different messages than girls? What is true love anyway? Having been through a divorce doesn't necessarily make it any easier to answer these questions. All parents fantasize about telling their children some magic secrets that will spare the children from being hurt or hurting someone else during the emotional turmoil of falling in and out of love. Everyone can remember feeling like the child on the other side of the table. For divorced parents the imperative to offer help seems even stronger, since for most, the pain and negative feelings they wish their children could avoid are their own dominant associations with romantic or sexual relationships.

Unfortunately, there are no such secrets. One reason these important parent-child conversations flounder is that precious few people move beyond the bitterness and anger of divorce to reflect on their own shortcomings and how they, rather than just their ex-spouse, contributed to the marital breakdown. Another reason is that the child discounts the parent's advice, knowing the parent couldn't make his or her own marriage relationship succeed. This distrust of parental wisdom is all too often reinforced by the adult's post-divorce behavior. Many parents leap from a broken marriage to another relationship or a series of relationships based on little more than the need for sexual gratification or the desire to prove they are still worthy of giving and receiving love (see Chapter 12). Parents and therapists often defend these casual liaisons as part of the adult recovery process, but what is OK for the childless thirty-year-old is not permissible for the parent of an impressionable adolescent or child.

Even parents who have gained some new perspectives on their contribution to the breakdown of the marriage may be reluctant to talk to their children about relationships when they know they themselves do not yet have a complete grasp of what went wrong. Answering the inevitable questions about what really caused the divorce, what would you do differently, what does fault mean in these circumstances, is never easy. Parents find themselves being less than truthful with the children because the parents realize these questions can't all be answered in a single conversation or that there is no single "right" answer. Rather than acknowledging they are still learning to understand what makes relationships last, many parents fear any discussion will expose flaws in their character or inconsistencies in their behavior. The risk is small since few, if any, children go through divorce thinking either parent is a saint. Parents who openly admit a few shortcomings make it easier for children to talk about their own confusions and their thoughts about sensitive subjects like dating.

Once the conversation about relationships starts, both generations often find themselves with similar insecurities. If the parent has told the child that the divorce occurred because "we couldn't get along" or "we don't love each other anymore," such remarks, rather than being reassuring, are quite unsettling (see Chapter 4). Everyone is left puzzled and threatened by the thought that love can suddenly vaporize. It can seem that every relationship is in daily danger of collapsing. The result is that adults and children continue to hunger for a relationship they believe will endure, but at the same time, constantly distance themselves out of the fear relationships have to end.

For these talks to provide not only hope but also guidance to your children, you will have to show some emotional maturity. That's easier to manifest if you have anticipated the difficult conversations about sex or individual commitments by having talked about relationships in a more general way as your children mature. Hopefully, you can establish guidelines modeled by your own behaviors or be prepared to discuss what happened when you veered away from those moral precepts. Without a previously built foundation, the tenser, more emotionally loaded conversations (such as might occur in the family depicted in these diaries) can easily collapse into a postmortem of the divorce, complete with finger-pointing at the absent parent. It's much better for each parent to avoid blaming the other parent and putting their children in the awkward and painful position of having to defend the absent parent.

Talking with your children may make you aware of your own flash points and intense feelings. Your feelings and biases can twist every message you give your children. Beware of your tendency to see all relationships through the distorted prism of your recent bad experiences. Adults who feel lonely or abandoned can begin to interpret everything their children tell them through that distorted filter. Consequently their advice can insidiously diminish their children's optimism about male-female relationships.

In hostile divorces, maintaining an understanding of your own foibles and failings is extremely difficult. Even in divorces where the anger, guilt, and resentment lessen, children may still get caught in their parents' snares. The mother in the diary resents being abandoned and thinks all men leave relationships without really trying to preserve them. The father, on the other hand, does not want to send messages to his own son that he himself didn't try or that it's forgivable to walk out when you have one relationship to replace another. Both parents also know that their teenager should probably experience at least a few romantic relationships and that some relationships will inevitably end. They both want to see their son learn to make relationships endure and satisfy. The ideal is to help Harry understand their experiences, without denying him the opportunity to learn from his own choices.

General Guidelines

- Even for the sanest of adults, there are times to postpone or limit these conversations. Immediately after the decision to separate and in the days following the granting of the divorce, people of all ages tend to act out. If your spouse just remarried and you are single or you just broke off or lost a romantic relationship, then your perspective on your child's social involvements may be skewed. Similarly, the parent who has no active romantic or sexual relationship may be overly reactive to the sexual awakenings of the adolescent.

- Dating and sexual behavior in adolescents has been and always will be a convoluted area. Every parent needs to struggle with making sure personal moods and needs do not make it difficult to listen to the child or unfairly influence whatever advice is given. When faced with a child's incomprehensible behavior, every parent tends to look at the actions of the other parent as the root cause. This explanation is even more tempting following divorce. Don't give in to it. Children, especially adolescents, rarely copy a parent without very good reason. In fact, being like Mom or Dad is usually one of the least attractive options in life.

- Some adolescents go through a time of rapid turnover of relationships, including ones where they have sexual involvement. Is the divorce the cause? Perhaps. But simply telling them to stop, that it is self-destructive and that they'll be hurt, will not have much effect.

- Children rarely act out against a parent or try to hurt a parent by manipulating their own social lives, so don't overpersonalize actions you don't approve of, like staying out late or seeing a new boyfriend.

- If, as a result of the divorce, a parent becomes suddenly more socially active or sexually liberated, or produces a new persona with a change of wardrobe, new haircut, etc., then children will implicitly feel they have the right to make similar decisions. If you don't think that's allowable, rethink your own behavior.

- In their efforts to imitate a parent, younger children will engage in very inappropriate behaviors, e.g., the nine-year-old daughter becomes very seductive with males of all ages, or the five-year-old son wants to be in control of everything and everyone. Such imitation shouldn't be viewed as flattery. If self-destructive behaviors are being imitated, e.g., drinking or drug taking, and talking with the child doesn't produce an immediate and dramatic change in the child's behavior, then outside advice should be sought.

- If a child is acting out socially or sexually because of the divorce, they most likely will verbally blame you or your spouse as a justification for their actions. Contrition or self-defense on your part will rarely make any headway, but focusing on their self-interest may get a dialogue started.
- Children are self-centered growing up, and consideration for others is rarely gained through hearing lectures.
- Your child isn't your spouse. Don't assign motivations or patterns of behavior that don't fit.

The Disappearing Parent

32

In which Sam, age ten, wonders why Dad has
gone to Las Vegas and hasn't come back
after two weeks

Child's Point of View:
Why Have You Disappeared?

Well, I know that Dad's OK, because he left a phone message, but he didn't say where he's staying or when he might be coming back. I guess he isn't planning to return any time soon, or he would have said so. I tried calling his apartment to leave him a message, but the telephone has been disconnected. Why couldn't he have left a forwarding number so I could at least talk to him? Mom says he doesn't want to talk to me because he's never going to come back, but I just don't believe it.

I was so miserable last night. I couldn't stop myself from crying, just thinking about what Mom said. I know he still loves me, because he said so, and he'll come back for me one day, even if he can't come now. But how could he do this to me? It's not fair. What parent just disappears like that without telling anyone? Mom says he hasn't sent any money for two months now. How does he expect us to live? He said in his message he was in Las Vegas—but why there? Does he think we will move there? What about school and my friends?

Mom's a basket case. She says she only has money to last until the end of the month. She has no job, and I don't know how we're going to eat or pay the rent. Maybe I should go live with Grandma to make it easier for Mom. Maybe I should run away so she'll have one less person to feed, but then I'd be leaving little Emily and she'd have no one to play with. Wish I could get a job. Wish Dad was here to tell me what to do. Wish he was here to just take me to the park and play ball like we used to. Who will I play with now?

Parent's Point of View:
That Irresponsible Loser!

That bastard. Of all the rotten things to do. He fails as a husband, a father, and as a breadwinner, then he disappears with no word to anyone. I suppose I should be thankful he called Sam to say he's in Las Vegas. At least the police can track him down if he doesn't start sending me support checks, but I'm already in big-time debt. Of course, he tells Sam he's going to make a million bucks in Vegas. Fat chance! He's been a loser all his life. Tells the kids he had to leave town and this is his last chance to make things right. I wouldn't be surprised if he's in trouble with the law already. The big-time gambler! Bet we won't see any of the winnings, even if there are any.

That telephone message was typical! As usual, he puts the kids in the middle of a situation they can't understand and tries to claim he's doing his best. Now I bet he's praying they'll believe him and won't be mad that he's abandoned them again. I don't think that will fly this time. I could hear Sam crying last night and it broke my heart to think he still believes his dad will come back for him. Maybe now I'll be able to convince him it's not me who gets in the way of his visitation with his dad, as Mark keeps telling him.

Poor Sam looks crushed. What do I say to him? Do I try to cover up? I'm sure that will only make it worse. But how can I tell him that if his father doesn't come back, we're headed for the homeless shelter?

Making Sense of It All

Running off is one of the least-defensible actions any parent can take. It doesn't matter how provocative the behavior of the other parent or the number of economic problems that seem insoluble, no rationalization suffices. To be abandoned as a child is to have one's worst fears realized.

Too often, debts and financial obligations are cited as the reason for becoming a deadbeat parent. For various reasons, deadbeat parents are usually men. Some of these men are simply greedy and irresponsible. Many feel pushed out of the family by custody and schedule arrangements that they feel favor women, and they come to resent having to devote so much of their income to supporting a wife they've come to hate and children they rarely see. Men are frequently unjustly subject to reflex condemnation by society when they leave a marriage and bias from the courts when they assert their equal parental rights. We have heard numerous stories of wives who do not spend the money they receive to pay for their children's necessities, and countless men tell of being denied the right to visit their children because of a late child-support check. Many have suffered much worse harassment: false accusations of sexual abuse, false accusations of spousal abuse, or the use of domestic violence restraining orders to make visitation more difficult. Many fathers endure the repeated use of excuses, such as birthday parties, sports events, etc., as reasons not to send the kids for a visit, or a systematic campaign to persuade the children that they would be better off not seeing Dad at all.

Any father would react negatively to such provocations. Under these conditions, many fathers consider giving up the struggle to maintain contact with their children. But as hard as the emotional and physical struggle may be, it is never justified to simply opt out and disappear. Running off and dropping support may offer a way to get back at a manipulative or vindictive spouse, or provide relief from overwhelming guilt, but inevitably the kids' lives are made much worse.

The long-term consequences of a parent abandoning his or her children are profound. That is not to minimize the immediate horror of being made homeless or going hungry, which is the fate of all too many families abandoned by the breadwinner. Although most kids survive physically, the research shows that they do not do well psychologically. The loss of contact with a parent is the single most powerful factor in determining a negative long-term outcome for children following divorce. That should surprise no one. When a parent leaves, especially since they usually run away, the children's loss of self-esteem and trust in others consequent to being abandoned is devastating. The longlasting emotional effects on children from the loss of the parent-child relationship when an adult abdicates or deserts, and the increase in risk-taking behaviors, especially in adolescents, have been well documented.

We recognize that many fathers who temporarily or permanently "disappear" may rationalize their actions by thinking they are doing the best for their children by allowing them to live a more "normal" life without the disruption of being pulled between two parents. Children never see it this way. If allowed to, they will make a unique relationship with each of their parents in ways that children of intact families may never have an opportunity to do. Even if they cannot visit with the absent parent, maintaining phone or written communication is essential.

We have heard many men say they cannot bear the remoteness from their kids and that they would rather cut off contact altogether to preserve their own emotional sanity. Experience shows that walking away does not solve problems for the one who leaves. It just creates new ones. The parent who ceases to share in the children's lives is inevitably the loser. No matter how you feel about your ex-spouse, it is endlessly draining and devastatingly lonely to try to forget your kids.

There's always a void. Reconciliations after years of separation can occur, but they're rarely the all-forgiving fantasy that justifies the suffering and burdens you and the children have to endure.

General Guidelines

- If you're thinking of leaving, even if you've convinced yourself it will be better for everyone, don't do it.
- If you left, go back.
- If you left because of an abuse incident or a history of domestic violence, get help. Then go back.
- When you go back, don't just show up. It's disruptive, self-centered, and as unfair as leaving without notice. Unexplained appearances are no more beneficial than unexplained leavings.
- Come back with a plan to establish support. Financial responsibility should be reestablished and a time commitment to see the kids honored.
- Many men worry they will be punished, even put in jail or denied any contact with their children, if they return after a lapse. By all means consult with an attorney if you can. Fortunately, society has learned from the debtors' prisons of centuries ago that locking people up only prevents them from earning sufficient money to pay back their debt.
- If you are willing to resume your financial responsibilities for your children, you will reestablish credibility as a parent who is to be trusted to look after the interests of a child. Running off may temporarily cost you time with your kids after you return—the court may want you to prove that you will stay around, before risking the kids' emotions as they get reattached—but enduring whatever it takes on your part is better for the children than a permanent absence.
- As kids get older, they find ways to spend time with the people playing significant roles in their lives, regardless of what the courts or the divorce decree says.
- Remember that the longer you avoid communication, the greater the psychological damage to the children.

- Children who are abandoned by a parent carry the trauma with them throughout their lives—no matter how loving or attentive the remaining parent is. These children have difficulty forming lasting relationships or friendships and have a higher divorce rate. Next time you look in the mirror, ask yourself if you want to be responsible for that.

Long-Distance Parenting

In which Tom, age seven, arrives with his reluctant
siblings for a summer vacation with Dad

Child's Point of View:
I'm Going to Have a Great Time . . .

This is so great! I've been wishing for the summer to come. I've been counting down the days on my calendar and now I'm really here. I can't believe Dad remembered to buy those chocolate-chip muffins I love, and the stuffed alligator I won at the fair was still sitting on my bed to greet me after all these months! I love having those red crates in my room for all my stuff! Much easier than the bureau at home—and Dad doesn't mind if I leave clothes on the floor. Yeah! Tonight we're going to start making the model plane Dad said he had bought for me, and by the end of the vacation we'll be able to fly it.

Kaitlin is being a pain as usual. Thinks because she's ten she should be the one who tells everyone what to do. She's bossy at home but worse here, and Dad is getting really mad with her, which doesn't help. She's hardly looked at him since we arrived yesterday and has been in her room with the door shut all afternoon. She was like this for the first few days the last time we came, so I hope she snaps out of it soon. It's such fun here I can't understand why she acts like that, especially as last week she was all excited about coming too. I think she misses Mom, because she keeps asking me if I want to phone home. I don't really, but I will if she makes me.

Damon didn't waste any time; he's gone already. Went to find those big kids he was skateboarding with last year. Just grabbed a sandwich and walked out without saying good-bye. Dad shouted after him, but he just left saying he'd "be back." Dad looked upset, but Damon does that all the time to Mom at home, so it's no big deal. Anyway, with him out and Kaitlin sulking, I get Dad to myself—except right now he doesn't look in the mood to play.

Parent's Point of View:
Are We Going to Have a Good Time?

After four years I thought this summer might be different. I try so hard to keep in touch with the kids—E-mailing them, writing, phoning. I suppose it paid off—the last two seven-day vacations we spent together went spectacularly. But I want all that effort I made since

April to make an even bigger difference now that they're here for a whole month. Maybe I'm being unrealistic. I know it's only the second day, but I'm not sure whether this is going well or not.

Damon's taken off and I haven't had a chance to ask him anything about his plans for next year. Is he changing schools or not? It's unclear to me whether Finch High will take him back after the marijuana incident. And I really don't think he should have been allowed to get his tongue pierced—it's disgusting. Meanwhile, Kaitlin's barricaded herself in her room and says she's still mad at me for saying she couldn't stay home last Easter for her best friend's birthday party and that I never let her do what she wants. I think I'll never hear the last of that!

So that leaves little Tom, who has been hanging on me ever since the airport. He can't stop talking and won't let me do anything other than play with him. I've got stuff from work to finish and I haven't thought about dinner. The whole place seems such a mess with clothes all over the floor and Lego pieces underfoot. Doesn't his mother ever ask him to pick stuff up?

Going to get them from the airport, I was already anxious. They looked so different from last time, although it was only four months ago. I think about them all the time, but when it comes to actually being around them, I still don't feel like I want to feel. Why can't I just pick them up and *know* we're going to have a good time? Today has gone so slowly and nothing good has happened. Before I know it, they'll all be going home. I've got to make this fun. Uh-oh, Tom's looking as though he's going to cry.

Making Sense of It All

Living a long distance from your children is anguishing and lonely. Couples seldom anticipate that their divorce may result in not only living in a separate abode, but in a different zip code, a different state, or even a different country. Once you no longer live together in the family home, it is hard to recapture the feeling of being a "real" parent. You're just not around for the "events" and the "nonevents." A parent should be a constant presence in their children's lives, not a visitor or one to be visited. But that is often the fate of the divorced parent. Although your relationships with your children change when you don't live together full-time, they can simulate normal parental relationships if you are geographically close. Once you move 100 or 1,000 miles away, the relationship changes its character again. Indeed, the farther away you are and the more infrequent the visits, the more difficult it is to feel like a regular parent.

Yet the temptation to move as far away as possible can seem irresistible. Whether motivated by selfish interests or the well-founded belief that it will benefit the children to decrease the arguing and manipulation, many parents seek to put some distance between themselves and an obstructive or hostile ex-spouse. Others find that a new job and a big raise hold the promise of a better lifestyle for everyone—no small consideration in our consumer-oriented world. While it may seem paradoxical, there is also a certain allure to seeing your children for a few large blocks of time during the course of the year, when contrasted to the hassles and frustrations of maintaining a relationship dependent on once-weekly dinners and sharing part of every other weekend. Making that allure become a reality is difficult, but not impossible. In most cases, your change of address has to benefit everyone, and doing that calculation involves more than just the potential for a better lifestyle and more money.

So before you spring for the bigger bucks, the great new job, the career opportunity of a lifetime, or you decide you have to escape the spiderweb of an ugly divorce, consider the downside of leaving the kids behind—can you bridge the gap that's measured in something other than miles? If everyone benefits from your higher income, that is a definite plus, but it doesn't let you be anything more than the chancellor of the exchequer. Gifts, better clothes, funding more extracurricular activities, even freeing the kids from hearing the other parent complain about how selfish or cheap you are, doesn't in the end do much to maintain, let alone strengthen, your relationship with your children. They may feel gratitude, perhaps they will feel indebted, but is that all you want? The farther away you are, the harder it is to stay in contact. Not only aren't you there for the crucial events or performances, but the human contact is gone. Conversations on the phone become shorter and shorter when you have no faces to attach to their friends' names and no real sense of what has happened in their lives the day before. While you might be very interested in having them fill you in on the details, most children won't share your enthusiasm and quickly tire of that routine. Even the E-mail messages become terse when you're just not "with it"—and that exalted status is hard enough to attain when you do live in the same house.

To some extent, your success in maintaining contact will depend on the age of the child. Distance itself is a hard abstraction to get beyond; even for a mature seven- or eight-year-old, it simply reduces to "Daddy's not there" or "I can't see Mommy when I want to." The telephone may seem like a lifeline to you, but daily calls typically evoke sadness. From the kids' point of view the disembodied voice makes you seem more remote, rather than closer. Perhaps the self-enchanted adolescent who is "into life" may be happy to talk about "me," but younger kids run out of chitchat in a very short time. So when you strain to keep the conversation going by asking yet again, "What did you do today?" the answer will quite literally be, "Nothing." When you see the kids frequently, you know what the picture the art teacher decided to hang in the entrance foyer looks like, you know about the soccer game, you have good and recent memories to share, so the conversation flows more smoothly. There aren't the awkward silences terminated by your saying, "Hold it, hold it! Who's Fred?" or "I didn't know there was a bakery near the house." Those types of questions and your slightly off-base remarks don't make you seem interested and involved; they simply confirm you're out of touch. As divorced parents lose a sense of how their kids live and who they are, too many parents find that the saying, "Out of sight, out of mind," becomes true for both generations.

The electronic age does offer some bridges that weren't widely available a few years ago. Even kindergartners can use E-mail. It's private and quick, and, unlike lengthy or frequent telephone calls, is less likely to upset the parent the kids are with. Equally important, E-mail relieves the child of the nagging doubt, "Have I been forgotten?" and avoids the performance pressure of having to say something, which so often hinders telephone conversations. Information conveyed by E-mail can usefully set the stage for a later telephone conversation together. Words are only one device, however. Photographs, drawings, tapes, and even letters by snail mail share a "value" that doesn't get assigned to words on a computer or those spoken on a telephone since they are concrete and can be moved from place to place. Tapes can be sent back and forth; drawings or photographs can be edited, altered, even combined, and then exchanged by regular or electronic mail. Music can be used as a way to work on something together; or perhaps you share an interest in movies and can compare your personal reviews. Make predictions on sports games. Take lessons in the same thing, be it yoga or tennis, and compare the experiences. It's not the same as being there, but the options provide more opportunities to be part of the day-to-day life of your children.

And don't forget other more traditional sources of vital knowledge, like their hometown newspaper. Wait until it comes, before you call, so you know about the big game, the recital, or the fire at the neighbors' house. Have the school fax you the weekly calendar, the school newspaper, your children's best work—the expense to reimburse them for the costs is well worth it.

It surprises many relocating parents that the ultimate success of these efforts to maintain contact depends on the cooperation of the remaining parent. Moving away may not ease the hostility at all and may be seen as the ultimate act of irresponsibility. Even if there has been obstruction to visitation and multiple complaints about your involvement in the children's lives, leaving will just generate new friction—and if the remaining parent keeps the modem tied up or trashes the faxes before the kids see them, your efforts to keep in touch may be for naught. Such obstructive actions can be minimized by taking account of an important factor: when you move away, the other parent is faced with weeks or months with no "time off." It's wise to anticipate that the parent who lives with the kids most of the time will feel deserving of a break more often than the infrequent times the kids come to see you. So to keep the communication lines open, try to anticipate the logistic and financial costs of extra baby-sitters or whatever it will take to compensate for your absence—no matter how much "trouble" has been attributed to your proximity or how much resistance your presence has engendered before. Make economic provisions to cover the gap as part of the initial package, and your move away may not generate maximum antagonism and noncooperation.

All this effort to be involved with your kids will make the one-week vacations during the year go more smoothly, but it won't make them last longer. Nor does it eliminate the mixed emotions that arise in anticipation of the long time together, which typically happens in the summer. When you get that one chance all year to really be together as a family, everyone would prefer to transition from being apart without a glitch. It rarely happens, but how well you know each other lessens the anxiety of trying to create the feeling of being a "real" family. Being a real family requires not fixating on making the kids' time with you better than in their "other" life. That may be hard when vacations are really the only time you get together, and everyone wants to pack a year's worth of fun into a month or six weeks. But if you are honest, the family life you yearn for involves much more (or less!) than frantically running from theme park to movie theater doing "whatever the kids want to do."

Don't set your expectations too high. If your sixteen-year-old never spends much time with the other parent, don't expect much difference when the kid is with you. Many children like and need time to "veg-out" in front of the TV or downtime to lie on their bed staring into space! Your younger kids will be happy to build Lego cars with you or help bake cookies, so plan to do "normal" things. It actually helps to use the communication channels to plan not only what to do, but also to make sure you're up-to-date on what they like to eat, what each kid does to "chill out," etc. The multiple exchanges involved give each person a sense that "I'm being listened to" or that he or she is being taken care of, as well as a clear message that compromises are necessary from everyone, including the parent.

Unfortunately, you can't plan out all the emotional reactions that occur in the initial transition. In most families, the more needy the individual, whether it be the parent or the child, the more likely there is to be a push-away reaction in the first few days, combined with the clear hunger to be together. It is like the parent who, on the return of the lost child, is still so caught up in the loss that he or she has to ask, "Why did you run away?" or "Why didn't you stay where I told you?" rather than, "I'm so happy to see you." The child who hasn't seen you for months and seems to have withdrawn may not be able to get past the disappointment of the times you weren't there, or feels compelled to be rebellious and isolationist to show that "I don't need you, because I don't live with you." Such protective mechanisms are seen more often in older kids like Kaitlin, while the younger child, like Tom, may be so excited that they're uncontrollable. While most adults enjoy the latter for a while, it can't be tolerated for long. So the younger child needs limits enforced; the older child who seems rude and confrontational, especially about things that are ancient history to you, also needs limits.

Too often, however, the situation quickly gets out of hand. The parent ignores too much from the younger child or forbears so many comments from the older sibling, that anger ensues. It's easier to control the younger child—a few limits, combined with the judicious use of time-outs, and things settle down. With preadolescents or teenagers, however, it's more complicated. Often a child's words or choice of issues is all too reminiscent of your ex-spouse, and this may make you feel even more isolated, as it seems like the child identifies only with the ex-spouse. Even if you feel the mood has been "poisoned" by the attitude of the residential parent, try to stay cool. Be willing to talk about how hard it is to fit together when you haven't seen each other for months. Don't get discouraged because of behavior during the first hours or days.

Expect that the first few days may include listening to a list of your sins, even though the complaints are based on incidents you have regretted or tried diligently to prevent. You may want to explain some things the kids aren't aware of or have forgotten themselves, but it's rarely beneficial to attack the other parent—even though it may seem justified. Intensifying loyalty conflicts won't increase anyone's enjoyment. On the other hand, don't overdo it. Once the older child has had the opportunity to speak, emphasize your desire to enjoy the time together, not rewrite history. Explain your limits, since they may not be the same as those of the other parent. Then make the communication rules the same as they are when the kids are with the residential parent, so the rules about calling, use of E-mail, etc., are unchanged. The transition phase will pass if you handle it correctly; otherwise it can consume the whole stay.

Part of the planning process includes clarifying for the kids what the demands of your work will be and then doing everything you can to make sure work doesn't intrude excessively on your time with them. Equally important is protection for individual time with each child (see Chapter 23), as well as sharing the good times together as a group. If these efforts are successful, then the visit is likely to go well. Don't forget to use the time to anticipate the long absence that has to be endured. Is there new software you have to learn to use together? Are there projects like doll making, model building, etc., that, begun now, will help you stay in touch until the next time together? Find out whether the old mechanisms still work: is it necessary to use a new E-mail address, change the times for telephone conversations, or rework the ways you exchange tapes and faxes? When you're together it's tempting to ignore the distance that will soon separate you, but doing so only makes it tougher to span that distance when the children are gone. And don't leave these things to the very end, because there will be another transition period, perhaps as long as a couple of days, as everyone goes through the emotional preparation for leaving. Rather than casting a pall over the visit, facing up to the uncomfortable fact that you soon will be apart again will make the time a little more bearable and will likely make the next time together more fulfilling.

General Guidelines

When you live far away from your children, the task of improving their infrequent visits has multiple phases:

1. finding ways to stay in touch with their lives,
2. planning adequately before they arrive,
3. weathering the transition when they first arrive,
4. making the most of the family time together while they're with you, and
5. strengthening the old mechanisms or devising new ways to remain close before they leave and go back to their other residence far away.

Staying in touch often depends on the cooperation of the other parent. If there's resistance or interference, then E-mail is more reliable than the telephone, the mail, or a fax (see Chapter 13). Work out ways to contact your children at school or at a friend's; make sure they can contact you at the office or some other location during the school day or at times when they are not with the other parent.

- Develop projects that let you work together—creating art or editing photos, building models, writing stories, writing or performing music, or predicting sports scores.
- Find ways to exchange concrete reminders: letters, tapes, or photos are especially important to younger children, who need them to be assured of your presence in their lives.
- Stay "in the know" by getting the local paper and making arrangements for the school to fax you the weekly calendar or the

school newspaper. You also have to request duplicate report cards and teacher reports.

- Create a fail-safe system so you remember birthdays.

Planning the visit may seem artificial, emphasizing symbolically and literally how far apart you are, but it will make the long visit, and perhaps the short vacation as well, more enjoyable:

- Weeks before the children are to arrive, start an open discussion about what everyone wants to do during your time together.
- Make sure the kids know what your obligations are, especially if they are different than last year. Don't encourage false expectations of your availability.
- Build in individual time, and make sure older children have the latitude and the social contacts to "do their own thing," because they'll likely rebel if you expect them to be home whenever you are.

There will be a transition period when the kids arrive—for you and for them.

- Transition behavior requires parents to set limits and not over-personalize reactions.
- If one child is problematic, focus on the others. Don't let the isolationist, antisocial, or separatist behavior consume everyone's time and energy.
- Keep the communication guidelines and channels unchanged—what applies to you should work for the other parent as well.

The long visit is different than a vacation.

- Make it family time. Vacations don't have the same rewards.
- Continue the projects that serve to keep you in touch.
- The leaving transition starts before the actual moment the kids depart. Acknowledge that it will be hard, rather than try to overpower it or avoid it.
- Use your time together to build mutual closeness, trust, and respect.

Contact Information

For additional resources for parents and children, more information about divorce issues, and personal consultations, contact us at: http://www.childrenanddivorce.com or 1-800-422-6661.

Authors' Biographies

Dr. Jennifer Lewis has been in primary care pediatric practice in Brookline, Massachusetts, since completing her pediatric training in London and at Children's Hospital Boston and a subsequent fellowship with Dr. T. Berry Brazelton in child development. She has consulted for community groups, day-care centers, parent groups, and schools, while maintaining a practice in which she has incorporated a preventive approach to family conflicts and developmental crises within the traditional primary care model. She is the coauthor, with Dr. Sammons, of *Premature Babies: A Different Beginning* (Mosby & Co., 1985), which won two prizes and has subsequently been translated into Japanese. She and Dr. Sammons are child-development consultants to teachers in the American Montessori Society, and she currently maintains a behavioral pediatrics consulting practice. She is married and the mother of two daughters, ages fifteen and nineteen.

Dr. Bill Sammons started a pediatric practice in Wellesley, Massachusetts, following completion of pediatric training in Boston and a fellowship with Dr. Brazelton, where he and Dr. Lewis studied the behavior of premature infants and their families, as well as collaborated on a research study of sleep patterns in infants. He has published three books: *Premature Babies: A Different Beginning* (Mosby & Co.,1985), *The Self-Calmed Baby* (Little Brown, 1989; St. Martin's Press, 1991), and *I Wanna Do It Myself* (Hyperion, 1992). He has given numerous talks and presentations in the United States and abroad. He currently heads Red Tae Associates, a nonprofit group that has worked with thousands of families in all fifty states and fourteen countries abroad on a wide variety of issues such as adjustment to a new infant, discipline strategies, sleep disturbances, school readiness, and divorce. He is married and the father of a twelve-year-old son.

Dr. Sammons has been cited or quoted in dozens of magazine and newspaper articles, and has made numerous presentations to live audiences as well as appearances on television and radio.